A History
of Northern Botswana
1850-1910

A History of Northern Botswana 1850 - 1910

J. Mutero Chirenje

Rutherford • Madison • Teaneck
Fairleigh Dickinson University Press

London: Associated University Presses

© 1977 by Associated University Presses, Inc.

Associated University Presses, Inc.
Cranbury, New Jersey 08512

Associated University Presses
Magdalen House
136–148 Tooley Street
London SE1 2TT, England

Library of Congress Cataloging in Publication Data

Chirenje, J Mutero, 1935–
A history of northern Botswana, 1850–1910.

Bibliography: p.
Includes index.
1. Botswana—History—To 1966.   2.Tswana
(Bantu tribe) I. Title.
DT791.C49   968.1   74-194
ISBN 0-8386-1537-6

PRINTED IN THE UNITED STATES OF AMERICA

Dedicated to

Muchineripi waMurombo

of

Mudzimuirema

Contents

Preface 9
Acknowledgments 13
Abbreviations 16
Maps and Photos 17

1 Early Tswana Contacts with White Travelers and Agents of the London Missionary Society, 1800–1852   27
2 Tswana Intercourse with Traders; German Missionaries Come to Bechuanaland, 1850–1860   35
3 The L.M.S. Takes Over German Stations in Bechuanaland; Response to Missionary Work in Northern Bechuanaland, 1862–1880   81
4 Events Leading to Declaration of a Protectorate; Tswana Resistance to British Rule; Government Intervention in Tribal Affairs   123
5 "To Make a Book Talk": Problems and Progress in Tswana Education, 1880–1910   159

6	Boikgololo: Millenarians and Church Secessionists in Northern Bechuanaland, 1898–1910	201
7	More Aspects of Tswana Transformations	229
8	Conclusion	279

Genealogies 283
Bibliography 285
Index 307

Preface

RECENT WORKS ON TSWANA HISTORY HAVE TENDED TO BE preoccupied with political history, with the result that the gamut of forces that have shaped the history of Botswana (until 1966 known as Bechuanaland Protectorate) have been only partially revealed. This study seeks to shed more light on the history of northern Bechuanaland by taking into account some of the social and economic processes that beset that region in the nineteenth century.

From about the middle of the nineteenth century up to the turn of the twentieth century a host of external factors, in varying degrees, impinged upon social and economic institutions of the Tswana. And of these factors the advent of Europeans was the most significant; Europeans brought new ideas that interacted with those of the Tswana. The white newcomers also had tendencies to expand the British sphere of influence throughout southern Africa, a trend that resulted in the annexation of northern Bechuanaland in

1885. By 1910, British rule in Bechuanaland had become firmly entrenched.

A special feature of the interaction between the Tswana and the Europeans was that the latter group introduced its religious and secular ideas to the Tswana with an enthusiasm that was matched by Tswana reticence to abandon their traditional way of life in favor of an alien culture. Yet, in spite of their conservatism, the Tswana felt the impact of European ideas.

Even in a study that attempts to reconstruct a social and economic history of northern Bechanaland, it has been found necessary to include chapter 4, which deals with the creation of the Protectorate and indicates the extent to which the Protectorate Administration intervened in several aspects of Tswana life and how the latter group responded to some measures introduced by the new rulers. It is hoped that chapter 4, though largely dealing with political history, will enhance an understanding of Tswana history, for too often Tswana responses to government intervention mirrored the kind of responses that were evinced by the new social and economic ideas.

By the middle of the nineteenth century, northern Bechuanaland was dominated by four tribes: the Kwena; the Ngwaketse; the Ngwato; and the Tawana. These tribes occupied territories that were more or less coterminous with present boundaries, except that the idea of sharply defined boundary lines was imposed by British officials in 1899. Within each Tswana chiefdom were several subordinate groups, such as the Sarwa (so-called Bushmen) and the Kgalagadi, whose subservient status awaits a more extended investigation. In chapter 7 of this book I have merely indicated their marginal status during the nineteenth century, when the Tswana assigned to them a position in society verging on servitude.

The attention of readers is drawn to maps that are to be found at the beginning of the book: these show the position

Preface

of Botswana in relation to Southern Africa; the four chiefdoms dealt with in this study; areas of Tswana settlement in the nineteenth century; and the long-distance trade routes in the Tswana region. There are genealogies of rulers in four Tswana tribes at the end of the book. While I appreciate the assistance I obtained from many people, I alone am responsible for the assertions in the book.

J. Mutero Chirenje

Acknowledgments

THE PUBLICATION OF THIS BOOK HAS ENTAILED SO MUCH cooperation of tutors and friends that I can not name them all. Nevertheless, among them are some names that stand out above all others. In London I would like to express my gratitude to the following scholars who counseled me while I was a graduate student at the School of Oriental and African Studies, University of London: Mr. Anthony Atmore, S.O.A.S. and the Center for International and Area Studies, who was my tutor during my tenure as a commonwealth scholar at S.O.A.S.; and Professor Richard Gray of S.O.A.S. and Professor Isaac Schapera, emeritus, of the London School of Economics and Political Science, who both drew my attention to Northern Botswana and helped me in delineating the scope of this study. Professor Schapera's willingness to share his vast knowledge of sources on Tswana history is especially appreciated.

I also owe much to librarians and archivists in the various places I visited. Among them are Miss Irene Fletcher of the London Missionary Society, whose hospitality has been enjoyed by a generation of scholars; Mrs. I. M. Leonard of Selly Oak Colleges Library, Birmingham, England; Mr. I. C. Cunningham of the National Library of Scotland, Edinburgh; Mr. Eliatham Gwabini of the Botswana National Archives, Gaborone; and Mr. Crispin Tsara of Gaborone Secondary School, for making my stay in Botswana so pleasant. To this list must be added the staff of the British Museum; the Royal Commonwealth Society Library, London; African Methodist Episcopal Church Archives, New York City; Butler Library, Columbia University; and Mr. H. M. Reinfried of Zurich, Switzerland, who was a schoolmate of mine at S.O.A.S. and kindly translated into English for me Georg Haccius's work on Hanoverian missionaries to Southern Africa. Miss Leloba Molema of Royal Holloway College, and the Rev. Christopher Nteta of the Harvard Divinity School, both gave me valuable insights into Tswana life and culture.

Finally, I would like to record my thanks to the Association of Commonwealth Universities for awarding me a scholarship to pursue postgraduate work at the University of London, during which time I prepared a Ph.D. thesis on which this study is based; and to Harvard University for providing me with funds that enabled me to carry out research in Botswana.

A History
of Northern Botswana
1850-1910

ABBREVIATIONS

B. D. C.	Bechuanaland District Committee of the L.M.S.
B. N. A.	Botswana National Archives
B. S. A. Co.	British South Africa Company
C. M. M.	*Cape Monthly Magazine*
C. O.	Colonial Office
J. R. A. I.	*Journal of the Royal Anthropological Institute of Great Britain and Ireland*
J. R. G. S.	*Journal of the Royal Geographical Society*
L. M. S.	London Missionary Society
M. D. C.	Matebeleland District Committee of the L.M.S.
M. M. S.	Methodist Missionary Society
N. R. L. T. U. C.	Native Races and Liquor Traffic United Committee
P. R. O.	Public Record Office
S. A. N. A. C.	South African Native Affairs Commission, 1903–5
U. D. C.	United District Committee, comprised of the B.D.C. and the M.D.C. of the L.M.S.

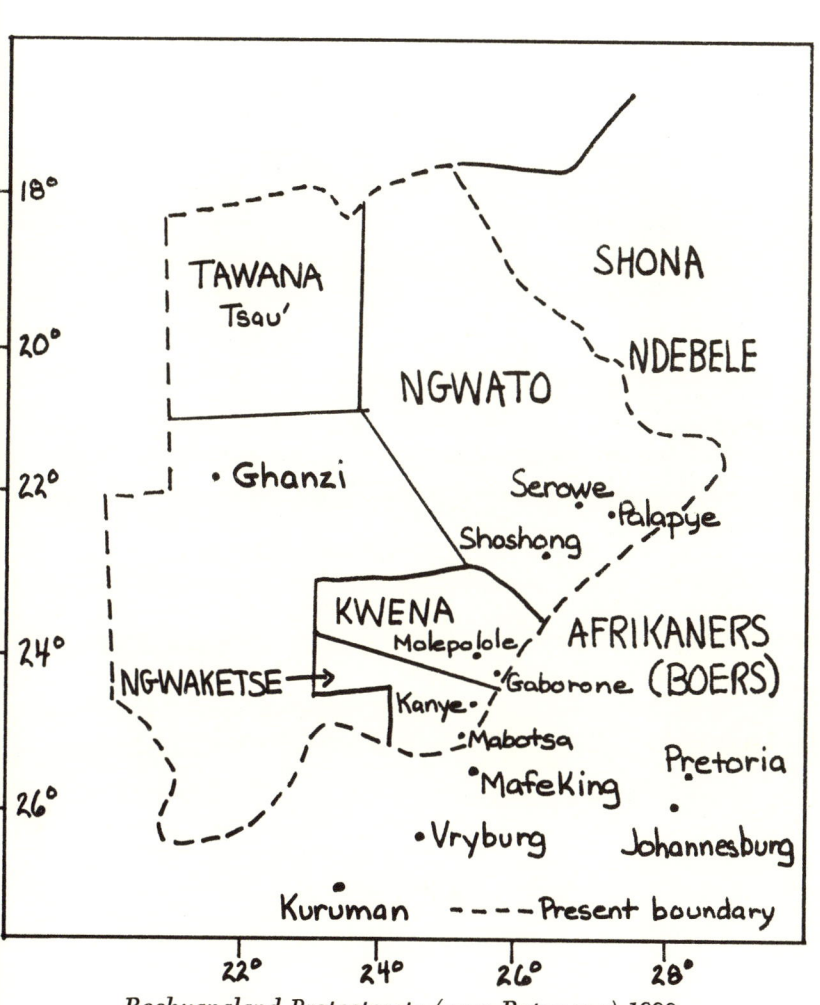

Bechuanaland Protectorate (now Botswana) 1899.

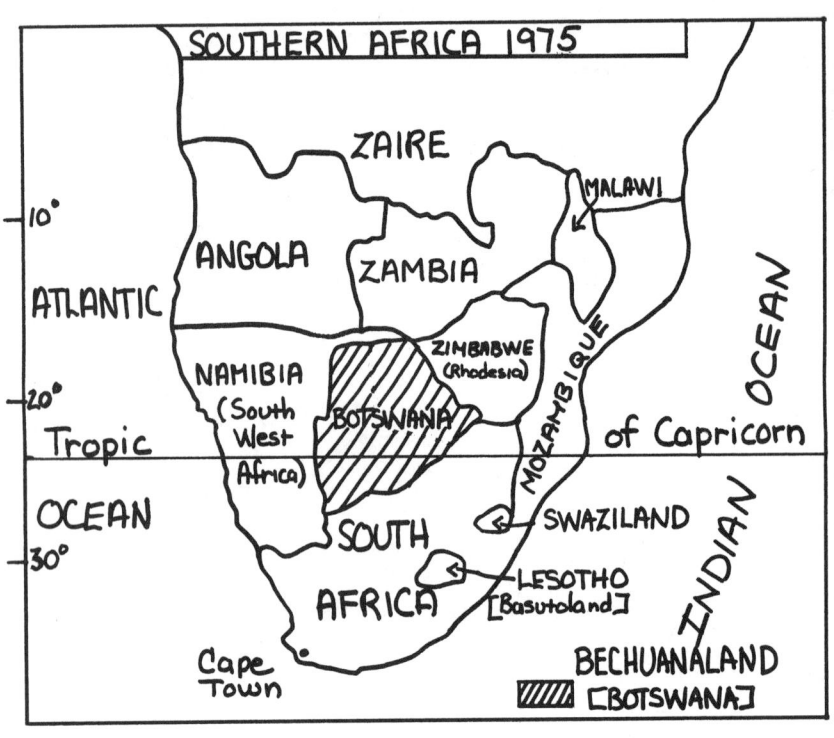

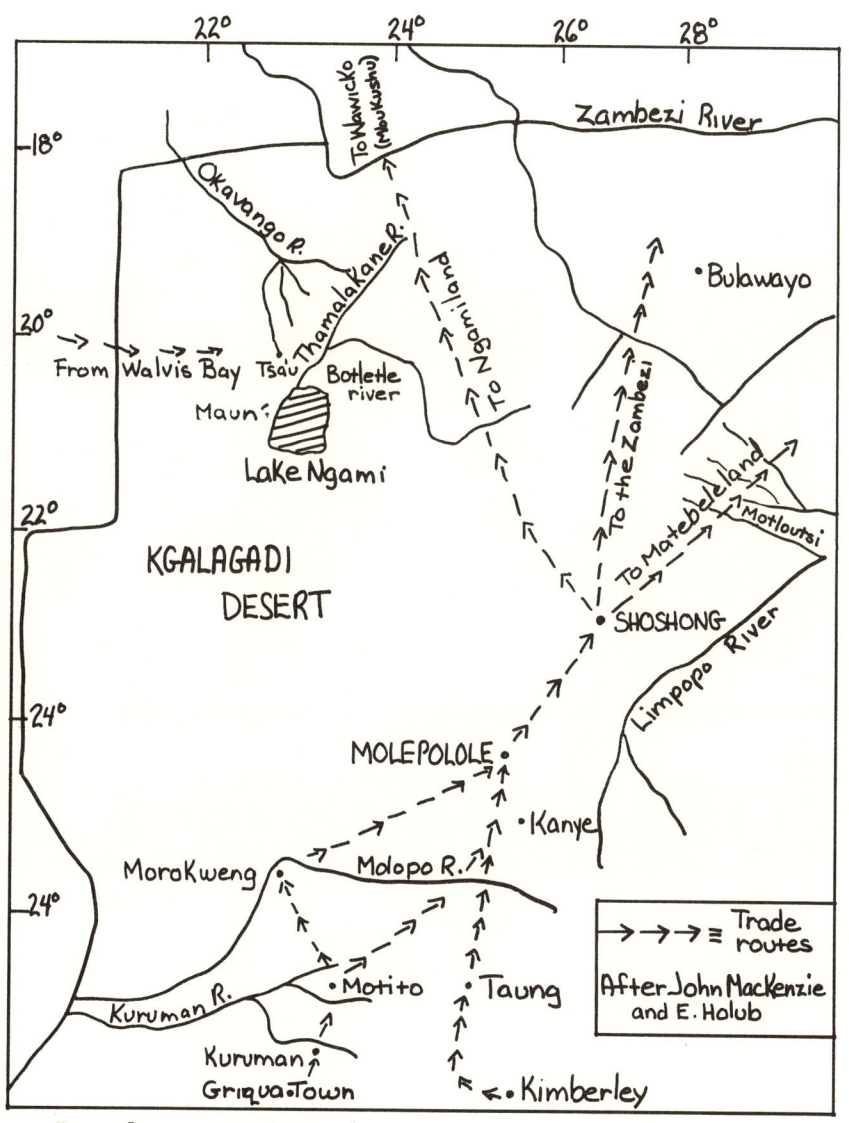

Long-distance Trade Routes in the Tswana Region, circa 1840–1890.

Chiefs Lentswe (Kgatla), Sechele I (Kwena), and Bathoen I (Ngwaketse). Background: a trader (unknown), Lentswe's brother, Segale, and Mr. J. Ellenberger. (From an old photograph, courtesy of Mr. V. E. Ellenberger.)

Chiefs Bathoen I (Ngwaketse), Sebele I (Kwena), and Kgama (Ngwato), in England, 1895. Background: Messrs. E. Lloyd and W. C. Willoughby. (From an old photograph, courtesy of the L.M.S.)

*Chief Seepapitso (Ngwaketse).
(Courtesy of Chief Bathoen II.)*

*Chief Bathoen II (Ngwaketse).
(Courtesy of Chief Bathoen II.)*

Chief Kgama III holding court, Palapye, 1890. (From an old photograph, courtesy of the Rhodesian National Archives.)

Kgama III of Botswana.

Kgama III in about 1890.

1
Early Tswana Contacts with White Travelers and Agents of the London Missionary Society, 1800-1852

IN 1800, WHEN THE LONDON MISSIONARY SOCIETY (L.M.S.) SENT two agents to evangelize the Tlhaping, a southern Tswana tribe, they had in fact opened an overland corridor for the white man's "road to the north";[1] hitherto, Europeans had relied on ocean routes via the Cape of Good Hope to reach the east coast of Africa and for that reason the African hinterland had remained largely unaffected by the traffic of whites who plied between Europe and the Orient. Now a new epoch had been unleashed by the opening up of a land route to the interior.

The Tswana seem to have been the least prepared to deal with European encroachment at the turn of the nineteenth century, for they themselves were beset by political bickering and internal secessions of varying magnitude. Examples of the breaking up of tribes far exceeded tendencies to unite, even when the various groups were threatened by a common enemy.[2] Oral traditions and written accounts provide evidence for the fissiparous tendencies within Tswana society. It was among these strife-torn communities that white missionaries and laymen alike made their appearance.

I

The early white travelers to southern Bechuanaland widely reported the ravages of war and the impact of firearms in that region. One of the earliest of such travelers, Petrus Borcherds, was secretary to the Cape Government, Truter-Sommerville mission, that was sent to explore and befriend chiefs in the Tswana region. He was told in 1801 by Molehabangwe, the Tlhaping chief, how a tribe called the Korana had been victorious at war owing to their use of firearms. According to Borcherds, the Tlhapings' numerical superiority proved ineffectual because the Korana forced them to "succumb, owing to the inferiority of their arms."[3] The Tlhaping were impressed by the effectiveness of firearms and in due course sought them from any white traveler who visited their territory.[4] They also tended to be suspicious of white newcomers until the visitors established peaceful intents. In 1805, a party from the Cape colony, accompanied by the German university professor Dr. Henry Lichtenstein, was accorded a grudging welcome, Molehabangwe stating that "he had not the least objection to strangers visiting his country provided they came with pacific views."[5]

Between the Truter-Sommerville mission of 1801 and Lichtenstein's visit in 1805, the Tlhaping had separated from the Rolong.[6] Both groups sought assistance from white

Early Tswana Contacts

visitors so that they could attack neighboring communities.[7] These early visitors described the elaborate system of military awards and the prestige attached to these honors, which were indicative of the high value attached by the Tswana to warlike activities.[8] In 1813, the Reverend John Campbell reported that the Tlhaping referred to cattle raiding "as if it were a fortunate and commendable enterprise, that [the Tlhaping] came to a people who had no instruments of defense, killed many of them, and carried off a great many cattle."[9] Northern Tswana tribes, too, had their share of troubles.

At about the turn of the century (c. 1790–1800) the Tawana hived off from the Ngwato and went to live in Ngamiland. While the Ngwato-Tawana separation was not accompanied by fighting, the first few years of Tawana's followers' stay at Lake Ngami were marred by internal disputes. Tawana quarreled with his father, Mathiba, shortly after getting to Ngamiland, with the result that Mathiba returned to Shoshong, where he was turned away by his elder son, Kgama I, who was consolidating his position as chief of the Ngwato. Mathiba then found refuge among the Kwena, with whom he lived for the rest of his life. But the removal of Mathiba from Ngamiland did not bring the Tawana any lasting peace, because Tawana's son, Moremi, assassinated his father and took over the chieftainship.[10]

This unstable situation, partly the result of a general craving for new territory in Bechuanaland and partly owing to dynastic intrigues within the chiefdoms themselves, was greatly aggravated by the impact of nineteenth-century wars that are generically called the *mfecane*. Accounts of the destruction caused by the migrations of displaced tribes, such as the Kololo and other Sotho groups, were amply recorded by white missionaries and other travelers, though these reports tended to exaggerate the ravages of war. Nevertheless, all the principal Tswana chiefdoms went to war with the Kololo at one time or the other.[11] The Tswana were caught at a time when they were suffering from grave internal weaknesses. In about 1820, the Kwena Chief, Motswasele II, was assassinated following allegations of immoral conduct, and one of the arch conspirators, Morwakgomo, usurped the chieftaincy. Another contender, Segokotlo, was driven away by Morwakgomo and went to live with the Ngwato in the north at Seruli; he took with him the minor heir apparent, Sechele, and the heir's half-brother, Kgosidintsi—two figures who were destined to play prominent roles in Kwena politics for over half a century.[12]

When the Tlhaping were threatened in 1823 by the Kololo, their Chief, Mothibi, who had succeeded his father in 1812, did not hesitate to turn to Robert Moffat, the L.M.S. missionary at Kuruman, and the traveler George Thompson, for help. Both Moffat and Thompson persuaded the Griquas, who were mounted and armed with guns, to reinforce the Tlhaping, with the result that the Sotho groups were soundly defeated at Dithakong in June 1823.[13] Sebitwane's Kololo retreated into the Kgalagadi, regrouped, and attacked the Kwena, forcing them to flee from Dithubaruba. However, the Kololo did not remain long at Dithubaruba. In 1826, the Ngwaketse, whose Chief Makabe had been killed in an earlier fight with the Kololo, turned to two travelers, Andrew A. Bain and John B. Biddulph, for assistance, and the Kololo, whose memory of the battle of Dithakong was still green, were dislodged by the two whites merely firing blank cartridges in the air.[14] But the Ngwaketse under their new chief, Sebego, were subsequently driven by the Ndebele to Lehututu on the fringes of the Kgalagadi Desert. When shortage of food compelled the Ngwaketse to return to southern Bechuanaland in 1842, misfortune dogged their footsteps as they successively suffered military defeats at the hands of the Tlhaping and the Kwena. For some time, Sebego and his subjects had to be sheltered by the Kgatla, who in the 1820s were certainly a poor match for the then powerful Ngwaketse.[15]

Early Tswana Contacts

In northern Bechuanaland, the Ngwato, too, felt the impact of the *mfecane*. Kgosidintsi Motswasele, who, as has been seen above, had fled to the Ngwato for refuge after his father's assassination, gives an idea of how the Ngwato and some Kwena refugees bore the brunt of the *mfecane* between 1823 and 1830 when the Kololo took the offensive:

> and while there [with the Ngwato] a tribe of Basutos . . . came to disturb us. We then went across to the Makalakas [Kalanga] where the Matebele are today [1886]. The Basutos followed us, then we fled to another portion of the Makalaka's country. . . . Then Kgari made war on the Makalakas to try and take their corn, but our chief Khari was killed, and the tribe returned to [Ngwatoland]. . . . Sechele and myself then left the Bamangwato. We had a good number of Bakwena and were joined by the Bakaa. We settled in the present Bamangwato Hills. The Basutos again molested us. We left the hills with a large lot of cattle and came and settled at Lopepe.[16]

These disturbances during the first quarter of the nineteenth century considerably disrupted Tswana economic activities and severely undermined their political stability. Previously, the Tswana chiefdoms were in a position to trade among themselves in weapons and in manufactured ironware. Accounts of early white travelers show that Tswana communities obtained from them various commodities including beads, tobacco, mirrors, buttons, knives, brassware, and some food (especially bread and tea).[17] After 1840, there is evidence to show that Tswana chiefdoms concentrated on the acquisition of firearms and ammunition.[18]

II

The history of nineteenth-century Bechuanaland is linked with the agonizing adaptation of Tswana rulers to the changing circumstances that beset their chiefdoms. On whatever other topics they differed, early white visitors to

Bechuanaland were unanimous in their estimation of the power of the Tswana chief; he was a force to be reckoned with in his own territory. Those traders and missionaries who defied the chief's authority often paid heavily for their intransigence. Among the tribes themselves, a group whose chief could accommodate himself to, and cope with, the external pressures impinging upon tribal life, was saved. It could employ diplomatic skills to ward off external aggression, or blend the new ideas and institutions of aliens (more particularly whites) with its own traditional customs and laws. But a chief who did not adapt to the ever-changing social and political situations was a liability to his tribe, and invariably led to the unretrieved loss of political independence and to tribal fragmentation.

Traditionally, the Tswana chief was associated with various attributes that sustained tribal life as a whole. Accounts left by early travelers and missionaries suggest the chief's authority to have been divided into three main categories. The first category was his political role, which entailed convening meetings whenever the need for them arose and presiding over them in the chief's court (*kgotla*). The most important of these gatherings was the *pitso*, at which serious issues of the tribe were discussed; the others were the *phuthego*, which was held to discuss minor issues; and the *lechulo*, which decided issues pertaining to war.

Next to the chief's political role was his conduct of diplomatic and external affairs of the chiefdom. In that capacity, he was the commander-in-chief of the armed forces, declared war, sued for peace, and negotiated treaties and alliances. Only men were eligible to attend the *pitso*, *phuthego*, and *lechulo* meetings.

In the social and economic realms, the chief tried cases and redressed social injustices; he determined when his people should hunt, plow the fields, and eat the first fruits of the harvests; and his homestead was a hostel to strangers, whose persons were inviolate.

The chief was also the religious leader of the tribe, in which capacity he made rain or invited more veritable rain-makers to do so; he sanctioned initiation ceremonies, and he performed piacular rites. He intimately supervised the safe-keeping of hereditary charms that were used in anointing and sustaining chiefs.[19] The range of his responsibilities was wide, as is shown in the information given by the woman Thatalhone to the Rev. W. C. Willoughby in 1901:

> I have said that the chief is the centre of everything done in the Bechwana [Tswana] tribe. They called the chief their God. If the chief spoke to a person, he assented by saying, "Yes, my God." This is the assent of a mo [Tswana]. Their expression "my God" does not mean that the chief is really God, it means that he is their superior. . . . He is the one who can pray for them to God, because he is the first born.[20]

Although some early white observers portrayed the Tswana chief's powers as absolute, the weight of the evidence suggests that however great an influence he wielded over the tribe, there were mechanisms that restrained his power. The tribal councils (*pitso, lechulo,* and *phuthego*) were in many respects supreme over the chief, and they could overrule some of his proclamations, censure him, and even depose him. An indication of the power of the tribal council was given by George Thompson who attended a *lechulo* in 1823, at which the Tlhaping Chief Mothibi seemed to have an upper hand in haranguing soldiers in readiness for the impending Kololo attack. Yet not even the expediency of war could influence the chief to deprive the Tlhaping of their civic rights to discuss military strategy freely. Thus, Thompson reported Mothibi to have concluded his speech by saying: "I now wait to hear what is the general opinion. Let everyone speak his mind freely."[21] This aspect of Tswana democracy impressed the Rev. John Philip, the superintendent of L.M.S. stations in South Africa, who in a book published in 1828 observed: "The most remarkable feature in the *pitso* is the existence of two things hitherto deemed incompatible in many civilised countries, the exercise of arbitrary power in the head of the government, with a perfect freedom of debate." [22]

Yet another restraining influence on the chief were his mother and uncles. In "Kaga Mma Kgosi" ("concerning the mother of the chief"), Thatalhone observed: "She, also, has her own station. If a person has been beaten, or perhaps his cattle have been seized, if he takes refuge with the mother of the chief, he will be free even if he is in fault, and will not be molested." [23] It is certainly the strong voice of a mother that can sway a chief by charging him with "treating the people of so-and-so with levity," when "the chief may cease to hamper the people because of this word of his mother." [24]

Many of the London Missionary Society missionaries who arrived in Bechuanaland after the *mfecane* too readily concluded that Tswana institutions, including the chieftainship, were not deeply rooted. This was the result of misinterpreting the institution, or of being misinformed about it. More perceptive observers realized that such institutions had evolved over a long period of time.[25]

III

The Kwena, Ngwaketse, Ngwato, and Tawana received missionaries much later than their southern kinsmen the Tlhaping. The first L.M.S. agents to work among the Tlhaping, Rogers Edwards and John Kok, went to southern Bechuanaland in 1800. However, that mission was shortlived because Kok was killed by his African servants over a quarrel arising from wages; while Edwards, who seems to have paid little attention to evangelization owing to his activities in ivory trade, withdrew to the Cape shortly after Kok's death.[26] A second attempt to send a mission to the Tlhaping was sanctioned by Chief Mothibi Molehabangwe in 1813, hardly a year after he succeeded his father. This followed a persuasive discussion the chief had with a visiting L.M.S. delegation led by the Rev. John Campbell. Initially, the Campbell delegation had been informed that the Tlhaping concerned themselves more with farming than with an alien religion. A little more effort on the part of the visitors persuaded Mothibi to allow missionaries to come and work in his chiefdom.[27]

However, when Evans and Roger Hamilton tried to take up Mothibi's offer early in 1815, Mothibi turned them away because he was then more interested in trade than in Christianity.[28] A year later, the chief was receptive to the idea of missionaries, and James Read was allowed to settle at Lattakoo (i.e., Kuruman or Dithakong).[29] His early reports to his Society are full of praise for the hospitality extended to him by that Tswana community. But the task of spreading the Christian gospel appears to have encountered many hurdles from the beginning. For example, an interpreter who was overwhelmed by one of Read's first sermons seems to have caused adverse effects on the Tlhaping congregation, for Read reported that they "knew not what to make of [that] proceeding, and particularly as they considered it disgraceful for a grown person to weep." [30]

A special feature of Tswana intercourse with whites in the nineteenth century is the lack of consistency in the responses of Tswana chiefs and their subjects to missionary endeavors; this trait was fostered largely by the diverse personalities of rulers and their subjects and the influence of traditional religion.[31] Mothibi typified this genre of Tswana response to the advent of whites, as, for example, in 1821, when he threatened to expel Hamilton and Moffat from Kuruman for allegedly stopping rain from falling.[32] Yet hardly five months after this incident, Moffat reported that Mothibi had become a pleasant neighbor.[33]

The first few years at Lattakoo were far from being a

success story. In 1821, the Rev. Robert Hamilton reported that preaching to the Tlhaping was tantamount to addressing stones.[34] However, in 1833, the Rev. Bailie of Kuruman reported that five women were baptized in 1832.[35] While his report did not say to which tribe those converts belonged, a joint report for the Kuruman district submitted by Hamilton, Moffat, and Edwards in the same year showed that there were no Tlhaping converts.

> It is also worthy of remark that of all the members and candidates there are strictly speaking no [Tlhaping] among them, their being composed of the following interior tribes: Kwena, Bashoota, Barolong, Batau, Bagathla, and some Batlaru who were formerly in Mothibi's jurisdiction. The gospel was first sent to the Batlap [ing] and to the palace of the king but Mothibi and his tribe are now in a hopeless condition and far removed from the means of grace . . . and failing after repeated attempts to drive us from them, they have abandoned us themselves, and appear to be given over to a [life] of hardened impenitence.[36]

Melville (the Cape Government agent at Griquatown), an external observer of missionary work at Kuruman and other stations in South Africa, remarked that missionary reports to their societies were not always factual; he wished they could "confine themselves in their publications to a simple relation of facts," adding: "I am sorry to say this is not the case with many periodical publications—the attention of the world has been excited at the expense of truth and while people in England were rejoicing at what they supposed to be a great work going on in South Africa, we have been here mourning over desolation and the triumph of enemies." [37] In spite of Melville's pessimism, some missionary accounts indicate that some material gains were made; for instance, in agriculture an irrigation scheme was started at Kuruman, which seems to have benefited Tswana

Early Tswana Contacts

residents there. In 1826, Andrew Geddes Bain reported that Moffat and his colleagues had raised the waters of the Kuruman River for irrigation purposes, but observed that very few Tlhaping residents were taking advantage of the irrigation project.[38] However, in 1834, his report was laudatory, pointing out that "improvements at Kuruman since my last visit are truly astonishing! . . . What pleased me much, both here and [at] Mateto [Motito], was to see large fields of yellow wheat belonging to the natives vieing with the crops of the missionaries, having been well cultivated and irrigated."[39] Nevertheless, the impact of missionaries upon the Tlhaping as a whole up to 1843 was slight.

IV

In due course, L.M.S. missionaries established stations in central and northern Tswana chiefdoms. David Livingstone, who arrived in South Africa in 1841, was one of the architects of the L.M.S. expansion. From 1841 to 1843 he used Kuruman as a base while he visited Tswana communities to the north of that station. In 1844, he went to work among the Kgatla-Kga Mmanaana at Mabotsa, his residence lasting until 1845, at which time he moved on to the Kwena at Chonwane. His decision to leave the Kgatla was resented by the chief and commoners alike, in spite of the Kgatla disagreement with him in secular as well as in religious matters. That the Kgatla alleged Livingstone was abandoning them ("Loa re latla"),[40] even when evangelist David Molehani remained at Mabotsa, is largely due to a sense of security the presence of a white missionary engendered. The precedent that Moffat had set by aiding the Tlhaping during the Kololo war in 1823 and Andrew Bain's decisive aid to the Ngwaketse in 1826 had created a myth that white men's assistance was indispensable to victory;[41] the Kgatla, therefore, thought Livingstone's departure would deprive them of an effective deterrent and a regular source of firearms.

Unlike some missionaries who preferred to stay at one place in spite of meager gains, Livingstone believed that the missionary should, after a short stay at one station, move on to more distant fields of labor in order to reach the maximum number of non-Christians.[42] His expansionist policy was enunciated when he informed L.M.S. directors of his reasons for leaving the Kgatla: "To me those who never heard the gospel are greater objects of compassion than those who have heard it for . . . years and rejected it." [43]

The Kwena, among whom Livingstone worked, had earlier divided into two groups—one under Sechele and the other under Bubi.[44] Before he settled among Sechele's people, Livingstone visited the two groups on several occasions, thereby preparing the ground for his mission. During one visit to Bubi's town, Livingstone was pleased to see the chief working on an irrigation project on which he had earlier persuaded Bubi to cooperate in its construction. In one letter he said: "For this purpose, we have been obliged to raise a huge dam of earth and stones and dig a canal," a project in which the Kwena "were quite delighted with the idea that [he] could make rain." He hoped the irrigation project would discredit traditional rainmakers and enhance Christianity.[45]

But success seems to have eluded Livingstone on the crucial issue of conversion. In one report, he observed that part of the congregation readily laughed when Pomore, an L.M.S. evangelist, was preaching.[46] However, a year later, the prospects for his mission greatly improved when Sechele I's defeat at the hands of the Ndebele characteristically compelled the Kwena chief to be more receptive to Christianity.[47]

However, in deciding to welcome Livingstone, Sechele seems to have been influenced more by military considerations and less by religious motives: Sechele, like his neighbor Moseileli, wanted Livingstone to act as a deterrent against outside attacks. However, to Livingstone, who had not yet had a convert, Sechele's overture inspired optimism. If Sechele succeeded in concealing his motives from Livingstone, the chief was unable to convince his subjects about the utility of the white man's religion. Nor did Sechele succeed in persuading Kgosidintsi (his brother) to accept his newly found pragmatism. Nevertheless, Kgosidintsi assisted Sechele in ruling the Kwena.[48]

Once Sechele had decided to become a Christian, his enthusiasm to learn and to assist Livingstone was considerable. He is reported to have acquired a perfect knowledge of the Tswana alphabet in two days. However, Sechele had difficulty in learning to speak English, the handicap probably stemming from his age.[49] In 1847, Livingstone noted that Sechele was a very reasonable man, was a fluent reader in the vernacular, and was fond of his Testament; his wives, too, were giving a good account of themselves as some of the missionary's best students. Livingstone had another reason for liking Sechele: the chief was absorbing European habits of hygiene, being resourceful enough to look for local substitutes whenever he ran out of soap.[50] In an attempt to show his sincerity as a catechist, Sechele sometimes used his authority as chief to compel some of his subjects to conform to a Christian standard of behavior. In this regard, Sechele probably went far beyond what Livingstone expected, because in one instance the chief condemned a man to death whom he suspected of dabbling in witchcraft. Livingstone reported: "We of course had a great deal of conversation on the subject . . . he asked me, if an individual acted justly, fairly avoided fighting, and treated both his own people and strangers kindly, killed witches, and prayed to God, would be saved." [51] Livingstone does not seem to have reprimanded Sechele for giving credence to witchcraft.

Sechele's misfortune in all his early relations with missionaries was his inability to persuade the Kwena to move with him; this was a major handicap in a chiefdom in which the chief was supposed to be a religious leader. The Kwena were slowly becoming disenchanted with their ruler. They opposed Livingstone's recommendation to move the town from Chonwane to Kolobeng in 1847. Sechele, however, sided with Livingstone and ordered the removal to the new site.[52] Some members of the Kwena community did not approve of what appeared to be Sechele's unreserved acceptance of the new order. When a member of the Tlharo ruling clan visited Kolobeng, he questioned Sechele's wisdom in building a school in his town, and predicted that the Kwena would desert Sechele to lead their traditional life in the visitor's own town; Sechele retorted by equating the Tlharo guest with Judas Iscariot.[53]

Among the Kgatla, little progress was being made. During one visit, Livingstone was told how unimpressed the people were with Christianity, it merely going "in at one ear and out at the other"; the Kgatla could retain only those lessons bearing on their mode of existence, that is, cattle-keeping and hunting.[54]

V

At the core of relationships between the Tswana and the missionaries was the persistence of some traditional customs and laws, in spite of a chief's interest in Christianity, his conversion to the new religion, and even his renunciation of such old practices. Rainmaking, so vital to pastoral and agricultural pursuits in the semidesert conditions of Bechuanaland, was one of the most contentious issues. Livingstone's report to the L.M.S. early in 1847 that rainmaking was on the wane, certainly overstated the position.[55] Although Sechele had once expelled a rainmaker from his town, a more popular one came at a time when the Kwena badly needed rain and he promised them some relief. This was the Bididi chief. In a letter to his father-in-law, Livingstone reported, with a typical note of the bias against Tswana rainmakers: "The sly rogue" to have said rain was "in the chief's mouth, that he had only to give them leave to dig up a child which died [the previous] year. He opposed this for some time, but the people became very clamorous and he allowed them, but still no rain. They then had a meeting . . . Sechele made a noble confession of his determination to depend on God alone. The people gave a shout of hu or hoo, in derision . . . which might be heard a mile off." [56] The report reveals another factor militating against conversion to Christianity: the missionaries' belief that the Tswana Supreme Being was a lesser God, inelegantly embodied in the tribal and family spirits (Badimo), unlike the "real" Christian God. This led missionaries to begin their Scripture lessons from the premise that the Tswana did not have a religion, when in fact they had elaborate elements of religion. L.M.S. attitudes to non-Christian religions seem to have been shared by other missionaries over the centuries.[57]

Nevertheless, after Sechele conceded to the *lechulo* party,[58] the Bididi chief was unable to make rain anyway. Nor did that shake the Kwena belief in rainmaking. The confrontation with the Bididi (rainmaker) chief mirrored a conflict that was to recur throughout the nineteenth century. However, while Kgosidintsi consistently promoted rainmaking ceremonies and other traditional ceremonies, Sechele equivocated, sometimes taking part in these ceremonies and at other times condemning them. Another factor in the Bididi rainmaker encounter was the support commanded by the *lechulo* party. Livingstone's account to Moffat noted that the rainmaker's intransigence was succored by the support he mustered from the Kwena. After this disturbing event, Sechele is reported to have thought of going to England to study the Bible in peace.[59] The weight of custom, especially that relating to rainmaking, was reinforced by

Sechele's reminiscences later in life. He confided to Livingstone that giving up his rainmaking role was the most difficult decision he had had to make.[60]

In the middle of 1848, Sechele applied for baptism. Livingstone put him on probation to satisfy himself that the chief was a worthy candidate. Moshweshwe, the famous Sotho chief, learned of Sechele's decision to become a Christian from some Kwena merchants who had been sent to him to buy horses, arms, and ammunition. Moshweshwe advised against baptism. As a gesture of goodwill, he sent his distant kinsman ten herd of cattle, two horses, and some guns, gratis. He promised Sechele an unlimited supply of guns and ammunition if he refrained from baptism. According to Livingstone, the Sotho chief said:

> Tell him to allow his people to believe if they like, but he [Sechele] must never believe. "I am a King," said Moshweshwe, "and I won't put myself under the authority of another. . . . I have my kingdom as well as He, and people would laugh at me if I believed and put myself under the power of another. Tell Sechele that."[61]

Moshweshwe's advice went unheeded.

Kwena opposition to their chief's impending baptism was steadily mounting. On 7 August 1848, Livingstone's journal shows that there was so much commotion in Kolobeng that the chief was compelled to convene a *pitso* the following day. At the meeting, speaker after speaker condemned Sechele's decision, to no avail.[62]

When, in October 1848, Sechele was baptized, Kwena reaction was unfavorable, and even hostile. Some men openly wept, a thing they seldom did, even at a funeral. The fact that a rumor had been circulating to the effect that candidates for baptism drank men's brains aggravated a bad situation.[63] Some Kwena resented the fact that the chief had had to divorce four of his innocent wives to conform to Christian precepts of monogamy. Political considerations might have prompted the neighboring Kgatla chief, Moseileli, to propose marriage to one of Sechele's former wives.[64] When the proposal was rejected, the chief directed his vengeance at the doddering church in his territory, and summarily imposed an injunction against church attendance.

A few months after Sechele's baptism, Mokgokong, one of Sechele's former wives, became pregnant and the chief accepted responsibility. Livingstone immediately disciplined Sechele, the suspension lasting until 1889, when he was reinstated.[65]

The Kwena groups remained divided until 1845 when Bubi died and shortly afterwards a large section of his followers joined Sechele. The L.M.S. mission to Bechuanaland had started expanding in the early 1840s and by 1859 a station had been set up at Inyati among the Ndebele, while an attempt to start one among the Kololo in 1859 failed.[66] Among northern Tswana chiefdoms, the Ngwaketse had a Kuruman evangelist sent to them in 1848; while the Ngwato in the north and Tawana in the lake region had flying visits from Livingstone in the 1850s. In all cases, military strategy seems to have been the primary motive for these people's wanting missionaries. It was certainly for his military potential that Livingstone was warmly received by Chief Sekgoma I in Ngwato country in 1842. On that occasion, Sekgoma must have veiled his real intentions for persuading Livingstone to stay at Shoshong for a month, for it is difficult to believe that Sekgoma's reason, as he himself put it, was to enable him to watch Livingstone's figure for a whole month.[67] When he bypassed Sekgoma on another occasion, the chief's mother sent a message pleading with Livingstone to visit Shoshong again.[68] Livingstone's popularity among the Ngwato was enhanced when he cured Sekgoma of an ulcer in 1851.[69]

The Tawana in northwest Ngamiland region were visited by Livingstone in August 1849, but they were preoccupied with military matters, so that his preaching to them was of little consequence.[70] There, as among other principal Tswana tribes, tradition and custom seem to have been well entrenched. For example, according to a layman's observation of Tawana institutions, the rainmaker there possessed, at least in a religious sense, "an influence over the minds of the people superior even to that of their king." [71] The Ngwato, too, had an influential rainmaker.[72]

Livingstone's residence among the Kwena ended in 1851. The evangelist he left in charge of the station there, Paul Mebalwe, made little headway in the wake of another recurring theme in nineteenth-century Tswana history: the conflict between church and state. Apparently, Livingstone's departure rendered Sechele's suspension from the church ineffectual. The chief asserted his right to lead the Kwena church and did so with a measure of intellectual discipline and some flamboyance. The Ngwaketse-based evangelist, Sebobi, noticed certain flaws in the chief's conduct and recommended that he be stripped of his privilege to preach. According to Moffat, Sebobi was reported to have said, in effect, that "there was a strange and unholy mixture in a chief sanctioning wicked, heathenish customs among his people with impunity (*boomu*) and then standing up with the Holy word in his hand and preaching repentance, faith, and holiness." Sebobi enunciated a separation of church and state theory in which he pointed out that, just as it was unbecoming "for the Christian teacher to interfere with the politics of the Chief, neither was it right for a chief to assume the teacher's office." [73] On that occasion some comment from Moffat, who was then present, did not move Sechele. He asserted his right to preach on the grounds that he had studied the Bible exhaustively. Above all, if the Griqua chief, Andries Waterboer, could preach, Sechele deduced his right to preach as being logically tenable.

The quarrel between Sebobi and Sechele worsened when the evangelist equated Sechele's participation in ivory trade with sin. Sechele rejected such a theological inference and resolved "to do what he liked." [74] Sechele's wife is reported to have supported her husband but Sechele's family soon felt the weight of Tswana custom when the chief's daughters defied him and participated in initiation ceremonies (*bojale*). However, his son, Sebele, obeyed Sechele's command and stayed away from the *bogwera* (boy's circumcision) ceremonies. On that occasion, Moffat happened to be at Sechele's residence. When he asked Ope, one of Sechele's daughters, what she preferred, she emphatically chose initiation, and characterized her father's strictures as being oppressive ("Ra oa'mpathika").[75] Ope's defiance indicates the extent to which the majority of Sechele's subjects preferred traditional institutions to alien practices. To them, the new order was a gamble; to conform to its demands was to accept a way of life whose utility was questionable.

A more eloquent plea for an understanding of Tswana customs was advanced by a Kwena rainmaker in an exchange of views with Livingstone. When Livingstone advised the rainmaker to abandon rainmaking, he argued, inter alia, that his practice was religiously sound, its utility dating back to times immemorial. After Livingstone had put to the rainmaker: "But God has told us that there is only one way by which we can pray to him acceptably . . . by Jesus Christ," the rainmaker retorted:

> Truly, and he has told us differently. God has been very good to both white and black. To the white he has given the knowledge of guns, gunpowder, horses, and many other things which we know nothing about. He has given you wisdom, too. We see it. To us blacks, he has not been so liberal, but he has given us the knowledge of some things, too, and the most important is that of certain trees and plants which we use to make rain. We have the knowledge of rainmaking, you have it not. Now we don't despise those things God has given you, though we are ignorant of them. Nor should you despise what he has given us, though you don't know nor understand them.[76]

The rainmaker's caution underscores a point, namely, a sympathetic understanding of Tswana institutions, which eluded the attention of some L.M.S. missionaries to Bechuanaland,[77] an omission that tended to minimize the effectiveness of their mission.

VI

The social and economic history of northern Tswana chiefdoms was profoundly influenced by traders and hunters, especially during the last half of the nineteenth century. To Livingstone and to some L.M.S. missionaries, trade and evangelical work coexisted and were indispensable to African assimilation of Western civilization. In Livingstone's estimation, the promotion of trade and commerce was to be encouraged, since it "more speedily than anything else, demolishes that sense of isolation which heathenism engenders." He postulated that legitimate trade (in contradistinction to the slave trade) would make "the tribes feel themselves mutually dependent on and mutually beneficial to, each other." [78]

This preliminary examination of the missionary impact on Tswana chiefdoms up to 1850 has revealed small achievement. Although there was a marked decline in warlike activities among the African groups, sheer exhaustion from the wars of the *mfecane* probably militated against aggressive warfare. The missionary role in this development of relative calm was minimal,[79] and was often offset by increased conflicts between the Tswana and the Boers. In these conflicts, the missionary played a more definite part because Boers believed, however mistaken such a view might have been, that missionaries armed and encouraged Tswana chiefs to attack them.[80] In any case, Boers on the Highveld could readily expel from their territory any L.M.S. agents they thought to be accessory belligerents in their armed conflicts

Early Tswana Contacts

with the Tswana. A case in point was the expulsion of Rogers Edwards and Walter Inglis from Hurutsheland in 1852.[81]

Sechele's response to Christianity contains within itself a microcosm of the problems connected with the chief-missionary relations in nineteenth-century Bechuanaland. Contemporary accounts of Sechele differ in their characterization of him. Robert Moffat depicted him as being an enigmatic ruler.[82] An L.M.S. delegation to Southern Africa (1849) was impressed to find that the Kwena chief was a monogamist, worshipped with his family regularly, and wore European clothes; Freeman, like most white visitors to Kwenaland, assessed Sechele to be very intelligent.[83] In retrospect, Livingstone thought Sechele was initially well motivated when he chose Christianity. Although he suspended Sechele, Livingstone did not then think that the chief's relationship with his former wife (Mokgokong) was too serious a breach of the faith.[84] A recent work by a latter-day missionary has gone a long way to identify the conflict between custom and an intrusive culture; but the assertion that the Kwena chief's dilemma was due to a "double-souled heart" has no foundation in metaphysics nor indeed in the philosophy of religion.[85]

Thus, in terms of future contacts between the Tswana and whites, the year 1860 was in many respects a fateful one for northern Tswana chiefdoms, because the survivors of the L.M.S. mission to Barotseland returned to the Cape that year. They told stories of malaria-infested territories in and beyond the Zambezi Valleys and about tsetse flies whose bites were fatal to livestock and debilitating to humans, while the myth of unfriendly Africans (Kololo) persisted unchecked and contributed to create an impression that the trans-Zambezi region was an area to be avoided for many years to come.[86] In comparison, northern Tswana chiefdoms appeared to be fertile grounds for the planting of Christianity and with it white communities. At the same time, white traders were discovering the Tswana region to be a lucrative trading zone in ivory and other products. To the white men, the two factors clearely interacted to make northern Tswana chiefdoms attractive to both white missionaries and traders.

NOTES TO CHAPTER ONE

1. Robert Moffat, *Missionary Labours and Scenes in Southern Africa* (New York: 1850), p. 150; J. A. I. Agar-Hamilton, *The Road to the North: South Africa, 1852–1886* (London: 1937).
2. The four principal tribes with which this study concerns itself are the Kwena, Ngwaketse, Ngwato, and the Tawana; all have a common origin. For the traditional history of Tswana tribes and their customs, see Isaac Schapera, *The Tswana* (London: 1952); *The Ethnic Composition of Tswana Tribes* (L.S.E. Monographs on Social Anthropology, no. 11, London, 1952); *A Handbook of Tswana Law and Custom* (London: 1938; reprinted 1955, 1970); Anthony Sillery, *The Bechuanaland Protectorate* (Cape Town: 1952), pp. 104–94; J. Tom Brown, *Among the Bantu Nomads, a Record of Forty years Spent among the Bechuana* (London: 1926), passim; George Stow, *The Native Races of South Africa*, ed. G. M. Theal (London: 1905), pp. 404–59; John Mackenzie, *Austral Africa, Losing It or Ruling It*, 2 vols. (London, 1887) I, chapters 1, 2, and 3; Isaac Schapera, ed., *Ditirafalo tsa Merafe ya Batswana ba Lefatshe la Tshireletso* (Alice, South Africa: 1940).
3. Petrus Borchedus Borcherds, *An Autobiographical Memoir* (Cape Town: 1861), p. 84; Robert Moffat, *Missionary Labours*, p. 150. Tswana weapons of war (*see* George Thompson, *Travels and Adventures in Southern Africa* [London: 1827], p. 99) consisted of bows and arrows, assegais, battle axes, and shields made of skins.
4. *See*, for example, the Tlhaping response to a gun-trap that killed a wolf that had terrorized them: "Great was the astonishment of these people to find that such destruction was effected without the presence of any human being. Such was their abhorrence of the animal that each visitor administered it a stroke with a stick or a trap. . . ." (Borcherds, p. 83). *See also*, Henry Lichtenstein, *Travels in Southern Africa in the Years 1803, 1804, 1805, and 1806*, 2 vols. trans. Anne Plumptre (London: 1815); 2: 399, 400, who reported that Molehabangwe "wanted to see some specimens of our dexterity in shooting. Accordingly, a mark being set up, some of our marksmen . . . took their aim in his presence, and hit it very happily. He expressed very great astonishment, but begged that the ex-

periment might not be renewed, as the noise of the gun was very disagreeable to him."

5. Lichtenstein, 2: 368.
6. Ibid., p. 379; however, the major split between the Rolong and the Tlhaping must have occurred before 1800: *see* John Campbell, *Journal of Travels in South Africa; Among the Hottentots and Other Tribes in 1812, 1813, and 1814*, 2 vols. (London: 1815), 1: 258, 283–284; W. C. Willoughby, "Notes on the Totemism of the Becwana," *J.R.A.I.* 35 (1905): 303, in which he observed that the Tlhaping were an offshoot of the Rolong.
7. Lichtenstein, *Travels in Africa*, 1: 400.
8. Ibid., p. 416. *See also*, Borcherds, p. 204; George Thompson, pp. 106–107, in which he recorded Tlhaping preparations for war: ". . . the warriors sprung up to re-commence the war dance, in which the whole multitude occasionally joined, the women frequently snatching the weapons from the men, and brandishing them in the air, and people of all ages displaying the most extravagant and frantic gesticulations for a space of nearly two hours. Towards the conclusion, a messenger from the King delivered to each [headman] a sprig of the camelthorn tree, which conveyed an intimation that a private meeting of the warriors would be held next day in the mountains, in order to discuss some topics not fit to be made public in the presence of women and children and the lower class."
9. Campbell, p. 204.
10. Anthony Sillery, *The Bechuanaland Protectorate* (Cape Town: 1952), pp. 117–44; Schapera, *Ethnic Composition*, pp. 8–27; Oral Traditions recorded in No. 9 Folder 796, W. C. Willoughby Papers, Selly Oak Colleges Library, Birmingham, England.
11. In South African historiography, the forays of the Kololo have been erroneously associated with the so-called Mantatees. For accounts that identify more accurately the different ethnic groups involved in the *mfecane*, see Thornley Smith, ed., *Memoir of the Rev. Thomas Laidman Hodgson, Wesleyan Missionary in South Africa* (London: 1854), p. 70, where the "mantatees" are identified as the Tlokwa; D. F. Ellenberger, *History of the Basuto, Ancient and Modern*, trans. J. C. Macgregor (London: 1912); Marion How, "An Alibi for Mantatisi," *African Studies* 13, no. 2 (1955): 65–90; E. W. Smith, *Great Lion of Bechuanaland: The Life and Times of Roger Price* (London: 1957), pp. 367–410; W. F. Lye, "The Difaqane: the Mfecane in Southern Sotho Area, 1822–24," *The Journal of African History* 8, no. 1 (1967): 124–26.
12. E. W. Smith, p. 379, passim; Willoughby, Folder 737, Selly Oak Colleges, who observed: "I saw Mma-Kgama today (9 September 1915) . . . she said that Motswasele knew that his life was in danger, and had sent messengers to Sebitwane to come and avenge him after his death; and that he warned the Bakwena that Sebitwane would avenge his death . . . Sebitwane was then still in the South, but was coming North." While it is possible that Motswasele might have known about his impending death, it is very unlikely that Sebitwane could have undertaken

the costly wars just to avenge the death of a remote Kwena kinsman of his.

13. Robert Moffat, *Apprenticeship at Kuruman, 1820–1828*, ed. Isaac Schapera (London: 1951) pp. 73–77; Samuel Broadbent, *A Narrative of the First Introduction of Christianity amongst the Barolong Tribes of the Bechuanas, South Africa* (London: 1865, pp. 96–115; E. W. Smith, *Great Lion of Bechuanaland*, pp. 371–372; George Thompson, *Travels and Adventures in Southern Africa* (London: 1827) p. 90; J. D. Omer-Cooper, *The Zulu Aftermath* (London: 1966), pp. 93–99.

14. A. G. Bain, *Journals of Andrew Geddes Bain: Traveler, Explorer, Soldier, Road Engineer, Geologist*, ed. Margaret H. Lister, Van Riebeeck Society, no. 30 (Cape Town: 1949), pp. 51–70. E. W. Smith, *Great Lion of Bechuanaland*, p. 382. When the two hunters wavered at first, Sebego appealed to them on humanitarian grounds: "That cannot be, you have accepted of and given presents to us and we look upon you as our friends. If you are then what you pretend to be, you will join us against the common enemy of mankind." (*See* ibid., p. 53.)

15. *See* David Livingstone to Mr. and Mrs. N. Livingstone, 26 September 1842, in *Family Letters 1841–1856*, 2 vols., ed. Isaac Schapera (London: 1959), 1: 64–65; E. W. Smith, *Great Lion of Bechuanaland*, p. 384; Isaac Schapera, "A Short History of the Bangwaketse," *African Studies* 1 (1942): 9–10.

16. Parliamentary Papers, 1887, C. 4890, 59: 12; E. W. Smith, p. 386; John Mackenzie, *Ten Years North of the Orange River* (Edinburgh: 1871), p. 358; Sillery, *Bechuanaland Protectorate*, p. 118. The Tawana were attacked (c. 1827), and the young heir, Lecholathebe, was taken prisoner and grew up among Sebitwane's Kololo; he was subsequently released. *See* Lekoma's "History of the Mambukushu People," in Public Record Office, London, C.O. 879/79, African (South) Confidential, no. 717, p. 17, Milner to Chamberlain, 2 of 15 December 1902.

17. Borcherds recorded (*see* Borcherds, *Memoir*, pp. 77, 78) the Tlhaping response to the white visitors' wares as being that of "wonder and astonishment"; he also reported Chief Molehabangwe to have asked them to shave him with a razor blade and "when about half the face was cleared, he begged that his eyebrows might be also shaved."

18. However, in 1812, the Tlhaping Chief, Mothibi, obtained a gun from a white man. *See* William Burchell, *Travels in the Interior of South Africa*, 2 vols., ed. I. Schapera (London: 1824), 2: 287.

19. Willoughby Papers, Folder 798, Selly Oak Colleges.

20. Willoughby, Folder 798. The range of duties is confirmed by Isaac Schapera, *A Handbook of Tswana Law and Custom*, p. 62: "[the chief is] the symbol of tribal unity, the central figure round whom the tribal life revolves. He is at once ruler, judge, maker, and guardian of the law, repository of wealth, dispenser of gifts, leader in war, priest, and magician of the people."

21. Thompson, *Travels and Adventures*, p. 101.

22. John Philip, *Researches in South Africa*, 2 vols. (London: 1828), 1: 131. *See also* Lichtenstein, *Travels*, 1: 416; T. Smith, *Memoir of*

Hodgson, p. 62; R. Moffat, *Missionary Labours*, p. 171: the chief's power is ". . . controlled by the minor chiefs, who in their . . . pitshos, their parliament . . . use the greatest plainness of speech in exposing what they consider culpable or lax in his government."

23. "Kaga Mma Kgosi," Willoughby Papers, Folder 798.

24. Ibid. *See also* Rev. Edwin Lloyd to R. Wardlaw Thompson, 23 December 1903 (L.M.S.), where Chief Bathoen's banishment of evangelist Mothowagae was reported to have been vetoed by his mother "according to a very old native custom."

25. For a missionary who underestimated the depth of Tswana custom, J. D. Hepburn was typical (*see* Hepburn to Whitehouse, 7 June 1880, Box 40, Jacket C, Folder 3, L.M.S.): "We do not fight a system hoary with age and carrying its meaning down the stream of antiquity in elaborate and complicated symbolic imagery, or embodied and compacted in history . . . striking deep roots and reaching far . . . the South African knows nothing of it, to him it is but of yesterday. . . ." Cf. C. J. Andersson, "A Journey to Lake Ngami and an Itinerary of the Principal Routes Leading to It from the West Coast, with the Latitudes of Some of the Chief Stations," *The South African Commercial Advertiser and Cape Town Mail*, 22 May 1854, where he says of the Tawana chief: "Letcholathebe possesses great influence and power over his people, but I am inclined to think it arises more . . . from the force of custom, than from real regard for his person," an observation that was more perceptive than Hepburn's.

26. Robert Moffat, who claimed to have failed to persuade Edwards to come back to the L.M.S., observed (*see* R. Moffat, *Missionary Labours*, p. 151): ". . . their residences were several miles from the town of [Chief Molehabangwe]. They visited the colony and Cape Town when they had realized a sufficient quantity of ivory and cattle to be disposed of to advantage. . . . Edwards retired to the colony, purchased a farm and slaves. . . ."

27. Campbell, *Travels in South Africa*, 1: 209.

28. R. Moffat, *Missionary Labours*, p. 159, in which he observed that the headmen also opposed the L.M.S. mission.

29. The three names are used interchangeably and they refer to the same place. The 1815 mission was turned down, on the grounds that "it would be with us as with the people of Griqua Town, 'who,' they said once wore a 'Karos[s]' [garment made of skins], but now wear clothes; once had two wives, but now only one," in John Mackenzie, *Ten Years*, p. 68; *Journal of the Rev. James Read, 1816*, Incoming Letters, the London Missionary Society Archives, hereafter called L.M.S.

30. James Read, in *Quarterly Chronicle of the Transactions of the L.M.S. (1815–1820)*, January 2, 1817, L.M.S., p. 307.

31. I. Schapera, *Tribal Innovators, Tswana Chiefs and Social Change, 1795–1940* (London: 1970), pp. 119–23.

32. R. Moffat, *Apprenticeship at Kuruman*, p. 12.

33. Ibid., p. 17.

52   A HISTORY OF NORTHERN BOTSWANA

34. Robert Hamilton to Foreign Secretary, George Burder, 12 February 1821, Box 8, Jacket A, Folder 3 (L.M.S.).
35. J. Baillie to Burder, 3 January 1833, Box 13, Jacket E, Folder 4 (L.M.S.).
36. Hamilton, Moffat, Edwards, in "Progress Report," 30 September 1833, Box 13, Jacket E, Folder 4 (L.M.S.). By 1836, Lattakoo had 111 converts (46 men and 65 women), as reported by Robert Moffat to William Ellis, 23 November 1836, in "Schedule for Returns to be Made Annually by Missionaries in South Africa." The substantial increase in new members was probably due to more effort on the part of missionaries. However, the Tlhaping continued to be outnumbered, for out of 60 candidates for baptism in 1837 (Moffat to Ellis, 15 June 1837), more than half were Tlharo.
37. Extract of letter from John Melville, Cape Colony Government surveyor and agent at Griquatown, to a friend in London, 24 July 1821, Box 8, Jacket C, Folder 3 (L.M.S.). For Melville's appointment to the Griquatown, *see* R. Moffat, *Apprenticeships*, p. 62.
38. Bain, p. 12.
39. Ibid., pp. 153–154.
40. David Livingstone, *Family Letters, 1841–56*, 2 vols., ed. Isaac Schapera (London: 1959), 1: 142.
41. *See* Andrew Steedman, *Wanderings and Adventures in the Interior of Southern Africa*, 2 vols. (London: 1835), 1: 34, in which he observed that the Ndebele Chief Mzilikazi envied the Tlhaping for having missionaries.
42. A view that was criticized by his colleagues. *See*, for example, Walter Inglis, *Memoirs and Remains of the Rev. Walter Inglis, African Missionary and Canadian Pastor*, ed. William Cochrane (Toronto: 1887), pp. 206–23.
43. David Livingstone, *Livingstone's Missionary Correspondence, 1841–56*, ed. by I. Schapera (London: 1961), p. 150.
44. Ibid., p. 15, n. 3, 36 N. 1, 90; *Family Letters*, 1: 138.
45. Livingstone to Agnes Livingstone, 4 April 1842, *Family Letters*, 1: 53; Livingstone to Mrs. Sewell, 7 April 1842, MS 656, National Library of Scotland, Edinburgh.
46. Livingstone, *Family Letters* 1: 55.
47. Ibid., p. 69.
48. *See*, for example, James Chapman, *Travels in the Interior of South Africa*, 2 vols. (London: 1868), 1: 137: when Chapman arrived at Kolobeng in 1852, "Sechele the . . . chief, was absent. His brother [Kgosidintsi] . . . acted for him . . ."; C.O. 879/30, African (South), Confidential, no. 369, p. 12, Shippard to High Commissioner, 7 August 1888, enclosed in Robinson to Knutsford, 29 August 1888.
49. Livingstone, *Missionary Correspondence*, p. 152; Livingstone to Robert Moffat, 5 September 1845, *Family Letters*, 1: 143; cf. Mothibi's progress in reading, in Robert Moffat to Ellis, 23 November 1836, Box 15, Jacket D, Folder 2 (L.M.S.); early Sarwa response to education, in John Campbell, *Life of Kaboo, a Wild Bushman by Himself* (London:

1830), p. 32: "Many of us held down our ears to the book, to listen if we could hear it speak; but we heard nothing; no, not a whisper; on which we shook our heads at him, concluding he was telling us a fib."

50. Livingstone to Charles Livingstone, 16 March 1847, *Family Letters*, 1: 191.
51. Livingstone to Robert Moffat, 12 May 1845, ibid., p. 118.
52. Livingstone to R. Moffat, 13 August 1847, ibid., p. 203.
53. Ibid., p. 220.
54. Ibid., p. 228. *See also* J. J. Freeman, *A Tour of South Africa* (London: 1851), p. 276, who observed that Tswana communities wondered that "so much pains are taken to make them understand what they do not value, and to appreciate what they do not understand."
55. Livingstone to Tidman, 17 March 1847, in *Missionary Correspondence*, pp. 102–103. For rainmakers and Tswana belief in them *see* R. Moffat, *Apprenticeship at Kuruman*, pp. 12, 23–25, 39, 41, 65.
56. Livingstone to Moffat, November 1847, *Family Letters*, 1: 231.
57. Cf. Jessie G. Lutz, ed., *Christian Missions in China: Evangelists of What?* (Lexington, Mass.: D. C. Heath and Co., 1965); J. Mutero Chirenje, "Portuguese Priests and Soldiers in Zimbabwe, 1560–1572: the Interplay between Evangelism and Trade," *The International Journal of African Historical Studies* 6, no. 1 (1973): 36–48.
58. The use of "bantu balehuku" ("people of the book") for the Christian segment of Tswana communities, and "bantu balechulo" ("people of the hunt") for the non-Christian sector seems to have been fairly widespread; but *lechulo* in this context must have been associated with the hunt that precedes rainmaking ceremonies and not in the context of a "war council" (its second meaning), for Christians attended the latter together with non-Christians. For references on the use of the two epithets, *see* Mackenzie to Tidman, 27 June 1862, Box 32, Jacket A, Folder 5 (L.M.S.); Emil Holub, *Seven Years in South Africa: Travels, Researches, and Hunting Adventures between the Diamond Fields and the Zambezi, 1872–1879*, 2 vols., trans. Ellen E. Frewer (London: 1881) 1: 339; Frederick S. Arnot, *From Natal to the Upper Zambezi, Extracts from Letters and Diaries of F. S. Arnot* (Glasgow: 1883), p. 22: Christians ". . . are called . . . the people of the Word of God."
59. Livingstone, *Family Letters*, 1: 232.
60. David Livingstone, *Missionary Travels and Researches in South Africa* (London: 1857), p. 20.
61. Livingstone to Robert Moffat, November 1848, *Family Letters*, 1: 260, in which Sechele also is reported to have confided in Livingstone that "ki le Ka nyato, gone ga a itsa se ose buan, Ka a re Morimo Ki Khosi Ka ena" (I treated his message with disdain, because he did not know what he was saying, for he said, "God is a Chief like himself").
62. David Livingstone, *Private Journals*, ed. I. Schapera (London: 1960), pp. 298–300.
63. Livingstone, *Family Letters*, 1: 260–61, Livingstone to Robert Moffat, November 1848.
64. Ibid., p. 256, Livingstone to Moffat, 2 September 1848.

65. Livingstone, *Private Journals*, p. 304. The story of Sechele's reinstatement is in Howard Williams's *Annual Report for Molepolole*, 1889, Box 4 (L.M.S.).
66. B.N.A., MSS 1, *Holloway Helmore Journal;* E. W. Smith, pp. 411–25; Livingstone, *Travels*, p. 45; Ellenberger in Willoughby Papers, Folder 796, Selly Oak Colleges.
67. L.M.S. *Chronicle* (March 1843), p. 37.
68. Livingstone, *Travels*, p. 57.
69. Livingstone, *Private Journals*, p. 194.
70. Livingstone, *Travels*, p. 68.
71. Charles J. Andersson, *Lake Ngami, or Exploration and Discoveries in the Wilds of South Western Africa* (London: 1856), p. 458.
72. James Chapman, *Travels in the Interior of South Africa*, 2 vols. (London: 1868), 1: 42–43.
73. Robert Moffat, *The Matebele Journals of Robert Moffat, 1829–1860*, 2 vols., ed. J. P. R. Wallis (London: 1945), 1: 156.
74. Ibid., p. 158.
75. Ibid., p. 173.
76. Livingstone, *Private Journals*, p. 240. See also Livingstone, *Travels*, pp. 25–27.
77. Notable exceptions are Robert Moffat's son, John Smith Moffat, Albert Jennings, and Alfred Wookey.
78. Livingstone, *Travels*, p. 28; Moffat and Livingstone actually encouraged hunters to come to Bechuanaland for big-game hunting; see Gordon Cumming, *The Lion Hunter of South Africa* (London: 1904), pp. 181, 187, 250.
79. Traders and hunters of long standing seem to have been equally capable of forestalling Tswana punitive actions against their neighbors, as, for example, in 1852, when Chapman (*Travels in the Interior*, 1: 105–106) successfully persuaded the Ngwato not to attack the Boers.
80. See, for example, J. du Plessis, *A History of Christian Missions in South Africa* (Edinburgh: 1911), pp. 443–46; see also I. Schapera, "Livingstone and the Boers," *African Affairs* 59, no. 235 (1960): 144–56.
81. Walter Inglis, "Correspondence of Commandant P. E. Scholtz and Missionaries Edwards and Inglis," *Memoirs of Walter Inglis*, pp. 76–83.
82. See, for example, Robert Moffat, *The Matebele Journals of Robert Moffat, 1829–1860*, 2 vols., ed. J. P. R. Wallis (London: 1945) 2: 20, 25.
83. J. J. Freeman, *A Tour*, p. 281.
84. Livingstone to J. S. Moffat, 29 November 1860, in J. P. R. Wallis, ed., *The Matebele Mission: A Selection from the Correspondence of John and Emily Moffat, David Livingstone, and Others, 1858–1878* (London: 1945), pp. 121–22.
85. E. W. Smith, *Great Lion of Bechuanaland*, pp. 149–73. For more views on Sechele's character, see accounts by Roger Price and Howard Williams in *L.M.S. Chronicle* (February 1893), pp. 39–40.
86. See account in "No. 9 Ngami, Notes made by J. Ellenberger at Tsau, Ngamiland, in 1906," Willoughby Papers, Folder 796, Selly Oak Colleges; B.N.A., MSS 1, Helmore: *Letter and Journal*.

2
Tswana Intercourse with Traders; German Missionaries Come to Bechuanaland, 1850-1860

THE DECADE THAT INTERVENED BEFORE THE L.M.S. AGAIN SENT a resident missionary to the Kwena after the departure of Livingstone, and also for the first time established permanent stations at capital towns in the north and northwest of the Tswana region, was marked by increased intercourse with white traders (and some Griqua traders). For brief periods toward the end of the 1850s and early 1860s, the Ngwato and the Kwena had German missionaries. Tswana contact with traders was gradually transforming their essentially subsistence economies into ones that were structured to meet external demands. Karosses (i.e., skin garments), ivory, and other products from Bechuanaland found their way to European markets,[1] via Cape traders and merchants, and Livingstone conjectured even a Chinese destination for some of their goods.[2]

I

Before this time the Tswana had relied upon a mixed agricultural and pastoral economy, and environmental conditions determined what staple crops were grown in the various chiefdoms. Most of Bechuanaland, especially the arid western regions, suffered from periodic droughts, and supplies of wild fruits and roots and small game, such as rodents, were limited.[3] In the more fertile eastern and northwestern parts of the country, the Tswana and their neighbors grew sorghum, millet, yams, melons, pumpkins, and tobacco,[4] in spite of the unpredictable rainfall; this work was largely performed by the women. Boys and young men, or members of the subordinate groups, herded the cattle, sheep, and goats,[5] the numbers of which determined the wealth of the chiefdoms. The Tswana manufactured domestic utensils, ornaments, agricultural implements, and fighting and hunting weapons from iron and copper ores. A traveler to Bechuanaland in 1844 observed:

> The Ba [Kgatla] work a great deal in iron, manufacturing various articles, with which they supply the neighboring tribes, and obtaining this ore from the surrounding mountains. This is smelted in crucibles, and a great deal of metal is wasted, only the best and purest being preserved.[6]

There is further evidence for domestic trade in ironware and other commodities,[7] though the extent to which this enterprise stimulated the economy in the various chiefdoms is subject to varying and even conflicting assessments.[8] There was sufficient diversity in the Tswana economy to enable a small class of specialists and entrepreneurs to form corporate groups within the main body of society.[9]

A vital item in the diet of the Tswana was meat, derived mainly from game rather than domestic stock. Thus, hunting was an important part of Tswana life. The economic necessity of cattle herding and hunting were sanctified by religious rites and ceremonies, especially during initiation, when their mastery was stressed. Status was measured by success or failure in hunting. In 1854 James Chapman noted:

> According to an old custom of the Bechuanas [Tswana], after the ceremony of circumcision, they go out at times in a body and scour the country for this purpose, and it is considered a disgrace to return from such an expedition without having dipped the point of their spears in the blood of a victim of some sort. Failing this, they are held up to public scorn and execration in the songs and dances at the *Khotla*. All the opprobrious epithets that woman can muster are unmercifully heaped upon the heads of the unsuccessful candidates for manhood and glory, as well as upon those who begot them.[10]

Large-scale hunting expeditions, made up of members of age-set regiments, were sent out by the chiefs, but a steady flow of meat and hides (a source of revenue) to the chiefdoms were ensured by the system of serfdom and taxation (*lekhetho*). An agent of the chief was placed among the subject peoples or serfs, and collected dues or tribute from them. One form of tribute, *sehuba*, was described by an informant in "Melao ea Kgosi" ("Rights of the Chief"):

> The breast of game is the chief's portion; and if killed far away, it must be taken, at least in [theory], to the chief or his nearest representative. But the nearest representative to the chief and the hunter will probably eat it together. If the hunter is out of reach, he will sometimes compound for it by taking a whole animal to the chief from nearer home.[11]

Part of the tribute was retained by the tax collector, while the chief received about half of it. The chief used this meat to feed his subjects when they attended tribal meetings or court trials; he also fed them in times of famine, provided hospitality for strangers, and armed the chiefdom with proceeds from its sale or barter. Their system of taxation was, in theory at least, regulated according to a man's economic situation.[12]

This social and economic milieu was significantly affected by the advent of European (including some Tswana and Griqua) hunters and traders, with their more aggressive and competitive practices, and their more technologically advanced arms and ammunition.[13] The trickle of white travelers to Bechuanaland increased in volume after 1850. Hunting trips extended further into Bechuanaland, ivory and ostrich feathers being the special lure into the interior.

Traditionally, ivory does not seem to have constituted a prominent part of the Tswana economy, though a few ornaments were carved from it.[14] As late as 1849 the Tswana were found piling rotting ivory;[15] and elephant tusks had always been used for making cattle byres.[16] Each Tswana tribe had hunting preserves within its own territory, but boundary lines were tenuous, often causing intertribal conflicts.

If game was plentiful in the beginning of the century, accounts left by hunters in the 1850s suggest that the supply was becoming scarce—an understandable consequence of an economic system that consumed ever-larger numbers of game without taking adequate measures for its preservation. The relative calm following *mfecane* encouraged population increase and dispersal,[17] which inevitably led to a heavier consumption of game meat. By the middle of the century, each chiefdom was obliged to dispatch regimental hunting expeditions, in many cases in convoys of wagons, deep into the northern lake region. The growing scarcity of game led to competition, which was often undeclared. This struggle for a limited economic resource became more acute when white ivory hunters entered the area in earnest. In the new circumstances, it is understandable that the routes used by each chiefdom became closely kept secrets, known to the chief and his hunting regiments alone. Hence the Ngwato Chief, Sekgoma, was reputed to have been

> acquainted with a route which he kept carefully to himself because the Lake country abounded in ivory, and he drew large quantities thence periodically at but small cost to himself.[18]

It was against this background that white hunters and traders intensified their search for ivory and ostrich feathers. Their encroachment upon the Tswana economy in the form of ivory hunting had the effect of enhancing the value of ivory and of enticing big-game hunting. But in the trade relationships that developed between white traders and Tswana chiefs and their subjects, white traders had more obstacles to overcome than their Tswana counterparts. The oxen they used to pull wagons were ill suited to travel and to survive the long distances in semidesert conditions.[19] Horses—even salted ones—had an equally high mortality rate. The authorities of the Cape Colony and of the Boer Republics attempted to control the movements of the traders into the interior because of the arms and ammunition they took with them. Clashes between whites and Africans across the frontiers of the various polities were frequent, and the white governments feared that firearms might be used against them by their African neighbors.

As a corollary to this fear—real or imagined—the Free State and Transvaal Boers considered the land between the Limpopo and Zambezi Rivers to be their own territory ("Onze Veld"),[20] and tried to regulate all travel to Bechuanaland and beyond. They were particularly sensitive to British subjects passing through their newly established republics. The Boers feared that British hunters and traders were the precursors of British annexation, as they had been in Natal before 1843. Thus, like the Tswana rulers, the Boers veiled the long-distance routes into the interior in secrecy.

In 1850 Boers on the Highveld were incensed by the activities of a British trader, Joseph McCabe. McCabe must have been naively ignorant of Boer feelings when, before he undertook another trip to Lake Ngami in 1850, he published in a Cape newspaper the account of his journey to Ngamiland in 1849 together with a map showing the route he had used. McCabe was subsequently arrested, tried by a Potchefstroom Landrost, and fined five-hundred rix-dollars (about £112) for

> having made known to the British government and its subjects the road through the "Emegrante Grengebiet," which they say they wished to keep secret as long as possible.[21]

When news of McCabe's imprisonment reached the Cape, the *Grahamstown Journal* condemned the action of the South African Confederacy ("Maatschappy") and appealed to the British Government to

> remove this obstruction and convince the refractory parties that though distant they [were] not beyond the reach of that control which every civilized state is required to exercise over its own subjects.[22]

It is tempting to correlate this Boer assertion of sovereignty with British diplomatic moves after the McCabe incident. In June 1850, Sir Harry Smith, Governor at the Cape, sent a letter to an English hunter, W. C. Oswell, then in the Lake Ngami region, conferring on him some diplomatic responsibility. Oswell was asked to explain to the chiefs that the British government rejected all acts of aggression over land, and was committed to a policy of establishing friendly relations with Tswana chiefdoms at the lake.[23]

Still another impediment on the activities of hunters and traders was that, although the Tswana chiefs resented the Boer restrictions, they themselves regulated the hunters and traders who operated in their chiefdoms. Even when traders had laboriously negotiated their passage by presenting "gifts" or tolls to Tswana rulers, there were still obstacles put in their way by the Sarwa and the Kgalagadi.[24] Traders who used the alternative Walvish Bay route found local reticence to guide them equally obstructive. A trader who used that route found that the Tawana were reluctant to guide him.[25] When Andersson visited the chief in his court, Lecholathebe gave him directions only after

> opportunely placing in his hand a double-barrelled pistol, which I had previously been informed he coveted excessively, and which I begged him to accept as a memento of my visit . . . [when] his visage soon beamed with delight and satisfaction, and we became excellent friends.[26]

Tswana-Boer relations, which since the 1840s had maintained a delicate balance of petty land disputes and cattle stealing, worsened when the Transvaal Boers attacked the Kwena capital, Dimawe, in August 1852. The actual *casus belli* is difficult to establish.[27] However, the attack is important because it resulted in a display of Tswana unity that had been weakened by the catastrophes of the early nineteenth century. In the wake of the Boer invasion the mercurial Sechele deployed Kwena envoys to all principal Tswana chiefs, urging them to avenge his losses by killing all Boers on sight. He coupled his diplomatic moves with an attempt to petition the British crown for protection, but his delegation to England abandoned the journey in Cape Town, when he ran short of money. Sechele's appeal to Tswana chiefs caught Boer hunters unawares. One of them,

Jan Van Viljoen, himself a field cornet in the Transvaal, found the situation tense at Shoshong, where Sekgoma threatened to kill him. The Ngwaketse and the Tawana do not seem to have responded to Sechele's call. Viljoen's life was spared in spite of the chief's verbal assault. His long and intimate connections with the Ngwato probably militated against summary execution. Other extenuating circumstances were James Chapman's admonition against such a reprisal, and Sekgoma's calculation that Viljoen would serve him better by warning his fellow Transvaalers against further aggression.[28] Nor was that the end of hostilities between the Boers and the Kwena. The Boers again attacked and killed three Kwena merchants in the Transvaal, whereupon the Kwena retaliated by killing three Boers they found hunting on the Kwena-Transvaal border in 1853.[29]

In 1854 two Kwena members of the ruling family gave Moffat their account of the state of race relations on the frontiers, an assessment that must have reflected Tswana sentiment on that issue. Sechele began the interview by complaining bitterly against the restrictions placed on the supply of gunpowder. He was reinforced by Kgosidintsi, who gave

> a statement of facts about the native tribes, the Boers, and the English, and deduced from these most logically that the Boers and the English were one, on one side, and the natives on the other, and asked most emphatically to whom they were to look, for the power and means of defense were with them only; that it was true what had been said, that if Sechele allowed traders and hunters to come, they the Bakwena, stood a chance to get some ammunition, but if they were entirely prohibited they would get none at all.[30]

Thus even the arch-traditionalist Kgosidintsi, who eschewed the white man's religion, was willing to associate with whites for purposes of trade.

II

If Kgosidintsi overstated the tenuous bonds of the Anglo-Boer *modus vivendi* on the South African frontier, his statement was perceptive on one important point: the Tswana perennial quest for firearms. Because of their newly discovered significance, it is difficult to exaggerate the role of firearms in business transactions in nineteenth-century Tswana history. Initially the gun had been received with reservations;[31] but once its effectiveness was demonstrated, Tswana demand for firearms was insatiable. Although firearms did not wholly revolutionize their military system, by the 1840s they became important in warfare; target shooting became an essential requirement of Tswana regiments. In 1844 Cumming noted Ngwato progress in marksmanship:

> Since I first visited Bamangwato [1843], and taught the natives the use of firearms, they have learnt to kill the elephant themselves; but previous to my arrival they were utterly incapable [*sic*] of subduing a full-grown elephant, even by the united exertion of the whole tribe.[32]

In Ngamiland the Tawana and their neighbors were in possession of firearms by 1850.[33]

The amount of ivory, feathers, and karosses that left Bechuanaland between 1850 and 1860—some bought from the Tswana and some of it hunted by traders themselves—must have been considerable. Those traders who have left written accounts give an indication of the brisk traffic between Tswana chiefdoms and Cape Colony. In 1852 James Chapman, who estimated the Ngwato to number 12–15,000, counted 100 wagons at Shoshong belonging to Griqua and Tswana traders;[34] their destination was Matebeleland. During his visits to northern Tswana chiefdoms between 1843 and 1847, Gordon Cumming bartered for ivory, ostrich feathers, and karosses, with beads, brass, copper wire, knives, hatchets, clothing, guns, ammunition, young cows, and she-goats.[35] From 1850 to 1854 Andersson, a Scandinavian adventurer, presented Chief Lecholathebe of the Tawana with "gifts" of beads, knives, tobacco, snuff, steel chains, rings, blue calico, red woolen caps, and trinkets of various kinds.[36] The Tawana chief is also reported to have purchased horses from passing traders.[37] In 1857 William Baldwin, who estimated the Kwena to number 20,000, thought that chiefdom had "no end of guns." [38] A year later Baldwin noted that Lecholathebe had an ample supply of guns and ammunition, while a traveler to the same area in 1861 put the Tawana chief's number of muskets at 500.[39]

The demand for ivory led to the destruction of game in huge proportions. A sample of the hunters of the 1850s gives an idea of the number of game that was killed. Baldwin's diary entry for the 16th of October, 1859, shows that he purchased 5,000 pounds of ivory during a single trip. He was informed by Jan Van Viljoen and Pit Jacobs, both residents of the Transvaal, that during their trip to Ngamiland they had killed ninety-three elephants.[40] However, the phenomenal gains in percentages of capital outlay computed by hunters and traders are distorted because they do not show the traders' expenditure in time, labor, and the wear and tear of their wagons and hunting equipment.[41]

In retrospect, it appears that the actual process of bargaining that went on between the Tswana and white traders was to prove a valuable diplomatic weapon after the 1880s, when the scramble for Africa entangled the Tswana chiefdoms. In this connection all written accounts of white traders depict the Tswana as developing or displaying shrewd business expertise. An early visitor to Ngwato country observed:

> They never conclude a bargain in a hurry, and always deem it necessary to ask the advice of nearly every one present before they can make up their minds; and should any one individual disapprove, barter is for the time at

an end. ... I have more than once been prevented from effecting a sale, which I had all but concluded, by some old wife, who happened to be passing at the moment, exclaiming that I was too high in my prices.[42]

An Ngamiland experience shows Baldwin to have had more than an inkling of Tswana business acumen.[43] In all cases of hard bargaining, the consultations carried out by chiefs before they purchased goods were a reflection of Tswana customary law, as free speech and consensus were the hallmarks of Tswana council (*pitso* and *phuthego*) proceedings.

However, attempts made by Tswana rulers to introduce monopoly practices failed due to the vastness of Bechuanaland. The Rev. John Mackenzie shows small-scale trade to have been carried out even at a chief's capital town:

While the chief or headman takes you in hand, and gets what he can as a "present," or for guides, his men are busy with your servants, doing the same thing on a smaller scale.[44]

While the era of big-game hunting lasted, the Kgalagadi and Sarwa enjoyed marginal gains. Although only a few of them conducted a clandestine trade with white hunters, large bands normally feasted on carcasses left by hunters. Baldwin observed:

There is no waste in the quantity of meat we have killed, as the poor Masa[rwa] light great fires by each animal, and cut and dry the last morsel. A whole batch of them moved their quarters to the three rhinoceros I shot.[45]

III

The Tswana were displaying their newly acquired goods as early as the 1830s and 1840s, and in some cases adjustments were made so that they could make full use of the new products. A traveler to Kwenaland found an innovation that was inspired by the advent of firearms, for Sechele is reported to have built a stone wall round the city

> with loopholes at intervals through which to fire upon the advancing enemy with muskets.[46]

Other Tswana communities do not seem to have emulated the Kwena contrivance. But luxury goods—some locally manufactured, some bartered—were widely used. In 1858 Baldwin commented upon the use of ornaments among the Tawana:

> their legs, arms, necks, and waists are ornamented with beads of every variety, and ivory, brass, and copper bracelets.[47]

In Ngwaketse country Chief Gaseitsiwe was reported by Emily Moffat to have developed a fondness for coffee and tea, adding

> the men are generally clothed with trousers and a Kaross. The women are but partially attired. Their beads are really pretty, and some of them are tastily [tastefully] arranged.[48]

Kwena neighbors, the Kgatla, seem to have made a colorful blending of the old and new modes of dressing, the Christian members of that community displaying their clothes on Sundays.[49]

The penal system of the Kwena had at least one innovation as a result of their chief's abortive trip to England. When he returned from Cape Town, Sechele adopted a mode of punishment he had found in vogue at the Cape, that is, making prisoners work on public roads.[50]

Another social practice that was being significantly affected by too frequent intercourse with traders was Tswana hospitality. Whereas hospitality to strangers had always been a traditional virtue, the changing socioeconomic circumstances partially vitiated that attribute. In Ngamiland a trader reported:

> What ever civility he [Lecholathebe] might have shewn to [infrequent] strangers in former years, he is now anything but hospitable. During my whole stay at the Lake, I never received as much as a handful of corn, or a cup of milk from him. On the contrary he was in the habit of begging for food from me. The arrival of several wagons at the Lake at the same time puts him in the highest glee, when he never fails to make his rounds, for contributions of bread from one, sugar from another, coffee from a third, meat from a fourth, and so on.[51]

After Livingstone's departure from the Kwena in 1851 and before the L.M.S. could send resident-missionaries to the Tswana in the 1860s, the traditional religion of the chiefdoms remained essentially unaffected except for a few Kwena Christian converts (or "inquirers") under the uncoordinated patronage of evangelist Mebálwe (i.e., Paul Molehani) and Chief Sechele; Sebobi was plodding on among the Ngwaketse.[52] Mebalwe's attempt to evangelize the Tawana was no more successful than Livingstone's in 1849. When he preached there in 1850, a layman reported:

> The service had not proceeded far, before they all burst out laughing; the chief amongst the rest endeavouring to ridicule the preacher for the strange doctrines, to them, that were being enunciated, terming it all nonsense.[53]

Among the Kwena, Christian morale is reported to have lapsed markedly after the Boer attack in 1852, and when Kgosidintsi was mauled by a lion, a witch was held responsible for the attack and executed. Only the desperate plea of evangelst Mebalwe saved the deceased man's wife and child, whose lives Kwena justice demanded.[54]

Not that Sechele relinquished his quest for an understanding of the Bible. But in this pursuit his studies deepened his doubts about the moral rightness of the injunction against polygamy. On a Sunday in 1854 he

> gave Mr. Moffat a text, and asked him to preach upon it, as his people, to whom he had been reading, were puzzled to know why the missionaries had made him discard all but one of his wives, while Solomon and David had so many wives and concubines, and were still "men after God's own heart." [55]

Moffat refused to take up the challenge and, according to Chapman, who was present, gave an unsatisfactory explanation. The Ngwato chief, Sekgoma, seemed fearful of the implications of having a resident missionary at Shoshong. Although he persistently invited L.M.S. missionaries to come and stay at Shoshong, the marriage issue troubled Sekgoma all the time because he had six wives. Chapman reported Sekgoma to have said:

> I should like to have a missionary, and to become a Christian, if I could be allowed to keep my wives. I don't want any more. I have transgressed, and nothing can ever undo that which has once been done; but I cannot turn my wives and children out. All men's hearts will be against me; I shall be alone on the earth. To have my wives disgraced, and my legitimate children branded with a false and ignominious name, would bring overwhelming ruin and trouble without end upon me.[56]

Whatever quarrels Sechele might have had with the L.M.S. on religious affairs, it was his good fortune that white visitors to Bechuanaland were impressed with his display of European influences. J. Leyland thought that Sechele was a very intelligent chief, and that he lived a truly Christian life.[57] And when Sechele was returning from a hunting trip to Matebeleland, he followed such a rigid

Christian routine that the hunter, Baldwin, was frankly incredulous.[58]

The presence of hunters and traders in northern Tswana chiefdoms had economic as well as social consequences. Their activities did not always conform to the accepted mores of Tswana society. Their ignorance of these mores led to the violation of taboos. Thus, when Chapman brought a dead crocodile into a Ngwato village in 1853, it caused resentment and some commotion because the animal was venerated there.[59] And traders' sexual relations with Tswana women brought all whites into disrepute. The non-Christian elements among the Tswana always blamed the presence of whites for rain failure and any other misfortune that beset the tribe; and the traders' relations with Tswana women without undertaking marriage obligations provided non-Christians with ready ammunition to retort to missionary sermons:

> Look at your brother, white man; your preaching must be all nonsense; they [traders] take our native women up into the country as wives and are not married to them.[60]

IV

Sechele's early contacts with a variety of traders, Boers, and missionaries placed him in a better position than his northern kinsmen; Gaseitsiwe was equally at a disadvantage because his chiefdom did not lie on the main long-distance routes to the interior. Sechele had, therefore, a much more accurate perception of the South African political scene than the other three principal chiefs. It was the calculations of a shrewd statesman that persuaded Sechele to call upon the head of the South African Republic to play a part in the affairs of his chiefdom. This was made in 1857, when Sechele invited President Pretorius to find missionaries who could reside among the Kwena.[61] This overture is crucial for an understanding of nineteenth-century Tswana history: it was made scarcely four years after the Kwena had suffered a decisive defeat in 1852 and subsequently lost three Kwena merchants at the hands of Boers in 1853. In spite of his oft-repeated dislike (and even hatred) of the Boers,[62] why did Sechele invite his archenemy to have a say in an issue that touched the social and political life of the Kwena so deeply?

During the first half of the nineteenth century, one external group after another had attacked or interfered with the Tswana communities: the Kololo, the Ndebele, the Boers, white hunters, and traders. Viewed against this background, Sechele's diplomacy was a move to forestall future Boer aggression, no doubt arguing that the Republics would be less likely to attack a community to whom they had supplied missionaries of their own choice.[63]

Pretorius first requested Moravian missionaries to answer Sechele's appeal, but when they failed to do so, he turned to the Hermannsburg Society, a German missionary society that had been operating in Natal since 1854. The Society sent the Rev. Heinrich Schroeder to the Kwena in July 1857. A year later he was joined by Ferdinand Zimmerman and Heinrich C. Schulenburg. The latter moved to Shoshong in 1859.[64]

The German missionaries found themselves dealing with a chief who had resolved to use any white men he could to the maximum advantage of the Kwena and not to regard them as personal friends; Sechele nevertheless allowed the Germans to proselytize as a prize for the protection they afforded him. And Sechele had a wealth of experience in dealing with whites. Like any visitors coming to the Kwena for the first time, the German missionaries did not realize the complex character they were dealing with.

When Robert Moffat stopped at Dithubaruba on his way to Matebeleland in August 1857, Sechele implied that the

Germans, whom he thought to be Boers, had come to his chiefdom without his knowledge and that he did not know what they were doing. To some visitors he acknowledged their presence, but implied they were not an important factor in the religious life of the Kwena, for he judged them to be no wiser than himself. Sechele asserted that he was even wiser than the L.M.S. missionaries who had taught him to read and write; he maintained that his knowledge of Scripture was as good as that of any missionary. When Moffat announced his intention to remove Mebalwe because of the presence of German missionaries, Sechele said he would expel the Germans instead. Before he left Dithubaruba, Moffat had another brush with Sechele, when the latter prepared to preach to the youth in his town in spite of the suspension imposed on him.[65]

By 1858 the Rev. Schroeder was aware of some of the facets of Sechele's character, as is shown in Moffat's observation:

> Mr. Schroeder has had his troubles with Sechele. He said to me yesterday that, had they known all that they now know, they would certainly never have come.[66]

Sechele must have commended himself to the Germans sometime after Moffat's departure, because a year later (1859), when Sechele dabbled in Ngwato politics and successfully conspired to oust Chief Macheng from office, Schroeder defended him as "not only faultless but an honorable man."[67]

After Sechele had obtained German missionaries and, by that token, warded off Boer aggression, he seems to have been desirous to maintain good relations with Mzilikazi, who no doubt had surprised him by releasing Macheng. Sechele is reported to have visited Mzilikazi in Matebeleland in 1858 and was handsomely rewarded;[68] Sechele visited Matebeleland again in 1859 and achieved both diplomatic and religious success. Not only were Kwena-Ndebele relations amicable for some time, but Sechele even impressed Mzilikazi with his sermons. On that count he scored better than the L.M.S. mission later that year, which Mzilikazi placed on a year's probation before he allowed the missionaries to preach to the Ndebele.[69]

V

Between 1857 and 1865 Hermannsburgers founded, among other stations, Liteyana, Shoshong, and Dinokana (1858) in Hurutseland.[71] In trying to evangelize the Tswana, German missionaries found a situation similar to that found by James Read among the Tlhaping in 1816. Just as Read had found Chief Mothibi Molehabangwe to be reticent about conversion to Christianity, so did the Rev. Jensen find the Hurutshe Chief, Moilwe, equally impregnable. Among the Ngwato, Sekgoma refused to become a Christian even though he had invited Schulenburg. Sechele, true to his pragmatism, was more diplomatic, for he accepted the new faith superficially. On the whole, Tswana Chiefs were reluctant to become Christians. By 1865 German missionaries had realized the Tswana chiefs' resistance to Christianity. In one report Superintendent Behrens complained that a Tswana chief exerted little effort to learn Christian gospels.[71]

German missionaries paid more attention to teaching Scripture and less to formal education, believing as they did that evangelization was their most important duty. This aspect of mission work had something in common with the L.M.S. Thus, by 1865, Behrens could report that some Tswana children were

> able to read quite well and know the Bible and catechism from the beginning up to the end by heart.[72]

However, when the Hermannsburgers withdrew their missions from northern Tswana chiefdoms and settled in the Boer Republics, they started a few elementary schools there. Rev. Jensen started a school at Dinokana in 1865 where the ageing, bespectacled Chief Moilwe had changed his previous stand against Christianity and now was one of the pupils; he was assisted by Moremi, himself a Hurutshe. Although the Chief cooperated with missionaries in their work, his eldest son was reported to be hostile to missionaries.[73]

By 1861 Dinokana had twenty-three converts,[74] while Shoshong had twenty;[75] Bethanie had 115 converts (1864), while Matlare had seven converts by 1865.[76] During the Hermannsburgers' short stay in Kwenaland, Sechele showed his characteristic traits: in 1857 he built two huts for the Germans and was paid for that labor in gunpowder; and when the missionaries gave him a watch as a present, Sechele accepted it but returned it shortly afterwards, demanding that he be given some money instead.[77]

Meanwhile the Lutheran missionaries quarreled with their directors in Natal. Although it is difficult to establish the real cause of friction between the Tswana-based missionaries and their Natal headquarters owing to the partisan accounts given by both sides, superintendent Hardeland's account seems to be the more plausible. Hardeland dismissed them on the grounds that they were spending more time on trading than on mission work, a view that is supported by Robert Moffat.[78] On the other hand, Zimmerman and Schulenburg alleged that their Society had assumed "dictatorial methods," but do not cite instances to substantiate their allegation.[79] Whatever reason there was for the breach between the Society and its missionaries, there is no doubt that by December 1860, Hardeland had dismissed all Lutherans in Tswana chiefdoms from the Hermannsburg Missionary Society.[80] The dismissal of the Lutherans was certainly a boon to L.M.S. agents, who regarded the Germans as interfering in their sphere of missionary influence.

They could now consolidate their position without the nagging problem of dealing with a religious body whose creed challenged Congregational hegemony.

NOTES TO CHAPTER TWO

1. *See*, for example, E. Mohr, *To the Victoria Falls of the Zambezi* (London: 1876), p. 139: "I have seen specimens of them (karosses) at a furriers 'Unter den Linden' in Berlin." Mohr visited Bechuanaland in 1869.

2. The kaross was made by sewing skins of animals together, and according to Livingstone's estimates, 20–30,000 skins were made into karosses between 1840 and 1852. For destination of Tswana products, see David Livingstone, *Missionary Travels and Researches in South Africa* (London: 1857), p. 50; Henry Methuen, *Life in the Wilderness; or Wanderings in Southern Africa* (London: 1846), p. 146, who suggested that the Tswana traded with the Portuguese in Mozambique. See also Robert Moffat, *Matebele Journals*, 1: 18.

3. For wild fruit and rodents that could be had in the more arid regions of Bechuanaland, see Livingstone, *Missionary Travels*, pp. 48–50; Joseph McCabe, "The Great Lake Ngami," in William C. Holden, ed., *History of the Colony of Natal, South Africa* (London: 1855), p. 432.

4. Livingstone, *Travels*, p. 20: "they select with great judgment the varieties of soil best suited to different kinds of grain"; J. J. Freeman, *A Tour in South Africa* (London: 1851), p. 20; McCabe, "The Great Lake Ngami," Holden, ed., pp. 418–21.

5. Freeman, *A Tour*, p. 270; Livingstone, *Travels*, p. 20; R. G. Cumming, *The Lion Hunter of South Africa* (London: 1904), p. 7. Livingstone observed: "They are remarkably accurate in their knowledge of cattle, sheep, and goats, knowing exactly the kind of pasturage suited to each," in *Travels*, p. 22. Cattle were used for ritual purposes: the purification of warriors (*Go alafsha dintee*) and their dung was used in the reconciliation of estranged villages, when the headmen dipped their hands in the cow dung and chanted, "Re chwarang Ka moshwang" ("Our hands have met in the cow dung"). (*See* W. C. Willoughby, *J.R.A.I.*, 35 (1905): 305.)

6. Cumming, p. 187. See also Thornley Smith, *South Africa Delineated, or Sketches, Historical and Descriptive of its Tribes and Missions, and of the British Colonies of the Cape and Port Natal* (London: 1850), p. 184; Mohr, *To the Victoria Falls*, p. 266; Solomon Plaatje, *Mhudi* (Lovedale: 1930), p. 1; Livingstone to James MacLehose, 8 December 1841, MS 656, National Library of Scotland.

7. Livingstone, *Missionary Travels*, p. 50.
8. For example, I. Schapera, *The Tswana* (London: 1952), p. 29, restricts it to the village: a man with surplus "inquired among his neighbors until he found a customer"; Livingstone, *Missionary Travels*, p. 48, observed: "The [Kwena] sent trading parties every year to the Lake Ngami."
9. *See*, for example, John MacKenzie, "Bechuanaland and the Land of Ophir," (paper read to the British Association at Bath, September 1888).
10. James Chapman, *Travels in the Interior of South Africa*, 2 vols. (London: 1868), 1: 264; John Mackenzie, *Ten Years North of the Orange River* (Edinburgh: 1871), p. 377. For Tswana reluctance to dispense with their cattle, see Howard Williams, "Report of the Kanye Mission for Year ending December 31st, 1908" (L.M.S.): "His cattle are like Government stock which no holder will sell for the purpose of living on the capital unless he is forced to do so." *See also* D. Livingstone, *Private Journals, 1851–1853*, ed. I. Schapera (London: 1960), pp. 154–55: "The great object of the [*bogwera*] is to bind the bands so together that they must fight [and hunt] or be killed by their companions. If anyone fails in his duty he is insulted by his companions. . . ." Solomon Plaatje, *Mhudi* (Lovedale, South Africa: 1930), p. 1.
11. Willoughby Papers, Folder 798, Selly Oak Colleges. *See also* W. J. Burchell, *Travels in the Interior of South Africa*, 2 vols. (London: 1822, 1824), p. 216; I. Schapera, *Tribal Legislation among the Tswana of the Bechuanaland Protectorate* (London: L.S.E. Monographs on Social Anthropology, no. 9, 1943), p. 28.
12. Willoughby Papers, Folder 798: ". . . But he who has nothing that he can give is let alone, and has no fault. And the tax-gatherer takes half of these to the chief; and the chief takes half of them and gives the tax-gatherer the other half. And the chief takes weapons and dogs and gives them to a Mosarwa or Mokgalagadi who comes having killed something, some little profit out of the gains. And those people of ours [Tswana] who pay dues, something is due to them; they are given dogs, weapons, axes, tobacco that they may be contented. The saying is, they will become attached to their masters and bring them gain," observed Willoughby's informant.
13. There are references to Griqua and Tswana traders in missionary and travelers' accounts: in Wallis, ed., *Matebele Mission*, (pp. 132, 149), J. S. Moffat shows that Frederick, a Griqua trader, delivered mail between Kuruman and Inyati in 1861; that in the same year Merupe's Tswana party of three traders was detained by Mzilikazi for three months. Roger Price and John Mackenzie (in a letter to Tidman, 17 December 1862, Box 32, Jacket B, Folder 5) mentioned one Griqua trader, Sebehwe, whom they said traded regularly across the Zambezi. For a synthesized account of Griqua and Tswana traders who plied between Kuruman and Matebeleland, Ngamiland, and Barotseland, *see* Edward C. Tabler, "Non-Europeans as Interior Men," *Africana Notes and News* 13, no. 8 (December 1959): 291–96; Henry Bryden, *Gun and Camera in Southern Africa: a Year of*

Wanderings in Bechuanaland to Kalahari Desert, and the Lake River Country (London: 1893), pp. 343–44; McCabe, "The Great Lake Ngami," in Holden, *History of Natal*, p. 416.

14. Livingstone, *Missionary Travels*, p. 69.

15. Ibid. In *Journal of the Royal Geographical Society*, 21 (1851): 23, Livingstone says: "previous to our first visit [1849] the ivory was of no value; the tusks were left in the field with other bones . . . the Tswana would have preferred to sell a tusk for a few beads . . . they soon acquired a knowledge of the value of ivory."

16. Anthony Sillery, *The Bechuanaland Protectorate* (London: 1952), p. 26.

17. William Lye, "The Distribution of the Sotho Peoples after the Difaqane," in L. M. Thompson, ed., *African Societies in Southern Africa* (London: 1969), pp. 190–206.

18. C. J. Andersson, "A Journey to Lake Ngami and an Itinerary of the Principal Routes Leading to It from the West Coast, with the Latitudes of Some of the Chief Stations," in *The South African Commercial Advertiser and Cape Town Mail*, 22 May 1854; see also McCabe, "The Great Lake Ngami," in Holden, *History of Natal*, pp. 417–18.

19. Mackenzie, *Ten Years North of the Orange River*, p. 170: "I have since often observed that cattle bred by Bechuanas can stand thirst better than all others which come into the country. This is accounted for by the manner in which they are reared by their owners at their cattle posts. While colonial farmers make sure that water shall at all times be within reach of their herds . . . the Bechuanas teach their cattle to endure a certain amount of privation as to water"; Bryden, *Gun and Camera*, p. 339; Henry Methuen anticipated: "The introduction of the camel into South Africa will, at some future day, form an important epoch in its history." (See Methuen, *Life in the Wilderness; or Wanderings in Southern Africa* [London: 1846], p. 297.)

20. Thomas Baines, *Journal of Residence in Africa, 1842–53*, 2 vols., ed. R. F. Kennedy (Cape Town: 1964), 2: 309. See also Livingstone to Moffat, 18 January 1849, to Mary Livingstone, 14 January 1853, in *Family Letters, 1841–1856*, 2: 9, 200, for Boer claims to Tswana territory.

21. Baines, *Journal of Residence*, p. 309. For an alternative route to Ngamiland, see E. Tabler, "The Walvis Bay Road: Reitfontein to Lake Ngami," *Africana Notes and News* 12, no. 4 (December 1956): 123.

22. Baines, *Journal of Residence*, p. 308: "For were they to conduct themselves with prudence, it is quite certain they would continue independent in their own way."

23. W. E. Oswell, *William Cotton Oswell*, 2 vols. (London: 1900), 1: 221–22.

24. W. C. Baldwin, *African Hunting and Adventures from Natal to the Zambezi including Lake Ngami, the Kalahari Desert . . . , from 1852–1860* (London: 1894), pp. 304, 264; McCabe, "The Great Ngami," in Holden, *History of Natal*, pp. 417–18.

25. Charles J. Andersson, *Notes of Travel in South Africa*, ed. J. Lloyd (London: 1875), p. 429.

26. Charles J. Andersson, "A Journey to Lake Ngami and an Itinerary of the Principal Routes Leading to It from the West Coast, with the Latitudes of Some of the Chief Stations," in *The South African Commercial Advertiser and Cape Town Mail*, 22 May 1854. See also Alfred Dolman, *In the Footsteps of Livingstone: Being the Diaries and Travel Notes Made by Alfred Dolman*, ed. John Irving (London: 1924), p. 196.

27. J. Leyland, who was at Dimawe on 20 December 1851 (*see* Leyland, *Adventures in the Far Interior of South Africa* [London, 1866], pp. 111–16) observed that Sechele was attacked because he refused to expel Englishmen from his chiefdom and also to supply Boers with laborers. According to the account of Scholtz, commander of the Boers (*see* J. du Plessis, *A History of Christian Missions in South Africa* [Edinburgh: 1911], pp. 443–46), the Boers attacked Sechele after his refusal to surrender the Kgatla chief, Moseileli, with whom the Boers had quarreled.

28. Chapman, *Travels*, 1: 100–101.

29. Chapman, *Travels*, 1: 136–37. See also Livingstone, *Private Journals*, p. 98, where Livingstone reported: "The very first cases of cattle stealing from the Boers by Bechuanas took place this month (December 1852). The Barolongs of [Montshiwa] were the people, and they stole five lots [i.e., droves or groups]."

30. Robert Moffat, *The Matebele Journals*, 1: 168. For restrictions on the sale of firearms to the Tswana, *see* Anthony Atmore, "Notes on Firearms among the Tswana and Ndebele" (African History Seminar paper, Institute of Commonwealth Studies, University of London 22 January 1969). Sue Miers, "Notes on the Arms Trade and Government Policy in Southern Africa between 1870–1890," *Journal of African History* 12, no. 4 (1971): 571–77.

31. All early travelers to Bechuanaland show how sceptical the Tswana were at first. See, for example, Dolman, *Footsteps of Livingstone*, p. 157. *See also* chapter 1.

32. Cumming, *The Lion Hunter*, p. 254.

33. Andersson, *Notes of Travel*, p. 194.

34. Chapman, *Travels*, 1: 42–43; McCabe, "The Great Lake Ngami," in Holden, *History of Natal*, p. 416.

35. Cumming, *The Lion Hunter*, pp. 7, 254. For Ndebele monopoly on ivory trade, *see* R. Moffat to Sir George Grey, *The Cape Argus*, 21 November 1860: ". . . but it is to be regretted that there exists nothing like free trade. That of ivory and cattle is entirely in Moselekatse's own hands."

36. Andersson, *Notes*, p. 436.

37. McCabe, "The Great Lake Ngami," in Holden, *History of Natal*, p. 427; Andersson, "A Journey to Lake Ngami."

38. Baldwin, p. 165. See also Dolman, p. 196.

39. Thomas Baines, using estimates of William Baldwin, in Thomas Baines, *Exploration in South West Africa* (London: 1864), p. 432.

40. Baldwin pp. 343–44.

41. For example, Gordon Cumming (*see* Cumming, *The Lion Hunter*,

p. 254) who calculated his gain to be 3,000%. In the 1840s (ibid., p. 187) ivory was sold in the Cape at 4/6 a pound; karosses at £1–£3 each, and ostrich feathers at £5–£6 per pound. See also Methuen, p. 146.

42. Cumming, p. 251. *See also,* Dolman's diary for 26 May 1849, p. 158: "the Kwena in bargaining . . . are uncommonly sharp."

43. Baldwin, p. 251; "We arrived here [Ngami] on Friday, the 11th [June 1858], not until I had received messages from the Captain [chief] to make haste and be the first wagon at his state; since which time we have been haggling and wrangling about the price of two horses, till my interpreter and I were utterly exhausted, the former drinking half my cask of sherry to keep his throat moist, till today [15 June 1858] I gave in and let the Captain have them for thirteen teeth of ivory, and a saddle and bridle into the bargain."

44. Mackenzie, *Ten Years,* p. 179. See also Mohr, p. 157; Cumming, p. 250.

45. Baldwin, p. 191; J. Mackenzie, *Day-dawn in Dark Places* (London: 1884), p. 59.

46. Cumming, p. 336.

47. Baldwin, pp 266–67: He assessed Lecholathebe to be living in great comfort, asserting that "they say perfect happiness does not exist in this world, but I should say a Kaffir Chief comes nearer to it than any other mortal."

48. J. P. R. Wallis, ed., *The Matebele Mission,* p. 65. See also William Cornwallis Harris, *Narrative of an Expedition into Southern Africa, During the Years 1836 and 1837* (Bombay: 1838), p. 55, who said of the Tlhaping men: "little need be said, as they have generally adopted a rude imitation of the European costumes. The females . . . retain the garb of their ancestors."

49. Cumming, p. 331: "Sundry members of the congregation entered the Church clad in the most unique apparel; some of them wore extraordinary old hats ornamented with fragments of women's clothes and ostrich feathers, and these they were very reluctant to take off . . . one man sat with his beaver on immediately before the minister until the door keeper ordered him to remove it." See also Dolman, p. 158.

50. Livingstone, *Missionary Travels,* p. 121.

51. Andersson, "A Journey to Lake Ngami"; *see also* Dolman, p. 158.

52. For earlier reference to Sebobi, *see* chapter 1. See also Livingstone to Moffat, July 1847, *Family Letters,* 1: 201.

53. Leyland, p. 169.

54. Ibid., pp. 200–201. See also "Veritas," [pseudo.], "Secheli and the Boers," *Cape Town Mail,* 12 March 1853.

55. Chapman, *Travels,* 1: 220.

56. Ibid., pp. 220–21, 222.

57. Leyland, p. 135: "The people were married according to the rules of the land, to brand them as adulterers will turn all heathens against the faith which we are so anxious they should embrace. It is a pity that some middle course could not be found to remedy the evil [*sic*]."

58. Baldwin noted: "Sechele makes a great show of being very re-

ligious, saying a long grace before and after meat on every occasion; and he has been holding forth to his people and singing half [sic] the day. He will not allow a shot to be fired or any work to be done, and certainly sets a most praiseworthy example. He is most anxious to get home, but will not travel on Sunday on any account. I cannot tell whether he is sincere, or only does so through fear of Moffat, a Scotch missionary," (Baldwin, p. 295).

59. Chapman, *Travels*, 1: 230–31; see also Livingstone, *Private Journals*, p. 282: "The old superstitions cannot be driven out of their minds by faith implanted by preaching."

60. Leyland, p. 134. However, one of Sechele's daughters, Bitsang, was married to the English trader, J. H. Wilson, but Baldwin recorded on 6 June 1858, that Bitsang had deserted Wilson (*see* Baldwin, p. 264). The hunter, Gordon Cumming, was reported to have kept a Khoikhoi concubine (*see* Livingstone, *Family Letters*, 1: 217).

61. *See* account by Heinrich Schulenburg, in Willoughby Papers, Folder 795, Selly Oak Colleges; J. du Plessis, p. 375, Thomas Morgan Thomas, *Eleven Years in Central Africa* (London: 1872), p. 47. In contrast to Sechele's acquaintance with white people, Chief Nangoro of Ovamboland "positively refused to believe [in 1851] in the existence of any country which was inhabited by whites alone. He seemed to consider them as rare migratory animals of unaccountable manners but considerable intelligence." (*See* Francis Galton, *Narrative of an Explorer in Tropical South Africa*, 2nd ed. [London, 1853], p. 219).

62. There is ample evidence to suggest that Sechele and other Tswana rulers disliked the Boers (*see*, for example, Sechele's letter to Livingstone in Leyland, pp. 115–16). However, British officials and L.M.S. missionaries were mistaken in believing that this strained relationship was irrevocable; the political realities of the nineteenth century seem to have dictated that the Kwena and their neighbors have permanent national interests, not permanent friends or enemies.

63. *See* H. Schulenburg, in Willoughby Papers, Folder 795, Selly Oak Colleges; du Plessis, p. 325; Rev. Karl Hohls to Mackenzie, 8 September 1864, Box 33, Jacket B, Folder 3 (L.M.S.), writing from Dinokane, a Hanoverian station in Hurutsheland, suggests that his Society's mission in Bechuanaland had the approval of the Boer Republics: ". . . but it is a pity that the Boers will not have you." This is confirmed in the official history of the Hermannsburgers (*see* Georg Haccius, *Hannoversche Missionsgeschichte Insbesondere die Geschichte der Hermannsburger Mission* (Hermannsburg: 1910), pp. 321–25).

64. Schulenburg, Willoughy Papers, Folder 795; R. Moffat, *Matebele Journals*, 2: 30, 33; Haccius, p. 328.

65. R. Moffat, *Matebele Journals*, 2: 30, 33.

66. Ibid., 2: 148.

67. Ibid., 2: 179–80.

68. *See* Baldwin, p. 290, where Mzilikazi is reported to have given Sechele 40 oxen, 40 sheep, 40 goats, and some ivory.

69. Mackenzie, *Ten Years North of the Orange River*, p. 319. For

Ndebele response to Christianity, *see* Thomas Morgan Thomas, *Eleven Years in Central Africa* (London: 1872), passim; J. P. R. Wallis, ed., *Matebele Mission*, passim.

70. Haccius, p. 444.
71. Ibid., p. 410.
72. Ibid., p. 415.
73. Ibid., p. 420.
74. Ferdinand Zimmerman to Robert Moffat, 10 January 1861, Box 32, Jacket A, Folder 3 (L.M.S.). By 1865 they had risen to fifty-five.
75. Schulenburg, Willoughby Papers, Folder 795, Selly Oak Colleges.
76. Haccius, p. 444.
77. R. Moffat, *Matebele Journals*, 2: 35–36.
78. Moffat to Tidman, 20 February 1861, Box 32, Jacket A, Folder 3 (L.M.S.), where he deplores Lutherans for "trading with the natives to which the German missionaries seem . . . attached salaried or not salaried."
79. Zimmerman and Schulenburg to Moffat, 10 January 1861, Box 32, Jacket A, Folder 3 (L.M.S.).
80. *See* Hardeland's report, in Haccius, p. 413, where he calls them "renegades," "Merchant Jews."

3
The L.M.S. Takes Over German Stations in Bechuanaland; Response to Missionary Work in Northern Bechuanaland, 1862-1880

I

RELATIONS BETWEEN L.M.S. AND HERMANNSBURG AGENTS appear to have been cordial in spite of doctrinal differences on Scripture between their societies. The seeds of friendship—thanks to his ignorance at the time—were planted by Robert Moffat, himself a less compromising adherent of Congregational creed than other L.M.S. missionaries. The occasion was Moffat's fourth visit to Mzilikazi in 1857, when informants told him that Sechele had received the Moravian missionaries at Dithubaruba. Knowing that Moravians were less doctrinaire than Lutherans, Moffat welcomed the arrival of Heinrich Schroeder's party in Kwenaland, for he was aware of Sechele's requests for missionaries. Under the influence of this feeling of cordiality, Moffat seriously considered loaning evangelist Mebalwe—who was leaving Dithubaruba—to the new missionaries until they had learned to speak seTswana.[1]

By the time Moffat and his colleagues discovered the Hermannsburgers' real religious affiliation, friendly intercourse had been established between agents of the two societies. This had been facilitated by typically solid German hospitality, which Moffat was the first to enjoy.[2] The treatment he received at Dithubaruba led J. S. Moffat to conclude that the Lutherans' (Hermannsburgers') character was beyond reproach.[3] The Rev. Ferdinand Zimmerman, the Hurutshe-based Hermannsburg agent, must have treated Mr. and Mrs. Price well, for Mrs. Price was highly complimentary in her diary: "These people are extremely kind and hospitable—very homely and plodding."[4]

The cordial relations between the Germans and the British did not succeed in curbing for any length of time the expansionist ambitions of their societies, and it was inevitable that they would come into conflict in the execution of their societies' policies. L.M.S. agents were alarmed to find that their Lutheran counterparts were sending twenty-four agents to South Africa annually, a figure they could hardly hope to match. But they must have watched with interest the dispute that developed within the Lutheran Society in South Africa that resulted in the dismissal of all Hermannsburgers in Bechuanaland in 1860.[5]

As a result of their dismissal, the Hermannsburg agents were obliged to fend for themselves, which in their circumstances entailed trading with Tswana communities—an activity that interfered with their evangelical endeavors. Those Lutherans who wished to continue to work as full-time missionaries applied to the L.M.S. for vacancies, Zimmermann and Schulenburg being the first to do so in January

The L.M.S. Takes Over German Stations

1861. Zimmermann sent his letter of application through Robert Moffat, whom he regarded as "an experienced and fatherly friend." He assumed that Moffat was already acquainted with the unhappy developments within the Hermannsburg Society and confided to him the difficulty of having "to furnish ourselves as good as we can"; he also reported the difficulty he had faced to convert the Hurutshe, because the latter were reluctant to abandon their traditional beliefs.[6]

Schulenburg was even more forthright than Zimmermann. In his letter addressed to Moffat, Price, and Mackenzie, he alleged that the dispute with Superintendent Hardeland had let their society to take "many tyrannical steps against [them]." He noted that he was offering his services to the L.M.S. in defiance of a Hermannsburg order to return to Natal. He did not have as many converts as his Hurutshe colleague, having baptized only eight people, including two of Sekgoma's sons, Kgama and Kgamane.[7] Schulenburg decided to visit Germany, and asked Mackenzie, with whom he had stayed at Shoshong for two months, to take charge of the Shoshong station. Moffat, Price, and Mackenzie did not take the Lutheran offers seriously. In their joint letter to the L.M.S. they did not even mention Zimmerman's application but they grudgingly recommended Schulenburg, who they hoped might "prove to be an efficient labourer if he were to renounce [fundamentalist] tenets and trading with the natives to which the German missionaries seem ... attached."[8] According to Robert Moffat, their participation in trade had rendered them "not only ... unable to fulfil their duties as missionaries but [they also] lost caste with the people, who are keen enough to see the incompatibility of the two pursuits."[9]

The London directors had scarcely had time to consider Schulenburg's application when Moffat took the initiative in Bechuanaland. When it appeared to him that Schulenburg was not returning to Shoshong, he recommended that

Mackenzie, then on a short visit to Kuruman, be appointed to the Shoshong post on a permanent basis; the L.M.S. directors approved the appointment in February 1862.[10] But when Mackenzie hurried back to Shoshong he found there not only Price, who had been turned away from Inyati by Mzilikazi,[11] but also Schulenburg, who had not gone to Germany after all, but had decided to stay at Shoshong as a free-lance missionary. The three worked together until 1864, when Schulenburg again joined the Hermannsburg Society and went to work at Pata Le Tschopa in the South African Republic. Until the Lutheran left Shoshong in 1864, the three missionaries readily worked out a modus operandi:

> "Mr. Schulenburg chose that we should cooperate with him, sharing the public services of the Sunday, and teaching certain classes in the school. . . . The arrangement, however, was carried out very harmoniously; and we all found scope and verge enough for our teaching in the cardinal truths of our religion, upon which we were truly agreed." [12]

The London directors were not as enthusiastic about the occupation of the Kwena mission. Their attitude was no doubt influenced by the number of adverse reports they had received for over twenty years regarding Sechele's standing as a Christian (see chapter 2). In addition, Kwenaland did not command the same strategic importance as Shoshong (see chapter 2). Nevertheless, events that occurred in the early 1860s seemed to strengthen Sechele's leverage in his quest for agents. The Rev. Schroeder and the lay-worker, Herbst, both died in 1863.[13]

If the surviving missionary (Bakeberg) had any illusions about his continued stay among the Kwena, they were soon dashed. In January 1863 Sechele and two of his brothers, Kgosidintsi and Basiamang, jointly appealed to the L.M.S. for a resident missionary at Molepolole:

The L.M.S. Takes Over German Stations

> We ... being the chiefs of the country of Bakwena, in the presence of the teachers Bakeberg and Price, make it known to them that we do not desire the teaching of the Germans and will receive the teaching of the English alone. It is we who speak this and they, Bakeberg and Price, have heard how we have spoken.[14]

Late in 1863 Price was given the discretion to choose between Molepolole and Shoshong, the directors nevertheless pointing out that "Sechele's sincerity can be little depended on";[15] and Price chose to work at Shoshong.

Meanwhile, the Hermannsburgers mounted their demand to have Shoshong vacated by the L.M.S., a move that was strongly resisted by Mackenzie and Robert Moffat.[16] Both men insisted that the Germans hand over all their mission stations to the L.M.S., since they did not have as long a connection with the Tswana as the L.M.S., who had worked among the southern Tswana since 1816. In response to these requests, Karl Hohls, the local superintendent of Hermannsburg stations in Bechuanaland, gave the Kwena station to the L.M.S. but demanded that Shoshong be vacated "with man and mouse."[17] The demand seems to have been ignored, and L.M.S. agents instead mustered Ngwato support to let them remain in their town. When Keyser and Ferdinand Zimmermann tried to reoccupy Shoshong for their society in 1864, they were turned away by the Ngwato who preferred to have the L.M.S.

In Kwenaland the years 1864–66 were decisive in Sechele's endless quest for a resident missionary, for not only did the Hermannsburg complete the formalities ceding the Kwena station to the L.M.S. during that time,[18] but Sechele also expelled the remaining Germans from his country. In addition, Karl Hohls assured Mackenzie that Dithubaruba was indeed vacant because their remaining agents had been expelled.[19] Sechele, on the other hand, was covertly playing on the perennial rivalry between Boers and

Britons to induce the latter to act quickly. In October 1865 he wrote:

> My soul's grieved that the German missionaries who came from the Boers should be the teachers of my people; why then do you English refuse to give me teachers? As to them [the Germans] some died at my place, the rest I told to depart; for I said, I shall ask the English for missionaries because you do not teach.[20]

Sechele's relentless struggle was rewarded only after another appeal, when Price was sent to Molepolole in 1866.

The Ngwaketse, the neighbors of the Kwena to the south, commanded an even less strategic geographical location than either of their northern kinsmen. Since the late 1840s they had had to be content with an African evangelist, Sebobi, for their chief's requests for a white missionary went unheeded. Sebobi (*see* chapter 1) had taught Chief Gaseitsiwe to read and write, the Ngwaketse ruler professing to Moffat in 1860 that he was "grateful for Sebobi's services, in . . . visiting them every Sabbath, preaching twice and teaching them." [21] But in spite of this service, Sebobi could not be a substitute for the all-important white missionary and Gaseitsiwe, though not as persistent as Sechele, made his wishes known whenever the opportunity arose. In 1870 he invited the Inyati-based missionary, Thomas Morgan Thomas, to make Kanye his permanent station and not to proceed to Matebeleland. When that invitation was turned down, the Ngwaketse chief next turned to the more pressing needs of his tribe, pleading that "he would . . . be much obliged if [Thomas] would give a little gun powder. . . . I believed in his sincerity, and gave him what he wanted. . . ." [22] The Rev. James Good was subsequently sent to work at Kanye in 1871.

The mission to the Tawana was linked with the evangelical progress made at Shoshong, a station that had been founded to act as a channel for the society's expansion into the interior of Central Africa. Since Livingstone's first visit in 1849, the Tawana had had more intercourse with traders than with missionaries, the most significant contact with the latter group having been made with the ill-fated L.M.S. mission to the Kololo in 1859. Lecholathebe's humane treatment of the survivors of the Kololo mission in 1860 commended him to L.M.S. directors and agents alike;[23] and when Mackenzie arrived at the lake to take the survivors of the Kololo expedition to Kuruman, Lecholathebe lost no time to plead his case for a missionary: "I desire instructions for myself and my people; I should persecute no one for believing; at any rate I have shown that I would not eat the missionaries up in my own town, as Sekeletu has done."[24] To emphasize the importance of a resident missionary agent as against the infrequent visits of Livingstone and some Griqua and Tlhaping traders, Lecholathebe observed: "We retained their instructions for a little time only; they soon faded from our memory. We should not so soon forget were a teacher living amongst us."[25] Even when Lecholathebe was presenting his case for a missionary agent, he, like all Tswana rulers in the nineteenth century, took some time off to barter with Mackenzie for arms and ammunition with the shrewdness of an experienced trader.

Lecholathebe did not live to see the first white missionary reside in Ngamiland. He died in 1874 and, after the regency of Meno and his son, Dithapo, was succeeded by Moremi II in 1876. The new Tswana chief had as much difficulty as Lecholathebe in persuading the L.M.S. to act in the matter. His efforts were rewarded only after he had appealed to Kgama to "obtain him missionaries like his own; also to teach his men to read, and to give them all information about the new teaching of the word of God."[26] In 1877 J. D. Hepburn and two Tswana evangelists, Kukwi Mogodi and Diphukwe Yakwe, went to Moremi's chiefdom to evangelize and, after a short spell back at Shoshong, the two African evangelists were again sent back to Ngamiland as permanent agents of the L.M.S. in 1878. This mission, like all attempts to work in areas where Tswana rulers had requested L.M.S. agents, had the full support of Chief Moremi. But as will be shown later in this chapter, the Ngami mission was destined to grapple with grave problems when Chief Moremi asserted his supremacy over the Church.

II

Tswana communities among whom L.M.S. agents worked in the 1860s and 1870s were fairly populous centers. The Ngwato at Shoshong numbered about 30,000, while Sechele's subjects around the Dithejwane hills numbered 60,000, of whom 35,000 were Kwena.[27] The first task of all L.M.S. agents to Bechuanaland, in the tradition of James Read at Dithakong earlier in the century, was to try to establish a cordial working relationship with each chief. In this regard agents who went to work among the Ngwato and the Kwena were initially inhibited, because they believed Tswana chiefs to be preoccupied with secular issues. The journal of Mrs. Price depicts the Ngwato chief, Sekgoma, as being obsessed with the acquisition of firearms: "It is all guns and ammunition with him . . . and Roger [Price], having a little taste in the mechanical line, is worried [sic] by Sekgoma for every broken gun which meets his eye. Roger mends one after the other and so earns most of our oxen, sheep and goats . . . sometimes very quickly."[28] However, the Prices easily befriended themselves to two of Sekgoma's sons, Kgama and Kgamane. To the newly arrived missionaries, the two brothers seemed to compensate for their father's reluctance to adopt Christianity; whenever they were guests at Price's home, their cleanliness, mode of dressing and general deportment strengthened the ties of friendship with the new missionary family. Mrs. Price was only too happy to find that Kgama and Kgamane were eager to learn new ideas.[29]

At Molepolole Sechele typically welcomed the Prices with a present of a fat ox.[30] However, in spite of the fine gesture, the missionaries' ignorance of Tswana customs, coupled with Sechele's trade practices, marred chief-missionary relations from the very beginning. The general tone of misunderstanding is reflected in Mrs. Price's letter to her sister at Kuruman in 1866, when she complained that Sechele begged "disgracefully, like the meanest of his subjects—and [when] transacting business will try and squeeze his unfortunate customer into the very smallest space ere he is satisfied."[31] But in due course there were some aspects of Sechele's life—notably his enthusiasm to teach in the Sunday school—that helped to reduce tensions between him and the missionaries. Sechele was eager to reassure Price that the Kwena field was a fertile ground for the planting of Christianity.

In July 1866 Sechele called a meeting at which he asked his brother, Kgosidintsi, to inform Kwena Christians and non-Christians alike what they were required to do for the missionaries. They were to build a house for the Prices and a school where they might be taught to read and write. Kgosidintsi, who himself refused to become a Christian for the rest of his life, saw some good in the white man's school; he urged disgruntled elements at the meeting to perform the assigned tasks without flinching, for "no one could be sure that he would not one day be in great earnest in frequenting [the school] and getting its knowledge—nor still less could they be sure that their children one and all would not be its devoted frequenters."[32] Nor was that the last of Sechele's gestures. In 1867 he paid builders generously to ensure the speedy completion of a church under construction at Molepolole.[33] The Ngwato, Tawana, and Ngwaketse rulers were just as eager to cooperate with missionaries during the incipient stage of evangelization. However, this initial cooperation between chiefs and missionaries was severely tested by demographic and political developments within the Tswana chiefdoms shortly after the missionaries' arrival.

III

Mackenzie had hardly established himself at Shoshong when catastrophe struck the Ngwato communities in northeast Bechuanaland. The advent of a smallpox epidemic (*sekoripane* in seTswana) there in 1862, which Mackenzie described in vivid if somewhat exaggerated terms, brought a head-on encounter between Ngwato traditions and the fledgling-white man's ideas. Mackenzie soon discovered that administering the white man's medicine was much more difficult than Sekgoma's prompt grant of permission had suggested, because the majority of Ngwato preferred local medicine men (*dingaka*) to Mackenzie's exotic ministrations of vaccination.[34] The chief himself refused to be vaccinated, on the grounds that 'because he had previously suffered from the disease, the white man's treatment would be ineffectual.[35] However, Mackenzie was able to vaccinate members of the chief's family and a few commoners. Although his accounts do not show the actual number of patients he treated, his efforts seem to have been rewarded; only one patient out of those he treated was confined to bed for any length of time, and the rest rapidly recovered. Those patients who refused to be treated by Mackenzie and those who were treated by Ngwato medicine men died in large numbers; others lost their eyesight. Mackenzie's account gives a terrifying idea of the heavy casualties claimed by the epidemic:

> At length the people seemed to weary of burying the dead, especially in the case of friendless dependants. A long thong was tied to the body of such, which was dragged by this means behind some rock or bush, or into the dry bed of a ravine, and left there. The hyenas and

tigers battened by night, the dogs and vultures and crows held carnival by day, on these exposed and putrefying corpses. Several times I stumbled over these hideous objects, and scattered the dogs from their revolting feast."[36]

In the aftermath, Mackenzie's success as a medicine man enhanced his missionary work, and some Ngwato medicine men even came to consult him professionally. For some time after the epidemic more people attended church services than before.[37]

Smallpox broke out among the Tawana (1862) when the trader, James Chapman, was in Ngamiland. He moved from village to village encouraging the Tawana and their neighbors to be vaccinated. But Ngamiland communities must have thought that the kind of treatment Chapman had in mind was similar to their own, for the response he got everywhere was very encouraging: he was greeted with flattering titles ranging from "son of my father," to "sweetheart," to "mate of the chief"; all villagers expressed a willingness to be inoculated if their chief permitted Chapman to treat them.[38] But Lecholathebe was unimpressed with the visitor's brand of medicine, for "when he found that it was to be inoculation, the tables were completely turned, and [Chapman] was heartily laughed at for [his] pains, not alone by him but all his tribe, who take their cue from their chief."[39]

At Molepolole Chief Sechele's approach to medical affairs seems to have been pragmatic, dictated by the efficacy of medicine and not by the religious background of those people who supplied it. To accomplish this end Sechele tried to strike a delicate balance by straddling between the practice of the Kwena *dingaka* and that of the white man, a process that invariably strained his relations with missionaries. But the elusive Sechele could always put up some outward show that suggested that he had abandoned witchcraft, as, for example, in September 1866 when he publicly condemned the use of charms in guns.[40] Not that this stricture received any universal approval, for Kgosidintsi offered a flat rebuttal. If the chief was embarassed by his brother's outburst, he must have found consolation in the applause that was given Price, after the missionary had supported Sechele's speech.

If Price imagined that Sechele had finally abandoned Kwena traditional practices, he soon experienced Sechele's pragmatism. The year following his condemnation of the use of charms, Sechele suffered from dropsy and thought it necessary to consult Kwena medicine men. The *ngaka* (singular of *dingaka*) prescribed the liver of a black sheep mixed with that of a crocodile, and Sechele requested a black sheep from Price and explained why it was urgently needed. This prompted a reproof from Price; whereupon Sechele retorted that whites, too, had medicine men who made mysterious compounds that the laymen did not understand but simply accepted in good faith. Sechele submitted that the Kwena, likewise, had doctors, "clever doctors, who could effect cures as well as [white doctors] . . . that one of these [medicine men] he had employed to cure his disease—that he earnestly desired to use [the medicine man's] prescriptions, but that this particular . . . part being needed, why should he [Sechele] murmur at the [medicine] man's notion for a black sheep." [41] On that occasion Sechele sustained his defense of Kwena medicine and left unrepentant.

When L.M.S. agents embarked upon the crucial task of converting the Tswana to Christianity, the obstacles they encountered were reminiscent of those of the pioneering endeavors of James Read among the Tlhaping in Mothibi's chiefdom.[42] The fact that Lutherans had worked at Molepolole compounded Price's problems: Sechele had been admitted into the Lutheran Church and had once more become a full-fledged preacher on Sundays. Price dissolved

The L.M.S. Takes Over German Stations

the Hermannsburg church membership and enforced Sechele's previous suspension of 1848.[43] A few months after his arrival at Molepolole, Price sent a rather pessimistic report on Molepolole Christians: "Sechele and the few of his people who are nominally Christians—I am sorry to be unable to say anything favourable . . . Sechele may yet be reclaimed, though he certainly has gone very far astray."[44]

At Shoshong Sekgoma repeatedly informed Mackenzie that he could not be converted to Christianity, which in his opinion was essentially a white man's religion. To Sekgoma conversion conjured up a host of uncertainties in his mind that only a military analogy could indicate, for he explained to Mackenzie when the missionary insisted that he be converted: "Monare [Sir] you don't know what you say. The word of God is far from me. When I think of "entering the word of God," I can compare it to nothing except going out to the plain and meeting single-handed all the forces of the Matebele."[45] While Sekgoma did not object to his children being taught by missionaries and would himself occasionally attend church services, Mackenzie concluded that "no new thing was so inviting to [Sekgoma] as the customs which had the sanctions of immemorial usage."[46]

The response of Tswana laymen to Christianity varied from one station to the next and was largely influenced by the chief's attitude to the new faith. In due course the Tswana mission had to grapple with problems of teaching catechists ways of praying to God. For example, one of the missionaries' oft-repeated requests—that catechists communicate directly with God in prayer—was a religious experience that often eluded beginners. A Molepolole youth confided in Price "how it was that whenever he tried to pray, a mist gathered before his mind's eye and he could not catch any idea or form any request."[47] Because of the mystical nature of the problem, Price could not be very helpful.

The little formal education offered during the early days

of missionary activity in northern Tswana chiefdoms was decidedly rudimentary, designed to enable young and adult students ("inquirers") to read and understand the Scriptures.[48] Crude school buildings were constructed with labor provided by chiefs; wagons, trees, and the chief's *kgotla* (courtyard adjacent to chief's residence) were improvised to serve as classrooms. Students used broken boxes, planks, and stone walls to write on.[49] Wives of missionaries conducted sewing lessons in their houses. Among Price's first students at Shoshong were Kgama and Kgamane; the latter proved to be a better student than his famous brother. In her assessment of the two brothers, Mrs. Price observed that Kgama lacked "application and talent [in] both being quite behind the others in school . . . but had the virtues of commonsense, firmness, and decision of character."[50] Molepolole, too, had its share of educational problems.

A year after Price settled at Sechele's town, he reported that he was unable to have a day school but taught his students in his house; one of the pupils was a blind man of over forty years, who had been taught by Livingstone in the 1840s.[51] By January 1868 Price had seventy-five students, and in March of that year he baptized four converts from the Ngwaketse chiefdom.[52]

At Shoshong Sekgoma's somewhat cautious honeymoon with missionaries ended when he found that Christianity compelled his children to discard some of the tribe's cherished customs. Open conflict with the two sons developed after they had resolved to reject Sekgoma's authority "whenever it interfered with their duty as Christians."[53] As a consequence, Sekgoma's attitude suddenly changed and in 1863 J. S. Moffat reported the Chief's opposition to Christianity.[54] Sekgoma's relations with Kgamane and Kgama worsened when they, unlike his other sons, refused to take part in initiation ceremonies. Tensions between father and sons built up until they culminated in the civil war of 1866.

IV

Although the post*mfecane* era was a relatively calm one, that quiescence only harbored old grudges inherited from the *mfecane* and from tribal and family feuds. In this respect neither the northern Tswana communities nor their southern neighbors experienced unbroken peace. They engaged in sporadic skirmishes with their neighbors and among themselves. As Sekgoma's analogy suggests, relations between the Ndebele and the Ngwato were always tense.[55] The Tawana in Ngamiland, too, had their conflicts with the Ndebele, the Wawicko (or Mbukushu) and the Kololo of the trans-Zambezi area in the north. In every Tswana community military preparedness and the acquisition of firearms continued to be an essential part of political life.

The traveler and prospector, Thomas Baines, gives an indication of Tswana responses to military demands. When he stopped at Lecholathebe's court in April 1861, a call for a war council (*lechulo*) was readily answered by about 200 to 300 men.[56] A year later, when Tawana spies warned Lecholathebe that the Ngwato were on the war path, elaborate *lechulo* proceedings were conducted at the chief's court. At that gathering Lecholathebe's uncle, Mokhalakgwe, among others, addressed the army on the Tawana imperative to defeat the enemy. He warned them against precipitate action on the battlefield, urging them to ascertain the strength of the enemy before they could make any moves. His address is reported to have been "greeted by cries of 'poola, poola' (rain, rain), a term synonymous in a dry country with refreshment or blessing."[57] However, the Kololo, and not the Ngwato, eventually attacked the Tawana, who in turn took full advantage of the swampy terrain, lured their enemy to unfamiliar environment, and soundly defeated them. The Ngwato had their share of military troubles, too, in the 1860s. Ngwato conflicts with the Ndebele were largely inherited from the 1840s when the newly arrived Ndebele nucleus in Kalangaland contrived to gain control of southern Zambezia largely by force of arms. By 1850 these clashes had resulted in the creation of an explosive no-man's-land area between the Shashi and Matlotsi Rivers, which both the Ndebele and the Ngwato sought to control.

In March 1862 Shoshong residents were roused one day when Ngwato sentinels reported the Ndebele to be advancing toward Shoshong. Sekgoma immediately ordered the evacuation of women and children to Shoshong hills and proceeded to issue arms and ammunition to his regiments. Kgama and Kgamane refused to observe some of the ritual that preceded war—for example, the reading of a dice—which they believed to be incompatible with Christianity.[58] This incident marked the first serious estrangement between Sekgoma and his sons.

Although the Ndebele were driven away in the 1862 conflict, the outbreak of that war presented Mackenzie with a new dimension of experience: was he to take sides or was he to steer a nonpartisan course? He decided to take the latter course, although it was difficult to sustain since his own life was in danger if the Ndebele should win the war. Mackenzie nevertheless prayed for a "blessing on those who fought for home and family and property; and . . . that God would frustrate the councils of the nation delighting in war." [59] Also, when he preached on a Sunday after the conclusion of the war, Mackenzie must have unwittingly absolved Sekgoma from any breaches of the right conduct of war. He defended the just war in the somewhat ambiguous tradition of Christian theologians and some international jurists. The theme of his sermon was that "God had given the man a stronger body than the woman, that he might work for her and defend her. A man's mother, or wife, or sister, ought to be reached by enemies only over his lifeless body." [60] Sekgoma must have, no doubt, concluded the Ndebele to be the aggressors, for he expressed his satisfaction in the sermon at the end of the service. When Mackenzie pleaded for the life of an Ndebele prisoner of war, Sekgoma readily rescinded the death penalty, but his message arrived too late to save the prisoner.[61]

In May 1863 the Ndebele were reported to have again raided Ngwato cattle posts in the Tati area, and, in the ensuing skirmishes with the Ngwato, one of Mzilikazi's sons was killed.[62] When the Ngwato retaliated by raiding Ndebele cattle posts in July 1863, they were repulsed and brought back a meager booty of goats.[63] Because of the tense atmosphere created by these forays, the Kwena raid on Ngwato cattle posts in 1864 was not seriously challenged—the Ngwato no doubt calculating the Ndebele threat to be imminently more serious than any damage the Kwena might inflict.[64]

Perhaps the most serious conflict that occurred in Ngwatoland in the 1860s was the civil war of 1866. Although the immediate reasons for its outbreak were associated with missionary activities at Shoshong, the underlying causes had their roots in Ngwato and Kwena dynastic history.

When the Ngwato chief, Kgari, was killed in battle with the Kalanga (c. 1826), he left two sons, Kgama and Sekgoma —the latter from a junior wife—who were both too young to assume the chieftancy. Kgari's nephew, Sedimo, became the regent and ruled until 1833, when he stepped down in favor of Kgama II. Meanwhile, Sedimo had exercised his prerogative as regent, and, in conformity with the law of the levirate, had taken for himself Kgari's chief wife (Mma-Kgama), who bore him Macheng. According to Tswana law and custom, Macheng was the heir apparent.[65] Kgama II's death in 1835 was followed by a succession crisis in which the Ngwato polarized between Sekgoma and Mma-Kgama (i.e., Kgama II's mother). Sekgoma triumphed and assumed the chiefship, while the defeated Mma-Kgama and Macheng fled to the Kwena for refuge. Nor was Kwenaland a haven of peace: a few years after their arrival in Kalangaland from the Transvaal, the Ndebele invaded the Kwena at Sokwane (c. 1841) and captured several prisoners of war, including the heir apparent Macheng, who was kept in Matebeleland for sixteen years.

In 1857 Sechele requested of Robert Moffat, who was visiting Mzilikazi, to persuade the Ndebele chief to release Macheng. Moffat succeeded and brought Macheng back. The Ngwato heir stayed with Sechele at Dithubaruba briefly before he went on to Shoshong, where he was installed as chief of the Ngwato in 1858.[66] Sekgoma went to live with Sechele.

Sechele had thus started on the intriguing role as kingmaker for the Ngwato. His motives in assuming this role are not as capricious as it at first appears and Mackenzie, who watched Sechele closely, ascribed the chief's ambitions to social and economic considerations:

> "The Kwena taking precedence of the Ngwato as to rank, it [had] been the life-long endeavor of Sechele to obtain such influence in the town of the [Ngwato] as would enable him to secure some of the treasures of ivory and ostrich feathers and furs which are brought from its extensive huntinggrounds, extending northward to the Zambezi." [67]

This observation is persuasive, for not only did Sechele receive some ivory for assisting Macheng to become chief, but he also successively received money and ivory for assisting contenders for the Ngwato chiefship between 1859 and 1875.

Macheng's rule soon became unpopular, for reasons stemming from his unfamiliarity with Tswana law and custom. In the meantime, he had not treated Sechele with the deference commensurate with the efforts the Kwena chief had exerted in elevating him to the Ngwato chiefship. This so annoyed Sechele that in 1859 he sent an army to Shoshong

The L.M.S. Takes Over German Stations 99

that deposed Macheng and reinstated Sekgoma. Macheng fled east and stayed with the Seleka-Rolong for some time before he was given asylum by Sechele at Dithubaruba.[68] In this instance, as in several others, Sechele the opportunist was ready to accommodate a fallen Ngwato ruler.

The Ngwato civil war of 1866 broke out against this background of dynastic intrigues. Once Sekgoma had been estranged from his sons, tensions between father and sons mounted until Shoshong was divided into two camps—one composed of non-Christians entirely supporting the chief; the other comprised of Christians and some non-Christians supporting Sekgoma's sons. Fighting broke out in March 1866 and went on intermittently until May that year, when the besieged forces of Kgama and Kgamane in the Shoshong hills accepted Sekgoma's offer of a truce.[69]

Meanwhile Sekgoma had invited Macheng to Shoshong so that, in the event of his forces becoming victorious, he would forestall Kgama's political ambitions by offering the chiefship to Macheng. Macheng arrived on the 26th of May accompanied by a Kwena force of one hundred fifty men.[70] Clearly Sechele was again playing his game. When, after the war, Kgamane and his father-in-law, Chukudu, sought refuge with Sechele, he readily offered them asylum. But the asylum turned out to be a fatal trap for Chukudu, who was killed on Sechele's orders upon his arrival.[71] It appears that Chuduku's undoing was the influence he wielded at Shoshong, which Sechele was determined to control at all costs.

If Mackenzie's nonpartisanship was difficult to sustain during the Ngwato war with the Ndebele in 1862, neutrality was even harder to maintain in a civil conflict where members of his young church were clearly facing more odds than their adversaries. But he seems to have stood by his principle, ostensibly to demonstrate to his pupils and church members what he conceived to be the proper role of a Christian minister in a civil disturbance. But white traders at Shoshong appear to have sympathized with Kgama and Kgamane: they foiled Sekgoma's plot to poison his adversaries' water wells by selling him marking ink instead of the lethal strychnine and three traders are reported to have fought on Kgama's side for brief periods.[72]

At the conclusion of the war Sekgoma forgave his sons but imposed slight fines on their followers. However, an attempt by Kgama to set up one exclusive section of the town for Christians was stopped by Sekgoma. For some time after the conflict, Sekgoma and Macheng shared the chiefship; the former then abdicated in favor of Macheng and, for the second time, Sekgoma readily found sanctuary at Molepolole. Mackenzie's relationship with Macheng was amiable for some time, but deteriorated when Macheng was found to be promoting initiation ceremonies.

Thus, it can be seen that pioneer efforts of L.M.S. agents in evangelizing northern Tswana chiefdoms, like their predecessors' attempts among the Tlhaping early in the nineteenth century, yielded minimal results. Tswana chiefdoms went to war in spite of or even because of the presence of missionaries. Even when their role as diplomatic agents for the chiefs was in the ascendancy during the 1870s, L.M.S. agents exerted little moral suasion to avert armed conflicts among Tswana polities.

V

The discovery of gold in the Tati in 1867 ushered in a host of problems for Tswana rulers. Hitherto they had had to deal with petty misdemeanors committed by transient traders and hunters and a handful of resident traders; now, the influx of white diggers created more complex interracial relationships. The Tswana chiefs do not seem to have attached any value to gold. Even a chief of Sechele's shrewdness had great difficulty in identifying ore, as, for example, in 1866 when he was obliged to seek the advice of a white

The L.M.S. Takes Over German Stations

trader. He withdrew the invitation only after Price warned him that he might be swindled, a warning that Kgosidintsi welcomed as "one of the benefits from having a moruti [teacher] amongst us." [73] After Karl Mauch's discovery of gold in the Tati area (1867), Mackenzie enticed more diggers by sending gold samples to Governor Wodehouse at the Cape and taking some samples himself to Potchefstroom in the Transvaal. On the strength of the gold samples, *The Transvaal Argus* of the 16th of July 1868, could report:

> We now declare, on the sacred word of our editor, that the said sample required but to be seen in order to dispel the strongest doubts of even the most sceptical. The "myth," as the gold discovery has been termed, has resolved itself into a stupendous fact.[74]

By 1868 there were over sixty diggers.[75]

Prospectors and diggers were quick to notice the no-man's-land status of the Tati River district and could always foment trouble between the two contenders for the area, Macheng and Lobengula, in the hope of seizing the territory for themselves. Rival groups competed to dominate the goldfields, and Mackenzie, who was already adopting imperialist tendencies, settled some of their disputes.[76] Another element was added to the Tati scene when the Transvaal government asked Macheng to cede his country to them in return for protection. Macheng declined the deal; instead, he invited the British to protect his country. Mackenzie's advice undoubtedly influenced the chief's decision to turn to the British. However, Mackenzie's published account contradicts his report to his society. In *Ten Years North of the Orange River*, he says: "I may just mention that the Chief, Macheng, was not advised by me, either directly or indirectly, to write to the Governor at the Cape, offering to the English Government the possession of the goldfields." [77] Yet in his report to the society he is unequivocal, asserting that he "had no hesitation in recommending, as one of two alternatives, that [Macheng] should seek the aid of the English Government rather than that of the Transvaal."[78] In retrospect this report shows the embryonic formation of Mackenzie's imperialist tendencies, which manifested themselves more fully after the first British occupation of south Bechuanaland (1878–81).[79] Macheng's request fell through.

The revenue accruing to the Ngwato chief from the miners must have been relatively small, because the Ndebele chief also collected a portion of the miners' rent from this disputed territory; while his neighbor, Macheng, who did not attach much value to gold as such, collected part of the revenue. But, as Edward Tabler has shown, Macheng charged (one shilling) 1/- per head for a six-month license not for the gold produced by miners in that period, but merely as "a compensation for water and grass consumed in his country."[80]

The task of maintaining law and order among the white miners whose mores and legal systems differed from those of the Ngwato soon became insuperable for Macheng. According to Mackenzie, Macheng "very seldom settled a dispute, and used to tell white men, when they came before him with a case [for litigation] that the matter was no business of his, and that they might settle it as best they cared." This laxity on the part of Macheng was largely a result of his ignorance of customary law, for having spent sixteen years in Matebeleland, he succeeded Sekgoma before he had had the time to learn the duties of his office.[81]

In the meantime, Kgama, who had veiled his real political ambitions at the end of the civil war in 1866,[82] had taken advantage of Macheng's unpopularity to engineer the latter's removal in order that he himself might become chief. Kgama was supported by Sechele, who demanded £1,000 for the use of his troops. In the transactions that followed, both Kgama and Sechele found willing emissaries in Price and Mackenzie.

When hostilities commenced in August 1872, Kgama sent Sechele goods that he believed to be worth £1,000, but Sechele and Price assessed them to be worth £700. In October 1872 Price informed Mackenzie:

> I must tell you about the political business I had to transact. I took Kgama's letter up to Sechele . . . should Kgama be willing to pay £300, his simplest way would be to get Francis and Clark [at Shoshong] to give him a Bill for the amount, payable at Taylor's [a retail store at Molepolole].[83]

Kgama must have yielded to Sechele's demands, for, according to his testimony to the Shippard Tribunal in 1887, he said he paid the balance of £300 "through Mr. Price and Mr. Mackenzie; he then demanded more. I sent him £30." [84]

After Macheng's removal, Kgama became chief but quarreled with Kgamane shortly after taking office. In 1873 he abdicated in favor of Sekgoma and went to live at Serowe; he later moved with his followers to the Botletle River in Ngamiland. Kgama's abdication was clearly a ploy to give himself ample time to stage a permanent revolution. Consequently, when he had developed his plans, he invaded Shoshong in 1875 and defeated the forces of Sekgoma and Kgamane;[85] he became chief that year and ruled until his death in 1923.

VI

Although L.M.S. agents consolidated their positions by performing political and diplomatic tasks for northern Tswana chiefdoms, their evangelical work advanced at a very slow pace. At Shoshong, the Rev. J. D. Hepburn thought political bickering was largely accountable for the poor response;[86] among the Ngwaketse, the Rev. James Good blamed Gaseitsiwe's indifference to Christianity and the chief's attachment to traditional ceremonies, especially initiation ceremonies, for the deficiency.[87] With the Kwena, Sechele was reported to have undermined missionary efforts to convert his subjects, for the chief repeatedly embraced Christian as well as heathen practices;[88] and Roger Price reported that cattle herding interfered with conversion because boys too often absented themselves from school to look after cattle.[89] These observations are borne out by progress reports. Thus, after the L.M.S. had been working among the Ngwato since 1862, Hepburn reported in 1873 that his church had only seven full members, including one Kalanga convert.[90] At Molepolole, Price baptized two Ngwaketse children in March 1868 and six Kwena adults the following May;[91] in 1870 he baptized fifteen candidates, including five candidates from a Kanye outpost.[92] The neighboring Kgatla church at Moshupa had only twenty-eight "inquirers" in 1870, although the chief there was an ardent supporter of Christianity.[93] By 1875 Charles Williams, who had succeeded Price, reported that some Molepolole church members had volunteered to evangelize the Kgalagadi, a community living in the Kgalagadi Desert.[94] But church attendance at Molepolole is reported to have declined sharply in 1876, when the Kwena went to war with the Kgatla.[95]

While early missionary reports suggest Tswana communities to have been divided into two simple compartments of heathens and Christians, Mackenzie's analysis of Ngwato reaction to Christianity is more subtle and is probably representative of all Tswana communities. Mackenzie divided the Ngwato of the 1860s into three main groups: the first was composed of devoted Christians; another group of enthusiastic followers regarded Christianity merely as a popular movement but did not understand what it was all about; and one third, comprised of the majority of the Ngwato, were die-hard traditionalists and rejected Christianity out of hand.[96] The last two groups seem to have held sway before 1880.

The L.M.S. Takes Over German Stations

Between 1862 and 1876 only twenty-six candidates were baptized out of a Tswana population of about 90,000. If the number of converts is a sad commentary on evangelical achievement, it is also indicative of the fact that the religious life of northern Tswana chiefdoms remained largely unaffected by the missionary influence during the pioneer period. Some observations of missionaries and laymen alike suggest that traditional religious practices were in vogue between 1862 and 1880. Thus, W. C. Willoughby's texts of some Tswana oral traditions show that a prophetess arose among the Ngwato in 1864, and was reported to have had a large following.[97] In the same year accusations of witchcraft sparked off fighting between the Kwena and the Ngwato: the Kwena took the offensive when they believed the Ngwato to have cast spells on their crops.[98]

Initiation ceremonies continued to be revered despite missionary efforts to stigmatize them. Soon after her arrival at Molepolole, Mrs. Price was informed that no girl was considered fit for marriage until she had been initiated.[99] Among the Ngwato, Mackenzie found that initiation was associated with the attainment of wisdom. A Ngwato elder was proud of the marks he sustained during circumcision rites and displayed them to Mackenzie with a sense of accomplishment: "Monare [Sir], you must, no doubt, have also observed my superior wisdom. You see, my father did not beat me so severely in vain."[100] In 1879 a missionary reported initiation ceremonies to be rife at Kanye.[101]

In 1869 a German traveler to Bechuanaland observed the sort of euphoria that resulted from initiation ceremonies in a Tswana village:

> When these [instructors] pass out of the village with their troop of young maidens wearing short petticoats of plaited rushes, all the men get out of the way. . . . Later, the young women are exhausted by excessive watching and dancing and made to carry water and heavy loads of wood to the village, by way of learning their future duties as wives.[102]

Another German traveler, Emil Holub, found initiation ceremonies venerated very much by Tswana communities in the 1870s. According to his account, *bogwera* initiates had an age range varying from nine to fourteen years. Holub noted that the *bogwera* did not

> universally or necessarily indicate the attainment of a state of maturity—it is rather an initiation into the system of hardening which every youth is required to undergo before he is considered worthy of the title of "mona" or "ra," which betoken a man's estate.[103]

He further observed that the bonds of friendship formed at these ceremonies lasted a lifetime, and were unaffected by any subsequent conversion to Christianity.[104]

Of the three northern Tswana chiefdoms, Chief Gaseitsiwe of the Ngwaketse organized initiation ceremonies, Sechele conducted a halfhearted campaign against them, while Kgama tried hard but in vain to legislate against them. In 1876 Kgama informed Holub that he was determined to ban initiation ceremonies forthwith, but in fact succeeded only in banning them from the chief's court (*kgotla*).[105] The chief must have taken the missionary's advice into account, for Mackenzie had cautioned him against the use of "force to put down rites which [had] a singular fascination for the people." [106] In contrast to Kgama's attempts to proscribe initiation ceremonies, the Rolong chief, Montshiwa, punished Christians who refused to take part in traditional ceremonies.[107]

The suspicious reserve with which some Tswana communities often responded to new ideas illustrates the faith they had in their own customs; the "turkey incident" at Shoshong is a case in point. When the hunter and prospector, Thomas Leask, stopped at the Ngwato capital in 1869, he conformed to Tswana protocol by presenting a gift, a turkey, to Chief Macheng. However, after Leask's departure

The L.M.S. Takes Over German Stations

from Shoshong, the turkey caused some commotion. Macheng suspected it to be a bad omen and summoned a *pitso*, where Ngwato councillors "accused the . . . turkey of being a personification of some new sort of witchcraft which was being perpetrated on them by white men." Assurances by one of the councillors and Leask's African servant, Saul, that turkeys were edible were rejected by the *pitso*. Although the fate of the turkey is not told, the suspicion it aroused was the subject of a lively discussion, which lasted the whole day until the *pisto* was "adjourned to meet next day, and Saul was ordered to attend, but, fearing the displeasure of his master, he gave them the slip and left them to come to their own decision." [108]

Among the Kwena, Sechele continued to pay lip service to his missionary, but in fact observed some of the practices he condemned. When again inflicted with dropsy in 1879, he was reported to be "trying his missionary's medicine—his trader's medicine—and his own native doctor's medicine, all in turn. The latter has ordered for him (medicine) composed of some minute portion of the inside of a zebra." [109] When drought threatened Kwena crops in that year, Sechele employed rainmakers to avert the disaster. Sechele's predicament in 1879, which had ample precedents in his life since the 1840s, was to reconcile Tswana traditions, especially those imposing obligations on him to fend for the tribe, with the demands of Christianity. His dilemma was appreciated by Mrs. Price, who, in spite of her strong objections to rainmaking, could well understand Sechele's resort to it because it was a "time of distress and dire necessity for him and his people and he is tempted to try anything which will bring rain." [110] However, when Sechele suspected that his missionary had been informed about his rain-making activities, he visited Price to plead his innocence.

Tswana systems of government and the administration of justice were largely unaffected by missionaries during the first two decades of their stay in northern Tswana chiefdoms. During his visits there between 1872 and 1879, Holub observed the position of the Tswana chief to have been paramount, but he was persuaded to conclude that the Tswana system of government was constitutional.[111] Among the Kwena, the restraining influence of the *pitso* was noted by Bailie in 1876, when he reported the Kwena government to be "a mild despotism tempered by a council"; he also noticed the Ngwaketse chief's power to have been checked by the *pitso,* and that Gaseitsiwe consulted his son, Bathoen, even on very small issues.[112] Missionary accounts tend to corroborate travelers' observations on the functioning of Tswana governments. While the exigencies of the war of 1876 had compelled Sechele to take summary measures that suggested that he had assumed dictatorial powers, a report of 1879 shows that he had subsequently restored constitutional government to the Kwena: "Sechele had a meeting with his people yesterday with a view to ask them to assist in purchasing corrugated iron roofing for the church. . . ."[113]

An idea of how the judicial process functioned is shown in Holub's account. He noted that when a theft was reported to the chief, the latter sent a "royal herald" through the town declaring his intention to punish the offender. Then witchdoctors assisted the chief through psychological intimidation and that night the unnoticed culprit invariably surrendered the stolen goods.[114]

The Tswana system of punishment was restitutive, meting light sentences to first offenders and severe ones to incorrigible criminals. Thus, a prisoner who was convicted of theft for the first time was liable to pay a fine two or four times the value of the stolen goods; a second or third conviction on the same charge was punishable by scalding off finger tips; and an incorrigible offender lost the whole hand. Murder was a capital crime, but the convict could redeem himself by paying a fine to the deceased's next of kin in cash or in kind.[115] A condemned criminal could be tortured before he was executed.[116]

The L.M.S. Takes Over German Stations 109

But the presence of traders and miners in Tswana communities necessitated some change in the judicial process, and in this regard the Shoshong missionary played a prominent part. Macheng's letter to Governor Wodehouse spelled out the core of the problems: he invited the British Government to occupy the Tati area because he himself "felt utterly unqualified to govern such a community as that of gold diggers.... These gold diggers are your people; therefore I invite you, and I beg you, to come and occupy the gold country." [117] When the British Government did not respond to his request, Macheng set up a special court for whites that was presided over by Mackenzie, the chief's presence at the court merely conferring legal validity to its decisions. When Kgama became chief, he attended the special court more regularly than did Machenge. All told, the Ngwato seem to have adjusted to the new two-tier court system fairly well, and Kgama's fearless administration of justice to blacks and whites alike enhanced his prestige.[118]

L.M.S. agents did not, until late in the nineteenth century, make any conscious efforts to promote the economic well-being of the Tswana. Although Roger Price is reported to have built a dam at Molepolole,[119] the venture must have been of little consequence, for successive reports from that station show drought and hunger to have been perennial. Charles Williams's annual report for 1873 is typical: "The people have been widely scattered searching for food." [120] Hunting remained a reliable source of food and wealth, although game resources were continually diminishing. Edward Mohr, who passed through Ngwatoland in 1869, noted that "elephants have now entirely disappeared from this neighborhood, driven away by ceaseless persecution. It is quite a mistake to imagine them to have been all killed; indeed, I was assured that they emigrated in small troops, most of them following a northeasterly direction." [121] To ensure adequate revenue for their chiefdoms, Tswana rulers issued decrees making the trade in feathers and ivory a monopoly of the chiefs. But the monopoly was difficult to enforce.[122] Enterprising Tswana hunters sometimes sought the assistance of professional white hunters. Thus, when in 1875 Frederick Hugh Barber combined with Ngwato hunters in Ngamiland, the group shot adequate game, so that "trees all round the wagons were red with meat, hanging up to dry, and their wagons were filled with biltong [jerked meat]." [123]

This assistance did not acquire white hunters any lasting favors or privileges, for Tswana rulers were keenly aware of the declining game resources in their chiefdoms. When Barber asked for Kgama's permission to collect young ostriches and to hunt elephants in 1877, the chief refused "saying that, as there were so few elephants left in his country, feathers were the only source of revenue left him; and if he allowed young birds to be caught, there would very soon be none to grow up into big ones to grow feathers for his hunters to shoot." [124] By 1878 Kgama had banned all professional hunters, preferring those who hunted for sport.[125]

By the late 1870s Shoshong had the biggest concentration of white traders: twenty-three adult males, six women, and thirteen children. They operated nine retail stores but complained that their annual turnover was declining sharply. And due to the civil disturbances at Shoshong, Ngwato population had fallen from 30,000 in the 1860s to about 10,000 in 1878; of these, 2,500 were soldiers divided into five regiments, each headed by one of Kgama's brothers. Patterson estimated the Ngwato to have possessed between 7,000 and 8,000 oxen and a considerable number of sheep and goats; he confirmed earlier accounts on the barrenness of farming land and the scarcity of water. Because of these disabilities Patterson concluded that Shoshong was not a safe place to live.[126]

The Kwena and the Ngwaketse had some six resident traders between them by the late 1870s. Although both groups bartered with itinerant traders, they tended to purchase more goods from resident traders. In 1876 the Rev. James Good reported that resident traders were happy to notice the new Ngwaketse purchasing habits, and that beads, clothing, and trinkets had become popular with Kanye residents. The introduction of plows was gradually affecting some aspects of Tswana life. Previously, agricultural farming was performed by women, but since plows were drawn by cattle, which women were not allowed to handle, men now had to do the plowing.[127] This taboo was bound to become obsolete because, during the last quarter of the nineteenth century, the mining industry of South Africa was expanding and required more men from neighboring countries, making it even more imperative for the women to attend to agricultural pursuits.

Resident traders seemed to be associating with Tswana communities in a way that disturbed the chiefs. In 1865 Sechele complained about their relations with Tswana women: "Hark! I know what they are doing now. They are giving beads to the young girls, for it is dark. They are corrupting the women of my people, they are teaching my people abominations of which even they [Tswana] were once ignorant, heathens as they [Tswana] may be." [128] Attempts made by L.M.S. agents to dissuade traders from having illicit sexual relations with Tswana women and to conform to Christian standards of living were sometimes resisted. Hepburn's experience with a Shoshong trader typified the problem: "He told me on Sunday evening . . . that he regarded that subject as too sacred and too private for the interference of a second party and he for his part resented my intermeddling with so sacred a thing as his duty between him and his God." [129] Nor were traders themselves regular churchgoers. In 1875 Hepburn thought he had succeeded in persuading Shoshong traders to attend Sunday services regularly in the chapel they had built for themselves but, as his review shows, "The service . . . continued until they could bear it no longer and they plainly told me not to come any more."[130] Gambling and drinking seem to have been the traders' most popular pastimes.[131] These shortcomings seem to have had no ill effects on the traders' personal relationships with chiefs and missionaries. Although their occupations appeared to be mutually irreconcilable, there is evidence to suggest that missionaries and traders worked out a *modus vivendi*.

In his review of twenty-two years' missionary work in Ngwatoland, Hepburn cited instances when he advocated fair business practices, as, for example, in 1880 when he severely reprimanded the Tawana chief, Moremi, for ill-treating white traders in Ngamiland. Later that year Hepburn could report that Moremi "made a very [big] improvement of his conduct . . . the traders say who are residing at the Lake. They can sell, and they are not plagued with continuous petty annoyances from his people as formerly."[132] This service to the traders was often acknowledged and rewarded in the form of small gifts to the missionary, but the traders' appreciation was more conspicuous when a missionary was transferred to another station, or when he went on furlough.

In 1875 traders at Molepolole forwarded a £25 check to L.M.S. directors that was to be given to Price, who was on furlough, "as a small recognition of the many acts of kindness we have received from him."[133] In 1876 the same traders were more specific in their indebtedness: "Those unacquainted with the history of South Africa but little know the vast amount of commerce that has in all cases followed the steps of missionary labour. Some 50 years ago but little was known north of the Vaal River."[134] And before Mackenzie went on furlough in 1868, Shoshong traders gave him £35 and pointed out that the money was presented in recognition of the good work he had done as a minister of religion and the high esteem all traders had for him as a person.[135]

The L.M.S. Takes Over German Stations

The sporadic conflicts between chiefs and missionaries were certainly offset by long intervals of mutual understanding, a condition no doubt necessitated by their social and economic interdependence in isolated communities separated by vast land masses. In this connection, the Molepolole trader, Henry Boyne, seems to have been one of a few traders who became intimate friends of any Tswana chief. Mrs. Price must have underestimated Boyne's relationship with Sechele when she equated it with their own tarnished relationship with the Kwena chief.[136] This was demonstrated in 1881 when Sechele had a marital problem to solve. After his wife's (Mma-Sebele) death in 1880, Sechele had hardly recovered from his bereavement when his flare to meddle in the affairs of neighboring chiefdoms was aroused by the arrival at Shoshong of Kholoma, one of Lobengula's runaway wives. Sechele wooed Kholoma by sending her lavish presents, and, after she accepted his marriage proposal, the chief assigned Boyne the onerous task of delivering her to Molepolole. Kholoma was safely brought to the Kwena capital in June 1881.[137]

Thus by 1880, in spite of some petty quarrels among them, a pattern of mutual coexistence between the Tswana, the missionaries, and the traders was emerging; frequent incursions on Tswana territory by the Boers tended to engender Tswana reliance on Britain. When the British developed schemes to expand their sphere of influence into the African hinterland, northern Tswana chiefdoms were a natural corridor to Central Africa and their annexation became inevitable.

NOTES TO CHAPTER THREE

1. Robert Moffat, *The Matebele Journals of Robert Moffat, 1829–1860*, 2 vols., ed. J. P. R. Wallis (London: 1945), 1: 11–13, 203. For doctrinal differences, see Robert Moffat to Tidman, 20 February 1861, where Moffat says of the Hermannsburgers: "Our teaching in reference to baptism is also to them heretical," Box 32, Jacket A, Folder 3 (L.M.S.).
2. R. Moffat, *Matebele Journals*, 1: 41; Thomas Morgan Thomas, in *Eleven Years in Central Africa* (London: 1872), p. 47: ". . . such a welcome, indeed, as the Dutch and Germans only seem able to give."
3. J. P. R. Wallis, ed., *The Matebele Mission*, p. 149; Inyati missionaries were "merry over the sacks of wheat [they had] been able to procure from the Hanoverian missionaries. . . ."
4. Una Long, ed., *The Journals of Elizabeth Lees Price* (London: 1956), p. 113.
5. J. du Plessis, *A History of Christian Missions in South Africa* (Edinburgh: 1911), p. 376.
6. Ferdinand Zimmermann to Robert Moffat, 10 January 1861, Box 32, Jacket A, Folder 3 (L.M.S.); Wallis, *The Matebele Mission*, p. 203.
7. Henrich Schulenburg to Moffat, Price, and Mackenzie, 10 January 1861, Box 32, Jacket A, Folder 3 (L.M.S.).
8. Moffat, Price, and Mackenzie to Tidman, 24 January 1863, Box 33, Jacket A, Folder 1 (L.M.S.).
9. Wallis, *The Matebele Mission*, p. 203.
10. Mackenzie to Tidman, 14 May 1862, Box 32, Jacket A, Folder 5 (L.M.S.).
11. For Ndebele threat to kill Price, see Wallis, *The Matebele Mission*, p. 179.
12. John Mackenzie, *Ten Years North of the Orange River* (Edinburgh: 1871), p. 250.
13. Chief Sechele to R. Moffat, 31 October 1865, Box 33, Jacket A, Folder 5 (L.M.S.); Thomas, p. 48; Long, p. 169.
14. Price to Tidman, 10 March 1863, Box 33, Jacket A, Folder 1 (L.M.S.).
15. Tidman to Price, 5 September 1863, ibid. (L.M.S.).
16. Mackenzie to Hardeland, 23 January 1863, Box 33, Jacket A, Folder 1 (L.M.S.).
17. Karl Hohls to Mackenzie, 17 July 1864, Box 33, Jacket B, Folder 3 (L.M.S.). In Haccius, *Hannoversche* (1910), p. 410, Hardeland says: "Our Christian love and prudence required us to leave the field for the London brothers."
18. A copy of the agreement between the L.M.S. and the Hermannsburgers on their spheres of missionary influence is in Mackenzie to Karl Hohls, 3 September 1864, Box 33, Jacket B, Folder 3 (L.M.S.).
19. Karl Hohls to Mackenzie, 8 September 1864, Box 33, Jacket B, Folder 3 (L.M.S.). Writing from Dinokane, the Hurutshe center, Hohls conceded: "It is certainly the case that Sechele will not have us now. . . ."

The L.M.S. Takes Over German Stations 115

20. Sechele to Moshete (R. Moffat), 31 October 1865, Box 33, Jacket A, Folder 5 (L.M.S.).
21. Moffat to Tidman, 5 November 1860, Box 32, Jacket A, Folder 1 (L.M.S.).
22. Thomas, p. 46.
23. See "No. 9 Ngami. Notes made by J. Ellenberger at Tsau, Ngamiland, in 1906," in Willoughby Papers, Folder 796, Selly Oak Colleges Library, Birmingham; E. W. Smith, *The Great Lion of Bechuanaland: The Life and Times of Roger Price* (London: 1957), Appendix B, pp. 411–25; Mackenzie, *Ten Years*, p. 180; Hugh Marshall Hole to David Chamberlain (Managing Editor of the L.M.S. *Chronicle*), 28 October 1932, letter kept in a copy of Hole's book, *The Passing of the Black Kings* (London: 1932), at L.M.S. Archives.
24. Mackenzie, *Ten Years*, pp. 210:11. Lecholathebe was obviously under the impression that members of the L.M.S. Kololo mission were poisoned by Sekeletu, a view that was shared by some missionaries, but was later refuted by Mackenzie, R. Moffat, Price, et al.
25. Mackenzie, *Ten Years*, p. 211.
26. J. D. Hepburn to Joseph Mullens, 28 October 1875, Box 38, Jacket A, Folder 1 (L.M.S.). *See also* Thomas Tlou, "A Political History of Northwestern Botswana to 1906" (Ph.D. dissertation, University of Wisconsin, 1972, University Microfilms, Ann Arbor, Michigan), p. 189.
27. *See* Emil Holub, *Seven Years In South Africa: Travels, Researches, and Hunting Adventures, between the Diamond Fields and the Zambezi, 1872–79*, 2 vols., trans. Ellen Frewer (London: 1881), 1: 314–15, who gave the following population estimates: Ngwaketse, 30,000; Rolong, 65,000. *See also* Wallis, ed. *The Matebele Mission*, p. 70; Price to Tidman, 15 March 1862, Box 32, Jacket A, Folder 5 (L.M.S.); Price to Tidman, 11 July 1867, Box 34, Jacket A, Folder 3 (L.M.S.).
28. Long, ed., p. 135.
29. Ibid., p. 77.
30. Ibid., p. 180.
31. Ibid., p. 110, For Tswana views on begging *see* ibid., p. 166, where Kgama's wife exclaims: "Ah, but you must not wonder at us doing it— for in our eyes it is an honour to be begged of— a token of our greatness and ability"; Mackenzie in *Ten Years*, p. 45, says: "To be begged from is one of the marks of chieftainship among the Bechuanas. A stranger will say that his chief is a great man; people come from all quarters to beg from him!"
32. Long, ed., p. 193.
33. Ibid., p. 263.
34. Mackenzie, *Ten Years*, p. 252. Smallpox seems to have spread from the Cape, where in 1858 it killed thirty-five people ("The Small-pox Epidemic of 1858," C.M.M. 5 [January 1859]: 14–19). According to Levaillant smallpox was introduced to South Africa by Dutch settlers (*Travels into the Interior Parts of Africa, by the Cape of Good Hope, in the Years 1780, 1781, 1783, 1784, and 1785*, 2 vols. [Perth: 1796], 1: 25).
35. Mackenzie, *Ten Years*, p. 253.

36. Ibid.

37. Ibid., p. 265. In 1869 Thomas Baines was invited by Kgamane to treat his eight-year-old son who had sore eyes, and in the process of applying an eye lotion was closely watched by the boy's old nurse (see Baines, *The Northern Goldfields Diaries of Thomas Baines*, 2 vols., ed. J. P. R. Wallis [London: 1946], 1: 38.

38. James Chapman, *Travels in the Interior of South Africa*, 2 vols. (London: 1868), 2: 310, 312.

39. Ibid., p. 312.

40. Long, ed., p. 225.

41. Ibid., p. 267.

42. See chapter 1.

43. Long, ed., p. 220: "Roger [Price] said . . . the Lutheran Church was dissolved—that those who sought to be received as members must come as entirely new. . . . "

44. Price to Tidman, 15 July 1863, Box 33, Jacket A, Folder 1 (L.M.S.).

45. Mackenzie, *Ten Years*, p. 409.

46. Ibid., p. 378.

47. Long. ed., p. 263.

48. Ibid., p. 255.

49. Ibid., p. 155.

50. Ibid., p. 145.

51. Price to Tidman, 11 July 1867, Box 34, Jacket A, Folder 3 (L.M.S.).

52. Price to Mullens, 15 December 1868, Box 35, Jacket A, Folder 1 (L.M.S.).

53. Long, ed., p. 143. Mrs. Mackenzie to Mrs. Thompson, June 1866, Box 33, Jacket A, Folder 5 (L.M.S.), in which Kgama is reported to have defied Sekgoma's order to divorce his wife.

54. J. P. R. Wallis, ed., *The Matebele Mission*, pp. 203–204; John Mackenzie, *Day-dawn in Dark Places, a Story of Wanderings and Work in Bechuanaland* (London: 1884), pp. 227–30; "Notes from the Bamangwato," enclosed in Wookey to Hawkins, 26 December 1914, Box 76 (L.M.S.).

55. For Sekgoma's views on his Ndebele neighbors, see Mackenzie, *Ten Years*, p. 409.

56. Thomas Baines, *Exploration in South West Africa: Being an Account of a Journey in the Years 1861 and 1862 from Walvish Bay on the Western Coast to Lake Ngami and the Victoria Falls* (London: 1864), p. 432: "A speech worthy of applause it seemed had just been ended, for as we entered the chief rose, and at the head of a dozen or twenty young men brandishing their spears or muskets rushed forward till they nearly met us." In 1863 Sekgoma advised Lecholathebe (Chapman, 2: 307) to "buy guns, buy horses; do not let a gun go back from your town if you have a tusk to buy it with."

57. For more exercises see *Baines*, pp. 434–36: "Then followed the sortie. A company of men, headed by its own petty chief, rushed forward with strange gesticulations, creeping along nearly on a level with the ground, and covered by the shield until the moment for a blow; then

The L.M.S. Takes Over German Stations

charging and curvetting like a prancing horse, thrusting with the short spear (not throwing it like the Kaffir assegai), sweeping with fantastically shaped battle axe, or poisoning the musket . . . and returning victoriously to the main body. . . . One man, referring to the expected coming of the enemy, reminded them of the strength of [Kgwebe], their rock of refuge where they had before so successfully resisted the invaders."

58. Mackenzie to Mullens, 2 September 1872, Box 37, Jacket A, Folder 1 (L.M.S.); Mrs. Mackenzie, extract of letter in the L.M.S. *Chronicle*, June 1866; Wyndham Knight-Bruce, *The Story of an African Chief: Being the Life of Khama* (London: 1893), p. 13.

59. Mackenzie, *Ten Years*, p. 272; Mackenzie's belief in participating in the just war was again spelled out during the Tlhaping uprising of 1878 when he asserted it to be "right in the highest sense for Christian husbands and fathers to defend those whom God had given them, and if need be, to die in their defense," in his book, *Austral Africa: Losing It or Gaining It*, 2 vols. (London: 1887), 1: 86.

60. Mackenzie, *Ten Years*, pp. 279–80. For the Christian conception of the just war over the past 2,000 years, see J. Von Elbe, "The Evolution of the Concept of the Just War in International Law," *The American Journal of International Law* 33 (1939): 665–88; A. Nussbaum, "Just War —A Legal Concept?", *Michigan Law Review* 42 (1943–44): 453–79. Even the most conservative of L.M.S. agents, R. Moffat, sanctioned the just war provided the wronged party did not kill innocent civilians. See R. Moffat, *Apprenticeship at Kuruman*, cd. I. Schapcra (London: 1951), pp. 51–52.

61. Mackenzie, *Ten Years*, p. 284.

62. Wallis, ed., *The Matebele Mission*, pp. 196-97: "[In trying to pursue retreating Ndebele forces, the Ngwato] found themselves completely surrounded by the main body of the enemy. A few who were on horseback managed to break through the ring, and by their efforts a portion of their followers were left to the mercy of the Matebele and of course were all killed."

63. Long, ed., p. 129.

64. Thomas Leask, *The Southern African Diaries of Thomas Leask, 1865–1870*, ed. J. P. R. Wallis (London: 1954), p. 61; Holub, 1: 384.

65. See, for example, Thomas Leask, *The Southern African Diaries of Thomas Leask, 1865–1870*, ed. J. P. R. Wallis (London: 1954), p. 50: "I don't understand the laws of these people but, however it is, Macheng, tho much a younger man than Sekgomi, is considered the chief, because he is a son of the head wife." This is confirmed by Sekgoma Khama, in "Kama's Life," 28 March 1925, B.N.A., S. 601/18. For the traditional history of principal Tswana tribes, see works cited in footnote two, chapter 1.

66. Willoughby Papers, "Macheng Kgosi ea Mangwato," Folder 795, Selly Oak Colleges Library; R. Moffat, *Matebele Journals*, 2: 115, 142; Baines, *Northern Goldfields*, 2: 303.

67. Mackenzie, *Ten Years*, p. 361; H. A. Bryden, *Gun and Camera* (London, 1926), p. 264.

68. Mackenzie, *Ten Years*, p. 363.

69. Mackenzie, *Day-dawn*, p. 264; Mackenzie to Tidman, 3 July 1866, Box 34, Jacket B, Folder 1 (L.M.S.).
70. Leask, p. 50; Holub, 1: 384; A. Sillery, *Bechuanaland Protectorate* (Cape Town: 1952), pp. 120-22.
71. Mackenzie, *Day-dawn*, pp. 257-58. An Irish trader and a Boer hunter (Piet Jacobs) were attacked during the civil war but escaped injury; see Leask, p. 51.
72. Mackenzie to Tidman, 3 July 1866, Box 34, Jacket 3, Folder I (L.M.S.). For accounts on the civil war, see Price to Tidman, 13 April 1866, Box 34, Jacket A, Folder One. Mackenzie's neutrality was confirmed by Ngwato elders in 1914: see "Notes from the Bamangwato," enclosed in Wookey to Hawkins, 26 December 1914, Box 76 (L.M.S.).
73. Long, ed., p. 202.
74. W. D. Mackenzie, *John Mackenzie: South African Missionary and Statesman* (London: 1902), p. 126. Mackenzie to Governor Wodehouse, Cape Town, 20 May and 3 November 1868, in "Mackenzie's Papers. Early Missionary Life Private. Tati Gold Papers Down to December 1875," on microfilm, Reel One, Rhodes House, Oxford; R. Moffat, *Matebele Journals*, 2: 157.
75. Edward Tabler, "The Tati Gold Rush and the Diary of Alexander Hamp," *Africana Notes and News* 12-13 (1956-59): 55. According to Edward Mohr, who visited the Tati in 1869, there were 30-40 diggers (*To the Victoria Falls of the Zambezi* [London: 1876], p. 152).
76. For Mackenzie's role in settling disputes between miners see Mackenzie to Thomas M. Thomas and Sykes (undated) and Mackenzie to Mr. Biles (also undated), whom he informed: "You will have the right to rule over your own party, but over none others," in "Mackenzie Papers," Reel One, Rhodes House; Francois Coillard, *On the Threshold of Central Africa: A Record of Twenty Years' Pioneering among the Barotse of the Upper Zambezi* (London: 1890), p. 49.
77. Mackenzie, *Ten Years*, p. 455; cf. Anthony Sillery, *John Mackenzie of Bechuanaland 1835-1899* (Balkema, Cape Town: 1971), in which Mackenzie is unconvincingly portrayed as a humanitarian.
78. Mackenzie to Joseph Mullens, 20 January 1869, Box 35, Jacket C, Folder 2 (L.M.S.).
79. Mackenzie's letter to Thomas and Sykes at Inyati (April 1868) shows his imperial interests, for he announced Macheng's decision to invite the British to have been his own idea, and equated his role in the affair with John the Baptist's influence on King Herod, in "Mackenzie's Papers," Rhodes House. See also B.N.A., H. C. 48/1/2, Mackenzie to Sir Henry Barkly, 2 May 1876.
80. Edward C. Tabler, "The Tati Gold Rush and the Diary of Alexander Hamp," *Africana Notes and News* 13, no. 2 (June 1958); 54.
81. Mackenzie to Mullens, 2 September 1872, Box 37, Jacket A, Folder 1 (L.M.S.). Richard Brown, "External Relations of the Ndebele Kingdom," in *African Societies in Southern Africa*, ed. L. M. Thompson (London: 1969), p. 277, ascribes Macheng's fall to "attempting to rule in Ndebele

The L.M.S. Takes Over German Stations

manner," an observation that does not seem to take into account Macheng's ignorance of Tswana law and custom.

82. After Kgama's defeat in 1866, he had declared: "I wish all the Bamangwato to know that I renounce all pretensions to the chieftainship of the Bamangwato." Mackenzie, *Day-dawn,* p. 259.

83. Price to Mackenzie, 29 October 1872, in "Mackenzie Papers. Africa. Personal. 2." (L.M.S.); Sillery, pp. 120–21. See also Sekgoma Khama, "Khama's Life," B.N.A., No. Serowe 337, S.601/18.

84. Chief Kgama's evidence, in Parliamentary Papers, Accounts and Papers II, Colonies and British Possessions, 1887, 59, C. 4890, p. 9.

85. J. D. Hepburn, *Twenty Years in Khama's Country,* ed. C. H. Lyall (London, 1895), pp. 14–34; Serpa Pinto, *How I Crossed Africa,* 2 vols., trans. Alfred Elwes (Philadelphia, 1881), 2: 212–14.

86. Hepburn to Mullens, 20 April 1875, Box 38, Jacket A, Folder 1 (L.M.S.).

87. Good to Whitehouse, 25 August 1879, Box 40, Jacket D, Folder 1 (L.M.S.).

88. Robert U. Moffat, *John Smith Moffat, A Memoir* (London: John Murray, 1921; reprinted New York: Negro University Press, 1969), p. 144; Price to Mullens, 15 December 1868, Box 35, Jacket A, Folder 1 (L.M.S.).

89. Price to Mullens, 30 November 1870, Box 36, Jacket B, Folder 1 (L.M.S.).

90. Hepburn to Mullens, 13 September 1871, Box 36, Jacket D, Folder 3 (L.M.S.).

91. Price to Mullens, 15 December 1868, Box 35, Jacket A, Folder 1 (L.M.S.).

92. Price to Mullens, 5 July 1870, Box 36, Jacket A, Folder 1 (L.M.S.).

93. Price to Mullens, 30 November 1870, Box 36, Jacket B, Folder 1 (L.M.S.).

94. Charles Williams to Mullens, Molepolole Annual Report for 1874, enclosed in letter of 6 January 1875; Reports, Africa-South. Box 1 (L.M.S.).

95. Williams to Mullens, 25 September 1876, Box 38, Jacket C, Folder 3 (L.M.S.).

96. Mackenzie, *Day-dawn,* p. 275.

97. See "Worshipping the Daft," in Willoughby Papers, Folder 770, Selly Oak Colleges Library.

98. Mackenzie, *Day-dawn,* p. 223.

99. Long, ed., pp. 128, 159, where a married woman is reported to have been initiated because "she was not a genuine woman until" initiated.

100. Mackenzie, *Ten Years,* p. 376.

101. James Good to Whitehouse, 25 August 1879, Box 40, Jacket D, Folder 1 (L.M.S.).

102. Mohr, p. 137.

103. Holub, 1: 398; J. Tom Brown, *Among the Bantu Nomads, a Record of Forty Years Spent Among the Bechuana* (London: 1926), p. 73; "The age is not a fixed one, for it is governed by the time at which a child or near relative of the chief is judged to be ready for the [circumcision] ceremony"; W. C. Willoughby, "Notes on the Initiation Ceremonies

of the Becwana," *J.R.A.I.*: 39 (1909): 229: "It is held every fourth year, but the chief will sometimes delay the bogwera or hasten it, for the sake of having a son of his own or, failing that, a nephew in the ceremony." See also I. Schapera. *A Handbook of Tswana Law and Custom* (London: 1970), pp. 104–117.

104. Holub, 1: 399–400; Parker Gillmore, *The Great Thirstland: A Ride through Natal, Orange Free State, Transvaal, and Kalahari Desert* (London: 1878), p. 300: "[Circumcision was] supposed to bind them firmly together for good or bad."

105. Holub, 2: 421; Mackenzie to Mullens, 20 April 1875, Box 38, Jacket A, Folder 1 (L.M.S.).

106. Mackenzie to Mullens, 18 August 1876, Box 38, Jacket A, Folder 1 (L.M.S.).

107. Holub, 1: 295–96: "Baffled on this occasion by the advice of his rain doctor, Montshiwa next required that followers of the new faith should take part in two ceremonies connected with rain-magic; first, in the letshulo-hunt appointed by the rain doctors for the capture of certain wild animals, part of which were employed in the incantations; and secondly, in turning up a plot of ground for the service of doctors, which was afterwards considered consecrated, and called "tsimo ea pu[l] a," the garden of the rain." See also Alexander Bailie's report, in Parliamentary Papers, 1878–9, 52 C. 2220, p. 76.

108. Leask, pp. 144–45. Cf. the Tlhapings' angry reaction to the killing of a crocodile, which they considered sacred (Read to Hardcastle, 15 March 1817, Box 7, Jacket 6, Folder 1 [L.M.S.]).

109. Long, ed., p. 368.

110. Ibid., p. 375.

111. Holub, 1: 393.

112. Alexander Bailie, Parliamentary Papers, 1878–79, C. 2220, 52: 76.

113. Price to Mullens, 2 July 1879, Box 40, Jacket C, Folder 1 (L.M.S.): ". . . after the meeting was over the chief sent his second son down to inform me of the willingness of the people to accede to his request . . ."; Charles Williams to Mullens, 8 May 1876, Box 38, Jacket B, Folder 3 (L.M.S.). For accounts on the war between the Kwena and the Kgatla, see Edwin W. Smith, *Great Lion of the Bechuanaland*, pp. 201–202; I. Schapera, *A Short History of the Bakgatta-baga Kgafela of Bechuanaland Protectorate* (Communications from the School of African Studies—University of Cape Town, 1942); Alexander Bailie, pp. 52–53.

114. Holub, 1: 396.

115. Ibid.

116. Long, ed., pp. 431, 481.

117. W. Douglas Mackenzie, *John Mackenzie: South African Missionary and Statesman* (London: 1902), p. 124. For a slightly different version of the letter, see Mackenzie to Wodehouse, 29 March 1868, "Mackenzie Papers," Reel One, Rhodes House, Oxford.

118. Captain Patterson's Report of July 1878, enclosed in no. 78, Governor H. B. E. Frere to Sir Michael Beach, 14 September 1878, in Parliamentary Papers, C. 2220, 52: 237: "Justice is administered in Sho-

The L.M.S. Takes Over German Stations

shong by the chief sitting in the Khotla, surrounded by the elders, his advisers. The law is one of custom, well defined and understood. . . ." See also Coillard, p. 49.

119. Long, ed., p. 209.

120. Charles Williams to J. O. Whitehead, 16 December 1873, Molepolole Annual Report for 1873, Box 1 (L.M.S.).

121. Mohr, p. 124. For diminishing game resources see also H. Hall, "Notes on Animal Life in South Africa," *C.M.M.* 1 (January 1857): 6.

122. Mohr, p. 157; Mackenzie, *Ten Years North*, p. 179.

123. Edward C. Tabler, ed., *Zambezi and Matebeleland in the Seventies* (London: 1960), p. 66.

124. Ibid., pp. 70–71; Holub (1: 389) estimated the Ngwato chief to have had an annual revenue of £3,000.

125. Patterson's Report, Parliamentary Papers, p. 237; Gillmore, p. 212

126. Patterson, p. 237. Yet Shoshong hills were sanctuaries in times of war, as was demonstrated during the civil war of 1866. See also Pinto, 2: 220.

127. James Good to Mullens, 28 April 1876, Box 38, Jacket A, Folder 3 (L.M.S.); Holub, 1: 339–40; Pinto, 2: 215.

128. J. S. Moffat to Tidman, 18 December 1865, Box 33, Jacket A, Folder 5 (L.M.S.).

129. Hepburn to Whitehouse, June 1880, p. 61, Box 40, Jacket B, Folder 3 (L.M.S.).

130. Ibid. See also Pinto, 2: 218.

131. J. D. Hepburn, *Twenty Years in Khama's Country*, ed. C. H. Lyall (London: 1895), p. 117: "And it is enough to make the heart of any man sad to recall how many an interior white trader has also been civilized off the face of the earth by [liquor]." See also Patterson, p. 237.

132. Hepburn to Whitehouse, June 1880, Box 40, Jacket B, Folder 3 (L.M.S.) See also Good to Mullens, 28 April 1876, Box 38, Jacket A, Folder 3 (L.M.S.).

133. Henry Taylor to Mullens, 25 January 1875, Box 38, Jacket A, Folder 1 (L.M.S.) In Long, ed., *Journals*, p. 237, three Boer hunters found poaching in Sechele's country had their fines reduced to half after Roger Price interceded on their behalf; such services rendered to traders and hunters cultivated lasting friendships.

134. Henry Taylor to Mullens, 9 August 1876, Box 38, Jacket C, Folder 3 (L.M.S.). See also Gillmore, p. 441.

135. Shoshong traders to Mackenzie, 19 November 1868, "Mackenzie Papers," Rhodes House.

136. Long, ed., pp. 393, 391.

137. Ibid., pp. 471–73; Boyne's task must have been a risky one, for Lobengula's spies had orders to capture Kholoma and send her back to the Chief's harem.

4
Events Leading to Declaration of a Protectorate; Tswana Resistance to British Rule; Government Intervention in Tribal Affairs

I

THE DECLARATION OF A BRITISH PROTECTORATE OVER NORTHERN Tswana chiefdoms was linked to white expansion in southern Africa throughout the nineteenth century.[1] In this development southern Tswana chiefdoms experienced white encroachment earlier than their northern counterparts because, situated as they were closer to white polities, they were exposed to the more daring white adventurers than were the northern chiefdoms. Nevertheless, the last quarter of the nineteenth century was destined to engulf northern Tswana chiefdoms in the tangled web of European imperialism.

Before the British started to extend their sphere of influence in earnest, northern Tswana chiefdoms had had several clashes with the Boers; the 1852 war between the Kwena and the Boers being one of the most serious conflicts.[2]

The Ngwato and the Kwena had another challenge to their territorial integrity in 1876 when a disaffected sect of the Dutch Reformed Church (also called the "Doppers," or "Gereformeerde Kerk Van Suid-Afrika") from the South African Republic resolved to go to Damaraland in southwest Africa through Tswana territory, with or without the chiefs' approval. The belligerent mood of this essentially fundamentalist Boer group was given by Parker Gillmore, a contemporary who stayed with the Doppers for some time on the Limpopo River. Gillmore observed:

> They [Doppers] consider themselves to be the chosen people of God, and are still in search of the promised land, which they profess to believe exists farther north in the interior of Africa. The heathen, they say, have been given [to] them as a heritage. . . . No kind look or even word here cheers the [Doppers'] task, for no bond of sympathy exists between the Dopper and the black man. His house he takes pleasure in, his cattle he is proud of, but a heathen merits not a thought.[3]

The threat of a Boer attack came at a time when Kgama had hardly consolidated his position as Chief at Shoshong and when Kgamane, now a refugee in Kwenaland after the break with his brother, was flirting with the Boers in the Transvaal, urging them to support him in an attempt to unseat Kgama.[4] In these circumstances, Kgama chose to rely more on diplomatic techniques than on military ploys to ward off the immenent Boer attack.[5] Thus, as soon as his sentinels reported the presence of Boers on the border, Kgama drilled his regiments for defensive purposes, while at the same time he mounted a campaign to pacify the Boers: he asked some of his councillors and the Rev. J. D.

Events Leading to Declaration of a Protectorate 125

Hepburn to contact the Boers on his behalf. Addressing them as "my friends on the crocodile river," Kgama offered the Boers advice on how to cross the formidable Kgalagadi Desert, pointing out that only small convoys of three wagons could hazard the journey at a time.[6] But the Boers ignored Kgama's advice and instead invited Kgama to come and discuss the issue with them on the Limpopo.[7] Kgama, who as head of state must have thought the invitation to be inappropriate, coming as it did from people of a lower rank than himself, refused to go and negotiations between the Ngwato and the Boers were shelved for some time.[8]

If the Ngwato were ill prepared to deal with emigrant Boers, the threat of Boer aggression found the Kwena at a most inopportune moment because the latter were at war with the Kgatla-baga Kgafela.[9] However, that conflict and the Boer threat were abated by the timely arrival of Alexander Bailie, a labor recruiting agent from the diamond fields of Griqualand West.[10] Bailie arranged a truce between the Kwena and the Kgatla in November 1876, which both sides agreed to observe until he returned from Matebeleland.[11] In this instance Bailie wielded more influence than L.M.S. missionaries who failed to stop the war and had to be content with merely passing a resolution deploring the conflict.[12] Sechele's disregard of the advice of missionaries is another illustration of Tswana diplomacy in the ninetenth century, when alliances with white groups was determined by the benefit the chiefdoms expected to get from them.[13] Sechele must have calculated that he would get British military aid more readily through Bailie than through the B.D.C. Hence, his acceptance of the truce. Nor was that the end of Bailie's influence: he succeeded in keeping the Boers off Tswana territory by warning them that Britain would intervene on the Tswana's behalf if they trespassed on native lands.[14] The warning was effective, for not only did the Boers postpone their journey, but the tone of their letters also became conciliatory: in one letter they assured Kgama that they had no intention of taking his country by force, and that they would not be accessories to Kgamane's conspiracy against him.[15]

Meanwhile, another diplomatic problem was unfolding across the Limpopo. J. D. Botha, a field cornet (sheriff) in the Marico District of the Transvaal, charged Kgama with having wrongfully impounded the property of one William Groening, a resident of the Marico District.[16] The charge was a sequel to a series of interborder clashes between the Boers and the Tswana, a common feature since the 1840s, that both groups had tried to resolve without success. What had actually emerged was an unwritten convention by which the Boers and the Tswana could mutually punish trespassers in their respective territories without any recriminations from the offenders' country of origin. It was on the strength of this understanding that Kgama had impounded Groening's property after the latter had been found poaching game in Ngwatoland.

Kgama rejected the charge and concluded that racial prejudice had impelled Botha to challenge his right to punish Groening:

> No opportunity is ever lost of making us know and feel how much you despise us because God has chosen to make us black and you white.[17]

He further submitted that Boer inconsistencies in their relations with the Ngwato undermined the latter's confidence in them.

Strategic and political considerations appear to have influenced the three chiefs' favorable responses to Bailie's request for laborers. Gaseitsiwe and Sechele agreed to supply Bailie with laborers after the plowing season was over, while Kgama provided him with fifty men. Although he needed the men for his army, Kgama must have known that the immediate loss of fifty men was also a tribal invest-

Events Leading to Declaration of a Protectorate 127

ment because it was calculated to win British friendship and protection. And when the three chiefs invited the British to protect them against Boer attacks, there were precedents to draw from. Just as they had invited German missionaries to forestall Boer aggression in the late 1850s, so did the same political expediency dictate Tswana alliance with the British in 1876. Even before Bailie had visited Shoshong, Kgama had written to "the great Queen of the English people" asking for protection:

> I wish to hear upon what conditions Her Majesty will receive me and my country and my people under her protection. I am weary with fighting.[18]

When the Boers renewed their request to be allowed to pass through Ngwatoland early in 1877, they unwittingly strengthened Kgama's faith in the British by asserting that their relations with the Ngwato were guided by Christian morality. To Kgama, who was himself a practicing Christian,[19] the Boer religious inference was clearly incompatible with their belligerent mood the previous year.[20] With these circumstances, the British had the credible appearance of promoting peace, while the Boers had a chronic record of conflicts with the Ngwato and could not discredit their image as warmongers. Kgama's retort to their claim to Christian morality was an uncompromising indictment:

> But I come now to speak of your own deceitfulness and treacherous conduct: you call yourselves Christians, and I also am a Christian, a member of a Christian Church. I am doing all that lies in my power to lead my people to give up their old and sinful [sic] customs . . . to serve the living God and His son Jesus Christ, who I believe died for white and black. . . . My missionaries have never taught me, and God's book does not teach me, that a man may write anything he likes today and do any other thing he likes tomorrow.[21]

Even though Kgama had had to punish British traders who contravened his laws, the British government's record in South Africa persuaded Kgama to believe that it was a more dependable nation with which to align than were the Boer Republics. Nevertheless, the Boers were allowed to pass through Ngwato territory.

The Boer sojourn on the Limpopo was another reminder to Tswana chiefs that their land was susceptible to foreign occupation unless the chiefdoms themselves defended its inalienability. At least one chief seems to have learned a lesson from the episode. In November 1876, Kgama reinforced Ngwato precepts on land tenure at a meeting of white traders at Shoshong. He asked all traders to sign a declaration in which they pledged that they would not sell the property or the land on which they operated their businesses. In this connection Mackenzie reported that

> Kgama recently proclaimed that the presence of Europeans in the country had not altered the [Ngwato] law as to land and houses: that the ground was inalienable; that no house could be bought or sold; but might be used by its occupant in the transaction of business, or as a residence, so long as he observed the laws of the country.[22]

The declaration seems to have been rigidly enforced by Kgama, and Captain Patterson's report of 1878 suggests that all Tswana chiefdoms observed the traditional law regarding land tenure:

> According to native law, all property is vested in the chief, who grants permission to build, and guarantees undisturbed residence to all the traders as long as the laws are complied with, but [he] will not permit such buildings to be sold.[23]

Thus by 1880, northern Tswana chiefdoms had suc-

Events Leading to Declaration of a Protectorate 129

ceeded in upholding their traditional land laws and, by accepting a vaguely defined protectorate from British officials, they also averted a major threat to their independence.[24] However, by the same token, Tswana chiefs opened a corridor for British imperial expansion to the north; a phenomenon that was destined to undermine the same independence the Tswana sought to preserve.

II

In 1876 Bailie reported a trend that struck him as characterizing all Tswana chiefdoms north of the Kuruman River. In his view, each consecutive chief to the north appeared to be more powerful than his immediate counterpart to the south:

> From the weak monarchy of the Batlapings the chief of each succeeding tribe assumes more and more power . . . showing . . . that the tendency of the natives being brought into contact with Europeans is to weaken the power of the chief.[25]

Although some Tswana chiefs, notably Kgama, used Europeans to strengthen their positions, there is some truth in Bailie's observation. Ever since Europeans had started coming to Tswana chiefdoms in relatively large numbers after 1840, they had in some ways contributed to the weakening of the chiefship, though some fragmenting within tribes was of the Tswana's own making. Again, because of their proximity to the Cape, southern Tswana chiefdoms experienced the ill effects of European encroachment earlier than their northern kinsmen. Thus, by the 1870s, a southern Tswana chief who had watched the fragmentation of his own chiefdom could complain to Mackenzie:

> There is nothing binding us together since the headmen have taken to live at their own places instead of in the

chief town. They are just small chiefs themselves, and take no notice of me or my laws. Divided as we are, we are at the mercy of any enemy.[26]

Most L.M.S. agents, Mackenzie among them, looked at the declining power of the chiefs as a happy development because they believed greatly centralized chiefdoms to be less responsive to evangelization. By the same token, all missionaries longed for the day when Tswana chiefdoms would come under British rule.[27] In 1876 Mackenzie urged the High Commissioner to expand the British sphere of influence as far north as Mashonaland.[28] The Tlhaping and their neighbors seem to have been aware of and resented the political activities of missionaries. Thus, during the war of 1878, L.M.S. agents were lumped together with other white laymen in the enemy camp, because they were believed to be working in league with British authorities. The Rev. A. J. Wookey, whose own home at Motito was looted by Tswana insurgents, informed his society about Tswana resentment of missionaries.

> I have been told again and again that we are deceivers and only trying as agents of the [British] government to get the country.[29]

Mackenzie also gives an account of his belated efforts to convince his Bible students at the Kuruman Institution that they should accept white immigrants and build up a multiracial society. The students rejected his plea and instead suggested that Queen Victoria should stop the flow of emigrants from Britain, especially that type of English man who engaged in freebooting activities.[30]

The rebellion of 1878 was swiftly suppressed because the Tlhaping and their neighbors failed to unite against British forces, a weakness that was engendered by perennial quarrels among the Tswana themselves. As a British officer noted, some chiefs "actively cooperated with [British]

Events Leading to Declaration of a Protectorate 131

troops in pursuing the refugee rebels; indeed, in several instances they captured some and delivered them up."[31] Sir Charles Warren, who led the British campaign, was therefore able to win a quick victory and, between 27 October 1878 and 1 January 1879, all rebel chiefs had capitulated; even those chiefs who had not taken part in the revolt asked to become British subjects.[32] The British occupation of what was then known as south Bechuanaland lasted until 1881.[33]

The withdrawal of British forces in 1881 left the Boers with little serious challenge to their plundering activities. And just as the British forces had taken advantage of Tswana disunity to contain the rebellion of 1878, so did the Boers accentuate rivalry between the chiefs in order to acquire land. In 1882 the Boers rallied behind opposing chiefs and set up two incipient republics in the Greater Molopo area. The republic of Stellaland was founded on land ceded to William Van Niekerk and his followers after the latter had supported the Koranna Chief, David Massauw, against Chief Mankurwane of the Tlhaping; their capital was at Vryburg. In the northeast, another group led by Gey Van Pitius supported the Rolong Chief, Moshette, against Montshiwa, Chief of the Tshidi-Rolong, and in return was ceded some land. They called their new community Goshen and their capital town was Rooigrand.[34]

Boer activities in the Greater Molopo area were an additional factor that spurred the British to step up their northern expansion; the Germans had earlier aroused British anxiety when they founded a settlement at Angra Paquena in Namaqualand, Southwest Africa, in 1883. In the wake of these threats to "the road to the north," Britain proclaimed a protectorate over south Bechuanaland in 1884 and, on the advice of High Commissioner Robinson, the Reverend John Mackenzie was appointed the first Deputy Commissioner of the Protectorate.[35]

The new mood of imperial expansion was reflected in

the attitude of L.M.S. directors toward the creation of the Protectorate and their response to Mackenzie's appointment. Whereas they had opposed his appointment to a government post during the first occupation of south Bechuanaland,[36] they now saw a necessary connection between their country's colonial expansion and the progress of their missionary activities. Hence, they "yielded to what seem[ed] to be a providential indication of the will of God in the disposal of the services" of Mackenzie and allowed him to join the new Administration;[37] their assumption was that Mackenzie would influence other government officials to augment L.M.S. efforts to evangelize the Tswana.[38] However, Mackenzie's tenure was short-lived, owing to the precipitate manner in which he dealt with Boers in Goshen and Sellaland as well as the indiscretion of proclaiming new British territory without consulting the High Commissioner. He was replaced by Cecil John Rhodes in August 1884.[39]

Meanwhile, Boers and Germans seemed to match Britain's expansionist policy. In January 1885 Paul Kruger annexed the Rolong Chiefdom of Montshiwa to the Transvaal. This spurred the British to declare a Protectorate over north Bechuanaland in January 1885.[40] Sir Charles Warren, Special Commissioner for Bechuanaland, was instructed to inform northern Tswana chiefdoms of the existence of a British protectorate.[41] Tswana responses to Warren's declaration varied from one chiefdom to another, ranging from Kgama's ready acceptance to Sechele's cautious reserve.

Among the Kwena, Warren's embassy had a protracted discussion with the *pitso* when he tried to convince them that a British protectorate was in their chiefdom's interest. As soon as he announced the existence of a Protectorate there on 27 April 1885, Sebele, who seemed to have inherited his father's (Sechele's) shrewdness, retorted: "What in us had brought this on, that the country should be taken from us." Warren's assurance that Kwenaland had not been taken by the British was rejected by Sebele, who insisted

Events Leading to Declaration of a Protectorate 133

that his interpretation of a protectorate was borne out by Cape Colony papers. He also protested that the Protectorate had been declared before the Kwena had been consulted [42] However, Warren found support from a most unexpected quarter, the councillor Kgosidintsi, who urged the acceptance of the Protectorate on grounds of logical consistency. He argued that the history of the Kwena in the nineteenth century had been marked by Sechele's endless search for a protective alliance with the British Crown, citing the Chief's abortive trip to England in 1852 and the expulsion of German missionaries in preference to British missionaries in 1864 as some of the proofs that the Kwena had always sought to become British subjects. Now that the protectorate had been declared, Kgosidintsi could tell Warren: "Yes, that is what we have always wanted." He went on to say,

> I hear nothing you have said today to make my heart sore. I hear merely the words which we asked for in olden time. I have no more to say but [that] I feel assured I am an Englishman.[43]

Sechele and Sebele stood their ground throughout the morning session of the *pitso*. However, after the lunch break, during which time Sechele consulted his councillors, Kgosidintsi seems to have swayed him, for when the *pitso* reassembled in the afternoon, Sechele conceded that he, too, had been "an Englishman" since 1852. But that fact notwithstanding, the Kwena preferred to judge Britain's sincerity first before they accepted the Protectorate; and the Kwena's testing ground was Ngwaketseland and Rolongland, where Britain had pledged to recover the looted cattle from the Boers. Only after the restoration of those cattle could the Kwena decide on the desirability of a Protectorate.[44] The British, however, in true colonial fashion, enforced their sovereignty in spite of Kwena reservations.

Gaseitsiwe accepted the protectorate after very little persuasion; he gave to the British government strips of land to the east and west of his chiefdom, but stipulated that his subjects be allowed to hunt in the western strip for as long as game might abound.[45]

At Shoshong Warren had a more receptive *pitso* during his two-day visit. On 12 May 1885 he easily persuaded Kgama to accept the Protectorate by enumerating the advantages that Kgama and his subjects would derive from it, namely, that the British administration could check treasonable activities of Kgama's brothers, that they would support Kgama's prohibition of the sale and consumption of liquor, and that they would stop German and Boer aggression.[46] Kgama's brothers and councillors accepted the Protectorate, but pleaded that the British administration respect their land laws. Gohakgosi, one of Kgama's brothers, said:

> We have heard the words of the Queen of England. This is our answer. We do not deny her; we do not oppose her coming into our country; but what we do say is that the Queen must not come into the country to sell it; for if it is sold, seeing that we are an agricultural and pastoral people, we shall not have room to sow our gardens or keep our stock.[47]

In his reply to Warren's speech, Kgama was much more accommodating than his councillors and brothers. He offered to the British government some land that lay between the Shashi and Motlotsi Rivers as the Ngwato estimation for what it would cost the Administration to protect their chiefdom. Kgama made more concessions:

> Further, I give to the Queen to make laws, and to change them in the country of the Bamangwato with reference to both black and white.[48]

Events Leading to Declaration of a Protectorate 135

When Warren wound up the *pitso* proceedings on 13 May, he was tactful enough to ignore the dissenting opinions of some of the councillors on the Protectorate issue, but highlighted Kgama's acceptance of the Protectorate. Thus, he informed the 2,000-strong *pitso* that their "chief [had] spoken as a chief ought to speak, in the interest of his people." [49]

III

Although northern Tswana chiefs did not wage armed resistance against British rule, they nevertheless expressed some reservation and even protest against the authority that British officials exercised in their chiefdoms. In December 1888, four years after the declaration of a Protectorate, Sidney Shippard, the Deputy Commissioner of the Bechuanaland Protectorate, toured northern Tswana chiefdoms. At Kanye, Chief Gaseitsiwe expressed misgivings about British intentions in regard to his chiefdom. Part of Gaseitsiwe's address to Shippard, which the Rev. James Good chose not to translate into English, wondered how the Commissioner could be "so unselfish as to seek to benefit others without demanding some recompense from them . . . [and as a result] whether the Deputy Commissioner, in return for the good he was doing to the Ngwaketse, would not in time demand a large grant of their land for himself." [50]

Shippard must have discerned the general tone of resentment to British rule throughout the Protectorate. He therefore convened a conference of chiefs at Kopong on 5 February 1889, at which he was to reassert British authority. But the outcome of the conference was disappointing to the Commissioner, because, except for Kgama's declaration of loyalty, all chiefs expressed the wish to rule themselves without British interference. Shippard closed the conference abruptly, a day after it started, for, as he reported, "the defiant attitude assumed by them—of which it is impossible to convey an adequate idea through the minutes of the meeting—left me no alternative but to adopt this course." [51]

The post-Kopong era witnessed further clashes between some chiefs and British officials, in spite of some attempts by L.M.S. agents to foster loyalty in the British Government. At Molepolole Sebele, who was virtually ruling the Kwena on account of his father's old age, had a brush with Shippard on an issue pertaining to British authority. When in June 1890 Shippard ordered Sebele to open a store the Chief had ordered closed, Sebele refused, saying it should remain closed because its owner, a Mr. Faulkner, had refused to purchase ostrich feathers on terms favorable to the Kwena.[52] Later that year Sebele refused Captain Carrington of the Bechuanaland Border Police permission to graze his cattle at Metsemalthabe because the Captain's cattle would interfere with the principal source of water for the Chief's cattle; Sebele further stated in the same letter that he wished to govern his chiefdom himself, "and not have it governed by white people." [53] In November 1890 Sebele wrote to the High Commissioner saying that he wanted independence for his chiefdom.[54]

Trouble flared again in 1892 when Assistant Commissioner, W. H. Surmon, closed two Molepolole stores because their Indian owners were not licensed. Sebele ordered the stores reopened on the ground that "he refused to allow any one trading on his ground to pay any license whatever; he was the man to whom licenses had to be paid, not the English Government." [55] On that occasion Sebele seems to have had the support of the Kwena. According to Surmon, "Kgosidintsi and several other leading members of the tribe, questioned the right of the Government to demand license money from any persons trading in their country." [56] In his report of 1892, Surmon included the license incident, observing that in another incident Sebele had actually prevented a peddler from paying for a trading license.[57]

Events Leading to Declaration of a Protectorate 137

Kwena illusions about the degree of autonomy they were entitled to enjoy in spite of the declaration of a British protectorate were soon dispelled when the Administration decided to punish Sebele for interfering with the police. On 16 February 1892 Jules Ellenberger and Surmon went to Molepolole to investigate a report that Sebele had prevented Lance-Corporal Lind from collecting license fees. Surmon and Ellenberger were unable to meet Sebele, but held an inquiry in his absence and determined that Sebele be fined twenty head of cattle or £60. Sebele actually paid ten head of cattle.[58] In June that year Sebele was encouraged to visit Cape Town so that he could, in the words of Henry Loch, the High Commissioner, appreciate the "difference between European and native civilization, and that the power and resources of the former might impress him to such an extent as would probably obviate any chance of his again acting in a manner likely to endanger the peace of the Protectorate."[59] Sebele went to Cape Town on 7 June 1892, accompanied by his son, Kebohula, and his interpreter, the Rev. Howard Williams. He was reported to have apologized to the High Commission for his quarrels with Protectorate officials and was impressed by the treatment he got from Henry Loch; the High Commissioner thought other chiefs should be encouraged to visit Cape Town.[60] However, Sebele's apology might have been a result of Loch's stern warning, rather than the splendor of Cape Town. The Rev. H. Williams reported the High Commissioner to have been "very firm with [Sebele] for which I was exceedingly glad. . . . I think he has come back a wiser man and must appear a much more insignificant personage than he had hitherto believed himself." [61] Neither Sebele's visit to Cape Town, nor that of Bathoen to the same city later in 1892, calmed the chiefs for any length of time.[62]

The period between 1892 and 1910 witnessed some instances in which Tswana chiefs tried to reassert their chiefdoms' political autonomy. However, these strictures were outweighed by measures that were introduced by the government to entrench British authority over the Protectorate. In some chiefdoms the chiefs' claims to sovereignty were, in fact, belied by their reliance on Protectorate officials to intercede on their behalf in domestic as well as external affairs. A case in point was Bathoen's quarrel with some Boers in 1894. When he learned that a party of Boers intended to go to Ngamiland through his chiefdom, Bathoen warned their leader, Isaac Bosman, in a letter to a newspaper:

> "My country is not in the power of other people; it is in the power of its owners . . . the Bangwaketse. . . . Bosman you must not pass through my country with your people, for you know yourself that I have no agreement with you in regard to my country. I told Mr. Surmon in the [land] Commission [1893] the words of my country, at Gaberones. I said, 'My country is ruled by myself.' " [63]

But Bathoen's warning was not matched by any concrete show of force, for when Bosman remained undeterred, the chief appealed to the Resident Commissioner for assistance, which he got, and only then was Bosman prevented from passing through Ngwaketse territory.[64]

Among the Tawana, Sekgoma Lecholathebe II had some quarrels with British officials, but his position as chief was vulnerable because he was merely a regent. This was a sequel to Chief Moremi's death in 1890, which created a vacuum because the heir apparent, Mathiba, was a minor and for that reason could not assume the chiefship.[65] Moremi's brother, Sekgoma, became regent in 1891, a position that, according to Tswana custom, he was required to relinquish when Mathiba became of age. In the meantime he seems to have consolidated his position so much that when Mathiba became of age, a large number of the Tawana wanted Sekgoma to continue to rule as chief. Before the

Events Leading to Declaration of a Protectorate 139

declaration of a Protectorate, usurpers of the Sekgoma brand might have succeeded, or else hived away with their supporters to form a new tribe. Now, British officials intervened to install the legitimate heir, Mathiba.

During his regency, Sekgoma's first clash with British officials occurred in 1896, when he claimed ownership of Ghanzi, an area that the High Commissioner wished to allocate as farms to Boer settlers. However, Sekgoma did not persist with his claim because he wished to be protected against outside attacks. As a consequence, he informed the Colonial Office that he was willing to renounce his claim to Ghanzi if the British could guarantee the protection of his chiefdom.[66] The Colonial Office offered him the guarantees and in 1897 the High Commissioner assigned 250,000 morgen (each morgen = 2.116 acres) of land to the Boers and assured them that they would be independent of Sekgoma.[67]

Relations between Sekgoma and British officials improved after the chief renounced ownership of the Ghanzi area. Because Sekgoma had given the British this land, Surmon informed the High Commissioner in 1900 that Mathiba's claim to the chiefship must be resisted and that Sekgoma could expel from Ngamiland two people who were suspected of plotting against the chief.[68] Nevertheless, Sekgoma's position became insecure when Chief Kgama III (who was immensely popular with the British) joined the campaign to end Sekgoma's regency in order to have his nephew, Mathiba, installed as Chief.[69] However, because of Kgama's support of Mathiba, the British administration was obliged to take a neutral stand in the conflict and to try to resolve the conflict through negotiation. A temporary truce was arranged by Commissioner Ashburnham early in 1901 when Kgama and Sekgoma agreed to solve their differences through peaceful methods.[70]

Between 1901 and 1905 Mathiba's supporters became more restless in their demands for the ouster of Sekgoma; the Rev. A. J. Wookey and the L.M.S. Church at Tsau turned against Sekgoma because the Chief had left the Church and promoted initiation ceremonies.[71] Another factor that militated against Sekgoma was the fact that the new Resident Commissioner, Ralph Williams, distrusted him. In his autobiography Williams, who took part in terminating Sekgoma's tenure, said:

> Sekgoma was a native . . . of a singularly crafty disposition. . . . There is no proof that Sekgoma ever definitely decided to cast in his lot against the British Government, but there was considerable reason to believe that he would do so. . . ."[72]

This unfavorable opinion about Sekgoma's character did not amount to much so long as Mathiba was still a minor, but when the heir reached the appropriate age, Sekgoma's regency became even more untenable.

Early in 1906 Sekgoma left Tsau to recuperate in the desert from an illness. During his absence, supporters of Mathiba, who was living with his supporter Kgama, mounted their campaign to have him installed. When in March 1906 Sekgoma went to Kimberley to consult a doctor about his illness, partisan supporters of the two protagonists almost fought each other during the Chief's absence. When news of this impending civil war reached government officials, Ralph Williams had Sekgoma trailed on the chief's return from Kimberley and had him detained at Serowe in an attempt to avert civil war at Tsau.[73] In May 1906 Ralph Williams went to Tsau to determine who the legitimate chief should be; his investigation satisfied him that Mathiba, not Sekgoma, was the heir apparent.[74]

A turning point came in December 1906, when the High Commissioner ordered Sekgoma's arrest and detention in Gaborone prison,[75] from which the Chief engaged lawyers to challenge his detention.[76] In October 1909 Sir Edward Carson initiated proceedings in England against Lord

Events Leading to Declaration of a Protectorate 141

Crewe, the Colonial Secretary, for a writ of *habeas corpus* for the release of Sekgoma. After lengthy litigations, the High Commissioner's right to detain Sekgoma was upheld in a ruling handed down on 14 December 1909. An appeal against the verdict was dismissed on 25 April 1910.[77] Sekgoma had thus exhausted all legal remedies to free himself.

Sekgoma's case dramatizes the extent to which British officials intervened in the affairs of northern Tswana chiefdoms. Between 1885 and 1910 British officials intervened in several other issues bearing on the social, political, and economic life of the Tswana. A sampling of cases from nothern chiefdoms gives an indication of the range of issues in which British officials played a part.

Among the Ngwato, the Tati area created a crisis in 1886 when three Boers (William Groening, John Meintjes, and W. A. Van Zyl) were found poaching game and using Kgama's *sarwa* (i.e., so-called bushmen). Kgama arrested two of them and impounded two wagons and some oxen belonging to Groening, who had escaped. In the precolonial era Kgama would have dealt with the offenders himself, but now he was not certain if he was competent to do so and consulted Shippard on the issue. Shippard informed Kgama that he had acted within his jurisdiction, but advised the Chief to free the two prisoners as a gesture of friendship to the Transvaal Boers.[78] Kgama took heed of Shippard's advice, but the overture did not ameliorate relations between Boers and the Ngwato for any length of time.

In December 1887 Kgama expelled three whites—William C. Francis, Edward Chapman, and J. G. Wood—from the Tati area for prospecting for minerals without his permission. The Protectorate Administrator, Shippard, reprimanded the prospectors and warned them not to foment trouble between Kgama and Lobengula again.[79] In 1888 the three prospectors came to Shoshong, where Kgama again deported them to the Transvaal. When in July that year Kgama sent a regiment to intercept them on the Limpopo,

Mokutshwane's regiment shot Piet Grobler and also a man by the name of Lottering, the former dying from the wound later in the year and the latter being permanently incapacitated. Shippard investigated the incidents and, after establishing that the Ngwato bore responsibility for the shooting, persuaded the Transvaal authorities to accept a settlement whereby the British Government paid Grobler's widow an annuity of £200, while Lottering received a lump sum of £250.[80]

Perhaps the most decisive intervention occurred in 1895 when the British Government reassured Tswana chiefs that they would retain the Protectorate status over the then Bechuanaland Protectorate. This was a sequel to rumors that had been circulating to the effect that the chartered company intended to annex the Protectorate to Rhodesia.[81] Although the charter granted to the British South Africa Company by the British Government in 1889 provided for the eventual cession of the Bechuanaland Protectorate to the B.S.A. Co., Tswana chiefs preferred to remain under the British Crown. By 1894 Cecil Rhodes had made up his mind to annex Bechuanaland. When it appeared to him that Sir Sidney Shippard was promoting the annexation of the Protectorate to south Bechuanaland, Rhodes wrote Shippard:

> "I find you have been warmly advocating the annexation of the Protectorate to Bechuanaland. You are aware that [Her Majesty's] distinct pledges have placed the ultimate destination of the country with the Charter. In return for which we have undertaken heavy expenditure. Your action is nothing more nor less than an attempt at public robbery from the Charter." [82]

Rhodes's attempts to bring Bechuanaland under chartered company rule were foiled by Tswana chiefs, who were no doubt kept informed about the company's intentions. For example, in 1893 John Smith Moffat reported that Palapye

Events Leading to Declaration of a Protectorate

residents were angered by rumors that their chiefdom might be annexed to Rhodesia.[83] This unhappy development became so acute that by 1895, Chiefs Kgama, Sebele, and Bathoen went to England later that year to lobby the British Government for support against any moves the chartered company might take to annex Bechuanaland;[84] they were accompanied by the Rev. W. C. Willoughby, who acted as the chiefs' interpreter and secretary. In England the chiefs were supported by L.M.S. directors and some philanthropic organizations;[85] they had an audience with Queen Victoria and Joseph Chamberlain, the Colonial Secretary, before whom they urged that Bechuanaland remain a British Protectorate. The visit of the chiefs was a success and the British Government pledged to retain the Protectorate.[86]

The Protectorate administration also intervened in several intertribal disputes and in disputes between chiefs and their next of kin. The tendency of Tswana chiefs' next of kin to want to unseat the ruling chiefs was a special feature of nineteenth-century Tswana history. In 1885 John Mackenzie observed:

> In every part of Bechuanaland, without exception, we find the actual Chief is ruling in spite of the fact that a claimant, or, as in some cases, claimants, for the chieftainship exert and put forward their claims more or less openly.[87]

Tswana chiefs were keenly aware of the danger of being removed from the chiefship; hence, when Kgama, Sebele, and Bathoen visited England in 1895, the chiefs asked the British Government not to make it easier for ambitious brothers to stir up trouble in their respective chiefdoms, for the latter were apt to say:

> I also am a son of my father. The chief cannot punish me as he would another man. I can appeal to the Govern-

ment. If I lose, the Government will still give me land and allow me to take my cattle. If I win, I become an independent chief.[88]

The tendency to secede was minimized after 1885, owing to government regulations. Professor Schapera has observed:

> The official demarcation of tribal reserves in and after 1899, coupled with enforcement of the rule that all inhabitants of a reserve must submit to the authority of the local chief, meant that rebels could no longer hope to establish independent chiefdoms either within tribal territory or on unclaimed land somewhere else. . . .[89]

Nevertheless, there were some instances when factions within a tribe seceded and in some of these secessions government intervention averted war. Thus, among the Ngwato, government intervention led to the peaceful separation both of the Mphoeng-Raditladi faction from the Ngwato in 1895–96 and also that of Kgama's son, Sekgoma, in 1899,[90] which lasted until 1922.[91] Boundary disputes were also settled by the Protectorate administration: in 1886 the Kwena and the Ngwato accepted Captain Goold-Adams's settlement of the ownership of the Lopepe wells,[92] in 1887 Shippard settled land disputes between the Ngwato and the Seleka-Rolong,[93] and in 1890 the Administration interceded on behalf of the Ngwaketse and obtained for the latter land that was claimed by the Hurutshe of the Transvaal.[94]

A more decisive intervention, with political as well as economic consequences, was taken in 1893 when the government set up a commission to determine the validity of land concessions that had been issued by Tswana chiefs. While part of the reason for the rather indiscriminate granting of land concessions by chiefs lay in the unfamiliar procedures adopted by some of the syndicates, the economic motive was compelling, owing to the ever-diminishing game resources and to the fluctuating prices of feathers and ivory.[95]

Events Leading to Declaration of a Protectorate 145

Syndicates or individual concessionaires persuaded chiefs, with or without the *pitso*'s approval, to grant them franchises.

The earliest concession to have been granted by any northern chiefdom appears to have been transacted in 1878, when Chief Lecholathebe of the Tawana allocated a farm at Ghanzi to H. M. Van Zyl. By 1888 the Administration became concerned about concession granting and issued a notice limiting the powers of chiefs in granting concessions.[96] This measure had little effect. By 1890 more than thirty mineral and land franchises had been granted to whites all over the Protectorate. Government anxiety over concessionaires was further caused by the latter's disputes over the ownership of their respective areas of operation or when, as in 1890, a syndicate operating in Ngamiland sought assurances from the High Commissioner that the tenure of their concession would remain valid even if the area came under the German sphere of influence.[97] In some instances concessionaries were even suspected of encouraging Tswana resistance to British rule. In 1890 the High Commissioner said:

> Chiefs are discontented at the restrictions placed on their sovereign rights, and their discontent is fomented by disappointed concession seekers.[98]

By 1891 the High Commissioner was even more dissatisfied with the issue of land concessions:

> There can be no doubt that the system of concession seeking which has grown up of late years, is most prejudicial to the best interests of the country, and that it would be a great advantage if all these concessions could be disallowed.[99]

Sir Henry Loch, nevertheless, realized that such arbitrary action might "raise a fierce opposition amongst the disappointed concession holders."[100]

The upshot of this concern was the appointment of a commission that was to enquire into and determine the validity of all concessions granted by Tswana chiefs and to make recommendations to the Colonial Office.

An examination of even only a sample of the claims that came before the Commission of 1893 suggests that Tswana rulers must have granted some of them under great misapprehensions, for example, in Ngwaketseland, Chief Gaseitsiwe was supposed to have given the Kanye Exploration Company a 999-year lease to build and operate twenty trading stations on one-square-mile plots at a yearly rent of £10 per station. In all cases economic considerations seem to have outweighed traditional land laws. Thus, even the more astute Sechele, whose business acumen was acknowledged by a whole generation of hunters and traders, appears to have been swayed by concession hunters until he gave away land indiscriminately. In June 1890 he was supposed to have given the Secheleland Syndicate a fifty-year land-lease with powers to make ordinances, to establish courts of justice, to set up a force of police, to regulate traffic in liquors, and to suppress slavery, all for a lump sum of £2,000.[101] Not unexpectedly, Kgama had been the most cautious of all Tswana chiefs, having granted only one concession to the Bechuanaland Exploration Company in 1887.[102]

One L.M.S. agent, the Rev. James Good of Kanye, appeared before the Concessions Commission to contest a claim to his farm, "Hilda Vale." Although Good had declared in 1888 that he had served the Ngwaketse but "had never accepted land or cattle of theirs or anything else belonging to them," [103] he had in fact accepted a 10,000-morgen (21,160-acre) farm granted to him verbally by Gaseitsiwe and subsequently ratified in writing by Bathoen on 9 January 1890.[104]

The Concessions Commission's terms of reference were weighted in favor of English law and reflected Tswana notions of land tenure only marginally.[105] In a political sense

Events Leading to Declaration of a Protectorate 147

the appointment of the Commission was also a way of asserting British authority, for its findings bound all parties concerned without any recourse to law courts.[106]

When the hearing started at Gaborone on 10 May 1893,[107] Sebele, who had succeeded to the chiefship after his father's death in 1892, challenged the competence of the tribunal to determine the validity of the concessions granted in Kwenaland because

> as sovereign of the soil, he [Sebele] . . . had full power to grant concessions in and over his country to whomsoever he pleased without his acts being questioned by any one.[108]

Sebele's protest was noted but ignored.

The proceedings of the Commission show that, besides the economic motive, military and political considerations impelled Tswana chiefs to give away land and mineral concessions; and this motive is a recurring theme in nineteenth-century Tswana history.[109] Gaseitsiwe, Sechele, and Kgama offered Commissioner Warren strips of land that were clearly buffer zones between their chiefdoms and their potential enemies. Kgama's military and political motive was discerned by Sir Hercules Robinson, the High Commissioner, who rejected the Shashi offer forthwith. Whereas Warren had reported the Shashi offer to be "magnificent," Robinson saw it for what it was:

> Khama's offer is nothing but an attempt to obtain a "buffer state" of English settlers between himself and his enemy, Lobengula.[110]

The Ngwaketse must have had military reasons for granting concessions because Chief Bathoen conceded under cross-examination that the concessionaires were supposed to prevent Boers from coming into his chiefdom.[111]

At the conclusion of the investigation, only seven out

of the forty-five claims were recognized, the rest being either rejected or deferred, owing to a paucity of evidence.[112] In the aftermath the Colonial Office suggested that the British South Africa Company compensate those chiefs who would lose much revenue as a consequence of the cancellation of their concessions. The Company agreed to pay the chiefs concerned, but at slightly lower rates than those suggested by the Colonial Office.[113] Under the Company's scheme the yearly grants to the chiefs were: Bathoen £150; Sebele, £225; Lenchwe (Chief of the Kgatla Kgafela), £70; and Ikaneng (Chief of the Lete), £50.[114] The chiefs accepted the grants and thereby placed themselves under more obligation to the B.S.A. Company.

The Commission of 1893 did not prohibit the granting of new concessions, nor did the Colonial Office issue any instructions on the matter, but the rules governing new land transactions were implicit in the Commission's terms of reference. On the whole, Tswana chiefs seem to have conducted their land transactions more carefully thereafter. Thus, when Chief Sekgoma of the Tawana granted some land to the L.M.S. in July 1893, he safeguarded its inalienability.[115] And when a formal deed of gift was granted for the same plot five years later, Sekgoma was even more explicit in his demands, the L.M.S. agent was required to promise that

> in building at Kgwebe, it does not mean that I am taking from the Botaona [Tawana] their country; the country is theirs, we are teachers only. . . . It is not my veldt, it is theirs.[116]

Bathoen, too, seems to have learned a lesson from past experience with concessionaires. When in 1898 he granted to the L.M.S. a piece of ground, he stipulated in the agreement that the society had no power to sell it.[117] The Ngwato, who had always been sensitive to land issues because of

Events Leading to Declaration of a Protectorate

Kgama's ascetic leadership and the trouble caused by white hunters,[118] had a more consistent land policy than their southern neighbors. When in 1897 the Rev. Willoughby quarreled with Assistant Commissioner J. A. Ashburnham over the use of a water well that the former wished to monopolize, Kgama ruled that both parties were entitled to use the well.[119]

A move that had lasting effects on Tswana tribes was the demarcation of boundaries to the chiefdoms. This was done in 1899 and the boundaries have remained in force to date. In the same year taxation, which Chiefs Kgama, Sebele, and Bathoen had accepted in principle during their visit to England in 1895, was introduced. Each Tswana hut was liable to a ten-shilling tax per year, the chiefs retaining 10% of the proceeds.[120] In 1904 the High Commissioner abolished the practice whereby Tswana chiefs were entitled to collect royalties from white hunters;[121] in 1907 an order was issued to prohibit the export of ostriches and ostrich eggs.[122] While these measures had the effect of entrenching British authority, they certainly curbed the revenue accruing to Tswana chiefdoms.[123] Yet, in spite of the worsening economic situation of the Protectorate, it took the L.M.S. and the Protectorate administration a long time to provide the Tswana with vocational training that was suited to their environment.

NOTES TO CHAPTER FOUR

1. *See,* for example, Eric A. Walker, *The Great Trek,* 4th ed. (London: 1960); E. A. Walker, *The Frontier Tradition in South Africa* (Oxford: 1930); Martin Legassick, "The Griqua, The Sotho-Tswana, and the Missionaries, 1780–1840: The Politics of a Frontier Zone," Ph.D. dissertation.

1969, University of California, no. 70–2230, University Microfilms, Ann Arbor, Michigan); C. W. DeKiewiet, *A History of South Africa: Social and Economic* (Oxford: 1941; reprinted, 1964), pp. 56–87. A Tswana chiefdom, *morafe*, was spread over a territory, although its boundaries were not always precisely defined; in the *morafe* were included wards and towns, agricultural land (*masimo*) and cattle posts (*mareka*), which were looked after mainly by serfs (i.e., the Sarwa and Kgalagadi). The collection of tribute from serfs and other subjects, even when exacted irregularly, was one of the methods used by a chief to exert sovereignty over territory. Thus, Chief Kgama III could claim the Tati-Shashi area on the grounds that ". . . at the Shashi there remained the Masarwa, who were our people. We have never been disturbed or seen anything to remove us from Shashi." In Parliamentary Papers, 1890, C.5918, 51: 67.

2. J. Leyland, *Adventures in the Far Interior of South Africa* (London: 1866), pp. 111–16; W. Inglis, *Memoirs and Remains*, pp. 76–83.

3. Parker Gillmore, *The Great Thirstland: A Ride through Natal, Orange Free State, Transvaal, and the Kalahari Desert* (London: 1878), p. 275. See also F. A. Van Jaarsveld, "The Ideas of the Afrikaner on His Calling and Mission," in *The Afrikaner's Interpretation of South African History* (Cape Town: 1964), pp. 1–30. For estimates of the number of Boers who camped on the Limpopo River, *see* Simon Ratshosa, who estimated that there were between 800 and 1,000 in "My Book. . . ," Rhodes House, p. 71; Henry A. Bryden, *Gun and Camera in Southern Africa: A Year of Wanderings in Bechuanaland, the Kalahari Desert, and the Lake River Country* (London: 1893), pp. 415–16, says there were seventy or eighty families.

4. Emil Holub, *Seven Years in South Africa: Travels, Researches and Hunting Adventures between the Diamond Fields and the Zambezi, 1872–1879*, 2 vols., ed. Ellen E. Frewer (London: 1881), 1: 36; Patterson, Parliamentary Papers, 1878–9, C. 2220, 51: 237; Mackenzie to Mullens, 18 August 1876, Box 38, Jacket A, Folder 1 (L.M.S.).

5. Ratshosa, "My Book. . . ," Rhodes House, pp. 218–19, says Kgama sent five messengers to talk to the Boers, namely, Rev. Hepburn, and councillors Mokomane, Lerobise, Tsheko, and Mokone, who were informed that the Boers would fight if Kgama intercepted their passage through Ngwatoland. Kgama's preference of diplomacy to war is a trait that observers of Tswana politics have amply recorded; *see*, for example, John Mackenzie, *Day-dawn in Dark Places* (London: 1884), p. 221: "But while Bechuanas sometimes fight with their spears, they decidedly prefer to do so with their tongues. . . . And so diplomacy played a prominent part in the public business in each little court. . . ."

6. Kgama to emigrant Boers, 6 and 23 March 1876, in Alexander Bailie's report, Parliamentary Papers, 1878–79, C. 2220, 52: 43.

7. J. M. du Plessis to Kgama, 26 March 1876; T. C. Greyling to Kgama: 26 June and 16 November 1876, and 27 February 1877 in Bailie, Parliamentary Papers, 1878–79, C. 2220, 52: 43–46.

8. Kgama to J. M. du Plessis, 11 March 1877, in Bailie, Parliamentary Papers, p. 46.

Events Leading to Declaration of a Protectorate 151

9. The *casus belli* was the Kgatla chief's refusal to pay tribute to Sechele (*see* Howard Williams to Mullens, 8 May 1876, Box 38, Jacket B, Folder 3 (L.M.S.), who predicted: "Sechele's power is almost done, and if he has to close his life as a fugitive, I shall not be surprised"; I. Schapera, *A Short History of the Bakgatla-baga Kgafela*, pp. 10–25.

10. Alexander Bailie to Commander of Emigrant Boers, 13 November 1876, Parliamentary Papers, p. 44.

11. Bailie to Administrator of Griqualand West, 6 November 1876, Parliamentary Papers p. 53.

12. B.D.C. to Mullens, Minutes of July 1876, Box 38, Jacket B, Folder 3 (L.M.S.).

13. Williams to Mullens, 8 May 1876, Box 38, Jacket B, Folder 3 (L.M.S.), who complained: "He [Sechele] asked my advice as to the war, and telling him it was the last time I would say anything about it, I advised him to make peace and act like a Christian . . . not five minutes after . . . he sent a message to his adversaries to the effect that they were to remove from his ground immediately after harvest . . . and almost upon the heels of the messenger a commando was despatched to attack them"; the B.D.C. to Mullens, Minutes of July 1876, Box 38, Jacket B, Folder 3 (L.M.S.).

14. Alexander Bailie to the Commander of Emigrant Boers, 13 November 1876, Parliamentary Papers, p. 44.

15. J. M. du Plessis to Kgama, 27 February 1877, Bailie, Parliamentary Papers, p. 44.

16. J. D. Botha to Kgama, 22 January 1877, Bailie, Parliamentary Papers, p. 44.

17. Kgama to J. M. du Plessis, 11 March 1877, Bailie, Parliamentary Papers, p. 45.

18. Kgama to Sir Henry Barkly, 22 August 1876, no. 4, Chief's Papers, in Willoughby Papers, Selly Oak Colleges; Hepburn to Barkly, 2 March 1877, Bailie, Parliamentary Papers, p. 42.

19. He had been baptized on 6 May 1860 (*see* H. Schulenburg, Register of Baptism, Willoughby Papers, Folder 795, Selly Oak College).

20. Question of Christian morality must have worried Kgama alone, for Sechele and Gaseitsiwe did not share the same convictions with Kgama (*see* footnote 13).

21. Patterson's Report, Parliamentary Papers, C. 2220, 52: 46; Holub, 1: 36–37; Bryden, pp. 415–16.

22. Mackenzie to Mullens, 18 August 1876, Box 38, Jacket C, Folder 3 (L.M.S.). See also Bailie, *Parliamentary Papers*, p. 54: "Yesterday the chief called a meeting of all white inhabitants. . . . The chief is anxious all should understand that building and occupying a house upon his ground gives no right to the person to sell or alienate the property, and that all buildings upon his ground belong to him"; proclamation concerning occupation of land by Europeans, 7 November 1876, Chief's Papers, in Willoughby Papers, Folder 7, Selly Oak Colleges Library.

23. Patterson, Parliamentary Papers, p. 237. *See also* I. Schapera, *Handbook of Tswana Law and Custom* (London: 1970), pp. 195–213.

24. Besides the military assistance implicit in the protectorate offered

the Tswana in 1876 and again in 1878, British terms of the alliance were not spelled out. Hence, Captain Patterson, one of whose duties during his tour of 1878 was to affirm the British offer of a protectorate, had no ready answer when Kgama asked him to define the protectorate: "He earnestly asked me to define 'British protectorate.' As this was far beyond my instructions, I declined" (Parliamentary Papers, p. 237).

25. Bailie, Parliamentary Papers, p. 76.

26. John Mackenzie, *Austral Africa, Losing It or Gaining It*, 2 vols. (London: 1886), 1: 76; Cape Governor Frere to Dr. Joseph Mullens, Foreign Secretary of the L.M.S., 13 June 1879, Box 41 (L.M.S.), said of the authority of chiefs: "The ancient authority of the chief, whether great or small . . . has been imperceptibly lessened.'"

27. Hence, when the B.D.C. assessed the effects of the 1878 war on tribes in the Greater Molopo area, they sent a detailed account to Governor Frere covering all facets of Tswana life but only casually referred to the chief's authority: ". . . as for the waning of the power of their chiefs, they will grow accustomed to that also, provided a good position is secured them as respectable subjects of the Queen"; B.D.C. to Frere, 25 January 1879, Box 41 (L.M.S.).

28. B.N.A., H. C. 48/1/2, Mackenzie to Sir Henry Barkly, 2 May 1876.

29. A. J. Wookey to Mullens, 3 September 1878, Box 40 (L.M.S.). See also J. Mackenzie, *Austral Africa*, 1: 80, 82; Ashton to Whitehouse, 1 September 1879, Box 41 (L.M.S.), who gives the main cause of the rebellion as the annexation of Griqualand West to the Cape Colony in 1871: "It was acquired upon a false issue, and that most unjustly because it was found to contain diamonds"; J. Tom Brown to Whitehouse, 5 September 1879, Box 41 (L.M.S.), traces the cause of the rebellion to the annexation: "The claims of the Bechuanas, who had lived in and ruled over part of the country, were treated with little less than contempt"; J. A. I. Agar-Hamilton, *The Road to the North*, p. 138; Eric A. Walker, *A History of Southern Africa*, pp. 330, 351, 356, 359, 372, 395.

30. Mackenzie, *Austral Africa*, 1: 80.

31. Parliamentary Papers, 1883, 49: 18, Captain Harrel to Administrator of Griqualand West, 27 April 1880.

32. Ibid., p. 7.

33. Mackenzie, *Austral Africa*, 1: 106.

34. W. J. Leyds, *The Transvaal Surrounded* (London: 1919), pp. 109–12, 180; Walker, *History of Southern Africa*, pp. 396–98.

35. Mackenzie, *Austral Africa*, 1: 79; A. Sillery, *Founding a Protectorate* (The Hague: 1965), p. 40.

36. John Mackenzie had served as an official assistant to Special Commissioner Warren from the beginning of hostilities until the middle of 1879. When Governor Frere asked the L.M.S. directors to allow Mackenzie to be officially appointed assistant commissioner for south Bechuanaland, they refused to do so because all members of the B.D.C. opposed the move. Ashton's letter to the L.M.S. (1 September 1879, Box 41, L.M.S.) was typical: "I think both the missionary position and influence of both

Events Leading to Declaration of a Protectorate

Mr. Mackenzie and all the rest of us would suffer by his accepting office." *Also see* Frere to Mullens, 13 June 1879; J. Tom Brown to Whitehouse, 5 September 1879; Mackenzie to Whitehouse, 25 September 1879, 10 September 1880; Frere to Whitehouse, 22 December 1879, Box 41, (L.M.S.).

37. The L.M.S. *Chronicle*, 10 March 1884, pp. 119–20.

38. Ibid.: "That through the development of a just and humane policy on the part of the British Government . . . there may be inaugurated a future for the Bechuana [Tswana] people, by which the first beginnings of civilization and the early lessons of the Gospel may be carried out in abundant prosperity . . ."; *also* in W. D. Mackenzie, *John Mackenzie: South African Missionary and Statesman* (London: 1902), p. 306.

39. Parliamentary Papers, 1885, 57: 61–62, Mackenzie to Sir Hercules Robinson, 19 August 1884, enclosed in Robinson to Derby, 29 of 20 August 1884. In the same communication Mackenzie formally resigned from being Deputy Commissioner; *see also* Parliamentary Papers, 57: 84, Earl of Derby to Robinson, 56 of 27 September 1884, in which Mackenzie's resignation was accepted and a gratuity of £300 allowed to him; Sillery, *Founding a Protectorate*, p. 40.

40. A. Sillery, *The Bechuanaland Protectorate*, (Cape Town: 1952), p. 53; S. M. Molema, *Montshiwa: Barolong Chief and Patriot* (Cape Town: 1966), pp. 155–64; C. O. 417/4, Robinson to Colonial Office, 123 of 8 April 1885.

41. C. O. 417/4, Robinson to Special Commissioner for Bechuanaland, Charles Warren, 5 January 1885.

42. Parliamentary Papers, 1885, C. 4588, 57: 37; C. O. 417/4, Sechele to Warren, 13 March, 1885, enclosed in Robinson to Earl of Derby, 132 of 15 April 1885, had instructed his missionary to inform Warren: "He says he is glad of your arrival . . . and feels confident you will settle this long disturbed country."

43. Parliamentary Papers, 1885, C. 4588, 52: 38; George Haccius, ed., *Hannoversche Missionsgeschichte Insbesondere die Geschichte der Hermannsburger Mission* (Hermannsburg: 1910), pp. 419–22.

44. Parliamentary Papers, 1885, C. 4588, 52: 41: There was no formal acceptance of British rule. Sechele said, "Go back and do the work you have in hand, and then we shall see the benefit of a Protectorate." In C. O. 417/4, Mokgosi to Warren, 123 of 23 March 1885, the Lete Chief had said: "We are anxious to place ourselves under the protectorate of Her Majesty's Government. We are close on the border, and are continually molested by the Boers."

45. Parliamentary Papers, 1885, 57: 48.

46. Ibid., p. 43.

47. Ibid. Rauwe, chief of the Khurutshe, spoke for the subject tribes of the Ngwato (ibid., p. 44): "We are glad of the Queen's message, but should be sad to see our country sold, as we live by cattle and corn."

48. Ibid.; Lloyd to Thompson, 4 July 1885, Box 43, Jacket C, Folder 1 (L.M.S.), reported Kgama's complaint about the 22° parallel limit of the Protectorate: "The word which I hear which speaks about 22° as

shown on maps ought to be taken away: I do not express thanks for it; it speaks of nothing which has existence. Boundary line there is none at 22°. It is to cut my country in two."

49. Parliamentary Papers, 1885, ibid., p. 44; Lloyd to Thompson, 4 July 1885, ibid.

50. Parliamentary Papers, 1890, C. 5918, 51: 152, Shippard to Robinson, 11 December 1888, enclosed in Robinson to Knutsford, 49 of 22 December 1888.

51. C. O. 417/28, Shippard's report, 6 February 1889, enclosed in Robinson to Knutsford, Confidential of 27 February 1889. *See also* C. O. 879/30, African (South), no. 372, pp. 63–65, where the B.D.C. sympathized with Shippard and regretted the failure of the Kopong conference: B.D.C. to Shippard, 6 February 1889, enclosed in Robinson to Knutsford, 24 of 25 February 1889.

52. C. O. 879/32, African (South), no. 392, p. 275, Loch to Knutsford, 251 of 2 July 1890, enclosure 1, Captain Carrington's telegram of 30 June 1890.

53. Ibid.

54. Ibid., Enclosure 2, Sebele to High Commissioner, 4 November 1890.

55. C. O. 879/36, African (South), no. 426, pp. 97–101, Surmon to Administrator, 18 February 1892, enclosed in Loch to Kuntsford, 92 of 16 March 1892.

56. Ibid.

57. Parliamentary Papers no. 8, 1892, 60: 44, "Report of the Assistant Commissioner for the Bechuanaland Protectorate, from 1 August 1890 to 31 March 1892."

58. C. O. 879/36, pp. 97–101.

59. Ibid., p. 238, Loch to Knutsford, 196 of 14 June 1892.

60. Ibid., p. 239.

61. Williams to Thompson, 10 June 1892, Box 49, Jacket A, Folder 2 (L.M.S.).

62. Parliamentary Papers, 1892–93, no. 100, C. 6857, p. 55, Report of the Assistant Commissioner for the southern part of the Bechuanaland Protectorate, 1892–93.

63. "Bathoen Protests," *Bechuanaland News*, 7 July 1894.

64. C. O. 879/40, pp. 393–413.

65. The Rev. Edwin Lloyd to Thompson, 1 June 1891, Box 48, Jacket C, Folder 1 (L.M.S.), who reported that Sekgoma was a young man of twenty-two years and that for that reason his uncle, Dithapo Meno, was acting for him; John Reid (a lay missionary) to Thompson, 9 August 1893, Box 50, Jacket B, Folder 2 (L.M.S.). According to Thomas, Tlou, Sekgoma Lecholathebe's installation as chief was delayed until 1891 because he had to undergo circumcision before becoming a chief ("A Political History of Northwestern Botswana to 1906" [Ph.D. dissertation, University of Wisconsin, 1972], p. 227).

66. C. O. 879/47, Sekgoma to Rosmead, 27 October 1896, enclosed in

Events Leading to Declaration of a Protectorate

British West Charlerland Company to Colonial Office, 565A of 27 January 1897.

67. C. O. 879/52, pp. 53–55, Milner to Chamberlain, 50 of 7 July 1897.

68. C. O. 879/68, African (South) Confidential, no. 656, p. 273, Surman to Milner, 18 October 1900, enclosed in Milner to Chamberlain, 170 of 31 October 1900.

69. C. O. 879/69, African (South) Confidential, no. 659, pp. 96–98, Sekgoma Lecholathebe to Surmon, 1 November 1900, enclosed in Milner to Chamberlain, 64 of 13 February 1901.

70. Ibid., pp. 98–99, Ashburnham to Surmon, 8 January 1901.

71. C. O. 879/86, African (South) Confidential, no. 763, p. 369, "Notes on the Batawana; Their History and Political Situation," by A. J. B. Wavell, enclosed in Selborne to Lyttelton, 25 September 1905; Jennings, Report of Serowe Mission for 1904, (L.M.S.).

72. Ralph Williams, *How I Became a Governor* (London: 1913), p. 339.

73. Ibid., p. 325; "Another Version: The Trouble in the Northern Protectorate. . . . The Story of Sekgoma's Arrest," *Diamond Field Advertiser*, 10 August 1910.

74. Williams, pp. 340–44; "Another Version"; A. W. Hodson, "The Ngamiland Mission, 1906," *Diamond Field Advertiser Christmas Number*, 1906.

75. C. O. 879/95, African (South) Confidential, no. 872, p. 71, Proclamation No. 25 of 1906, Selborne to Panzera, enclosed in Selborne to Elgin, 44 of 25 February 1907; Thomas Tlou, pp. 282–86.

76. J. M. Chirenje, "Chief Sekgoma Lecholathebe II: Rebel or Twentieth-Century Tswana Nationalist?", *Botswana Notes and Records* 3 (1971): 64–69. However, Mathiba's mother, not Sekgoma's, was Ngwato, contrary to the assertion in the article (p. 68, note 8).

77. C. O. 879/103, African (South) Confidential, No. 943, p. 245, passim; Proceedings, Judgments, Orders of the Court, and Affidavits in connection with an application for a writ of *habeas corpus* for the release of Sekgoma Lecholathebe, High Court of Justice, King's Bench Division, Royal Court of Justice, 19 October 1909, 25 April 1910.

78. Parliamentary Papers, 1887, C. 4890, 59: 111–12, Chief Kgama to Shippard, 6 September 1886, Shippard to Kgama, 28 September 1886.

79. C. O. 879/29, African (South) Confidential, no. 358, pp. 17–18, Wood, Chapman, and Francis to Lobengula, 15 December 1887, enclosed in J. S. Moffat to Deputy Commissioner, 26 December 1887, Shippard to Wood, Chapman, and Francis, February 1888.

80. Parliamentary Papers, 1890, C. 5918, 51, Shippard's tribunal report of 9 September 1888, enclosed in Robinson to Knutsford, 485 of 24 September 1888; Lloyd to Thompson, 25 July 1888, Box 45, Jacket C, Folder 3 and 28 September 1888, Box 45, Jacket D. Folder 3 (L.M.S.); Sillery, *Founding a Protectorate*, pp. 104–112.

81. Neil Q. Parsons, "The Visit of the Chiefs to England" (a dissertation for the Diploma in African Studies, University of Edinburgh, 1967); Par-

liamentary Papers, 1896, C. 7962, 59; W. C. Willoughby, Sundry Papers (L.M.S.); Sillery, *Founding a Protectorate*, pp. 212–34.

82. Rhodes House, Oxford, Manuscripts, Cecil John Rhodes, Rhodes to Shippard, July 1894.

83. C. O. 879/37, p. 84, Moffat to High Commissioner, 7 January 1893.

84. N. Q. Parsons, "Khama, Not Missionaries, Initiated Trip for Negotiations," *Kutlwano* (February 1972), p. 12, states that Chief Kgama III initiated the trip to England.

85. L.M.S. *Chronicle* (October 1895), pp. 251–53.

86. Sillery, *Founding a Protectorate*, pp. 212–31.

87. Mackenzie, "Disputed Chieftaincies," in Parliamentary Papers, 1885, C. 4588, 62: 66.

88. Parliamentary Papers, 62, Correspondence relative to the visit to England of Chiefs Kgama, Sebele, and Bathoen, p. 14.

89. I. Schapera, "Kinship and Politics in Tswana History," *J.R.A.I.* 93, no. 2 (July–December 1963): 163.

90. C. O. 879/47, pp. 37, 83, J. S. Moffat to Graham Bower, 5 February 1896, Ashburnham to F. J. Newton, 2 March 1896. For the group's settlement in Mangwe, Rhodesia, see C. O. 879/47, pp. 504–505, Earl Grey to Rosmead, 1 March 1897.

91. C. O. 879/57, Aprican (South) Confidential, no. 574, pp. 89–101, 157–158; B.N.A., Unit no. S. 42/3, Barry May to Acting Resident Commissioner, Francis Town, 17 June 1911, R. M. Daniel to Barry May 22 May 1911.

92. Parliamentary Papers, 1887, C. 4890, 59: 12–13.

93. Parliamentary Papers, ibid., C. 5070, pp. 7–18.

94. Parliamentary Papers, 1892, no. 8, 60: 44.

95. For declining resources, Captain Harrel's estimation in Parliamentary Papers, 1883, no. 12, 49: 18, which shows that by 1880 southern Tswana trade in ivory and feathers had dropped from an all-time record of £100,000 a year in the 1850s to about £50,000 in 1883. The declining trend was also reported in 1885 by Captain Goold-Adams when he noted that feathers fetched such low prices at the Cape that it was hardly profitable to send them there, and that a trader informed him that his yearly income from that trade had dropped by 50%. (Parliamentary Papers, 1886, C. 4839, no. 48, 58: 220).

96. Sillery, *Bechuanaland Protectorate*, p. 64 .

97. C. O. 879/32, African (South), no. 392, p. 33, Messrs. Fairbridge and Arderne to Imperial Secretary, 14 January 1890, enclosed in Loch to Knutsford, 17 January 1890.

98. C. O. 879/37, African (South), no. 441, p. 1, Loch to Knutsford, 1 of 24 November 1890.

99. Ibid., p. 2, Loch to Knutsford, 4 July 1891.

100. Ibid.

101. C. O. 879/50, African (South), no. 537, p. 19, Loch to Ripon, 7 October 1893.

102. Ibid., p. 33.

Events Leading to Declaration of a Protectorate 157

103. Parliamentary Papers, 1890, C 5918, 51: 152. Labouchere, a British member of Parliament and editor of the magazine, *Truth*, was the first to question if Good had not violated professional ethics by accepting land from the Ngwaketse. But the Rev. Good "looked upon it as a gift that a tribe or parish can properly give to their minister." The *Bechuanaland News* (6 December 1893) refuted Labouchere's objections on economic grounds: "[anybody who] occupies, utilizes, and improves land in this country ought to be allowed to keep it." The L.M.S. directors demanded in vain that Good return land to the Ngwaketse (in letters to Good, 9 December 1893, 15 December 1893, 3 March, 1894, L.M.S.). Good denied that there was anything unethical in accepting the farm as a gift: "I accepted it as such from them [the Ngwaketse], and not from any special value in the gift itself," In Good to Thompson, 15 January 1894, Box 51, Jacket A, Folder 1 (L.M.S.). John Brown (on 6 January 1894, Box 51, Jacket A, Folder 1, L.M.S.) informed directors that it was customary for missionaries to accept gifts from the chiefs.

104. C. O. 879/50, p. 9, Loch to Ripon, 1 of 7 October 1893.

105. Out of the twenty terms of reference, only three Clauses took into account Tswana law and custom; Clause I provided for the cancellation of a concession if it was granted by the chief without the approval of the tribe; Clauses 6 and 7 provided that a chief who granted concessions in a subordinate chiefdom had to prove that he received tribute from it in recognition of his paramauntcy, in C. O. 879/37, p. 78, Loch to Ripon, 24 January 1893.

106. Ibid., pp. 1–8.

107. The session at Gaborone adjourned on 23 May; the Commission resumed enquiries at Mafeking on 6 June and concluded on 7 June.

108. C. O. 879/50 p. 1.

109. *See*, for example, when German missionaries were invited to work in Kwenaland and Ngwatoland in 1857 and 1859, respectively (chapter 2).

110. C. O. 879/23, p. 10. On p. 15, the Colonial Office objected to Kgama's offer of the Shashi area (1855), "Because he wishes for the English settlers only, and this . . . would accentuate the division between Dutch and English, which it is most important to obliterate."

111. Bathoen's testimony to the Concessions Commission, MS at Selly Oak Colleges Library, Birmingham, in "With the Concessions Commission," (1893), p. 39.

112. C. O. 417/101A, Loch to Ripon, 422 of 7 October 1893.

113. The Colonial Office had recommended the following annual grants: Bathoen, £200; Sebele, £250; Ikaneng, £50; and Lenchwe, £70.

114. C. O. 879/50, P. 28, British South Africa Company to Colonial Office, 3 of 12 December 1894. The B.S.A. Co. readily agreed to compensate Tswana chiefs because they hoped Botswana would eventually come under the Company's control in accordance with the terms of the Royal Charter granted to them on 29 October 1889.

115. Wookey to Thompson, 13 July 1893, Box 50, Jacket A, Folder 2 (L.M.S.).

116. C. O. 879/53, p. 431, Agreement of 11 July 1893, L.M.S. to

C.O., 401 of 26 October 1898. The Foreign Secretary of the L.M.S., R. W. Thompson, noted Kgama's insistence that land not be alienated. He reported that while he was at Palapye he received documents "by which the chief and people have made over to the Society a plot of land on which the English community in that place had erected . . . a small place of worship. The deed of transfer . . . gives the land to the Society but without power to alienate it," in his *Report of the Deputation to South Africa (Confidential) January to March 1898*, p. 37. See also C. O. 879/53, p. 59, L.M.S. to Colonial Office, 21 January 1898.

117. C. O. 879/53, pp. 499–500, Milner to Chamberlain, 485 of 7 December 1898. The plot measured 150' x 310'.

118. Sekgoma Kgama, "Kgama's Life," 28 March 1925, in B.N.A., no. Serowe 337, S.601/18.

119. Kgama to Willoughby, 20 February 1897, Willoughby to Kgama 17 February 1897, Kgama to Willoughby 18 February 1897, Box 54, Jacket B, Folder 1 (L.M.S.). See also Thompson, *Deputation*, L.M.S., pp. 38–39.

120. C. O. 879/78, pp. 362–63, Goold-Adams to Milner, 3 July 1899, enclosed in Milner to Chamberlain, 320 of 29 September 1902; Sillery, *Bechuanaland Protectorate*, pp. 79–83. I. Schapera, *Native Land Tenure in the Bechuanaland Protectorate* (Alice, South Africa: 1943), p. 10.

121. C. O. 417/392, Milner to Harris, Minutes of May 1904.

122. H. C. Juta, *The Laws of the Bechuanaland Protectorate*, rev. ed., 3 vols. (London: 1949), 2: 907.

123. See, for example, Kgama to High Commissioner, Lord Buxton, 28 March 1916, Box 79 (L.M.S.).

5

"To Make a Book Talk":
Problems and Progress in Tswana
Education, 1880-1910

THE SECOND PHASE IN TSWANA EDUCATION, WHICH BEGAN IN the early 1880s, witnessed a significant change in the educational policy of the L.M.S. Hitherto, education had been largely literary, related mainly to the study of the Scriptures, but after 1880 Tswana parents were spurring L.M.S. agents to broaden the scope and content of the school curriculum; some chiefdoms started their own tribal schools to augment what they believed to be an inadequate L.M.S. school system. In deference to Tswana demands, missionaries belatedly reconsidered their approach to education until they discarded some of the society's concepts on the subject that had been in vogue since the formation of the society in 1795. However, vying with this transition to vocational education were fundamental problems that had been inherited from a system of education that James Read started at Kuruman in 1816.

I

A study of Tswana education between 1880 and 1910 shows that the major obstacle to progress was the missionary's philosophy of life. To them the most useful pursuit was man's preparation in this world for life after death. In pursuance of this view, evangelization took precedence over formal education, some of the missionaries actually equating Christianity with education. Hence, L.M.S. agents were satisfied if their pupils acquired a veneer of literacy to enable them to read the Bible. Nor were Tswana parents unaware of the limitations of such an education. To them, L.M.S. education enabled them merely "to make a book talk." [1]

Even when they had changed their educational policy, L.M.S. agents in Bechuanaland were not unnaturally preoccupied with evangelization well into the twentieth century. Thus, at an emergency meeting they held in 1904, the B.D.C. expressed a view not far removed from earlier attitudes: "We as a committee hold that education is not the primary work of a missionary society. We do it because the Government has not yet taken up its proper responsibility." [2] And yet in spite of their partisan attempt to educate the Tswana, L.M.S. agents laid the foundation upon which Botswana has built its present system of education.

By 1880 a thin network of schools had been built throughout northern Tswana chiefdoms, and the wagon-and-tree improvisations of the pioneer period had given way to pole-and-dagga (packed clay) classrooms; some school buildings were even built of bricks. Ngwatoland, with a population of about 20,000, had five schools in and around Shoshong; the Ngwaketse, who numbered about 10,000, had four schools, one situated at Kanye and three at the outstations; and all the schools were manned by Kuruman-trained evangelists.[3] In 1881 the Boys Boarding School at Kuruman, the society's sole supplier of evangelists, had an enrollment of five students, which was an increase of only one student on its annual student body since 1876.[4]

The Kwena, who by 1881 numbered about 15,000, had one day school at Molepolole with 140 pupils, including four Boer children; its head teacher was a Miss Wallace.[5] By 1887 school enrollment had dropped to 86 pupils (58 girls and 28 boys) and Miss Wallace was assisted by a moTswana teacher, Moshoboro.[6] However, by 1891 its enrollment had increased to 255, while the central school at Kanye had 500 pupils.[7]

Ngamiland does not seem to have benefited much from the service of Khukwe Mogodi, for soon after his arrival there in 1878, he paid little attention to teaching but reverted to his old occupation of trading in ivory. Khukwe probably traded in order to augment his irregular salary. The B.D.C., nevertheless, subsequently reprimanded him for what they construed to be misconduct and transferred him to Moshupa in Ngwaketseland in 1881.[8]

Missionary reports throughout the 1880s suggest that L.M.S. agents were generally satisfied with the type of education provided in their schools. For the majority of missionaries, learning by rote was the standard method of children-scholars acquiring new knowledge. Thus, Edwin Lloyd could report in 1887 with a sense of accomplishment that one of his best students was a blind Tswapong man who had "committed many passages of Scripture to memory."[9]

However, if learning by rote impaired the intellectual growth of many Tswana students, it did not seem to have had any ill effects on Chief Sechele. Ever since he had been taught to read and write by Livingstone in the 1840s, Sechele continued to make spectacular progress. Although part of the reason for his extensive study of the Bible was a reaction to his suspension from church membership, Sechele seems to have been a man of above-average intelligence. By 1880 his knowledge of Scripture and his ability to interpret it in the context of Kwena experience had become extensive. Thompson, who visited Molepolole in 1883, reported that Sechele could "quote Scripture in support of his own position with great aptness." [10] But the majority of Tswana students required a school environment that was conducive to learning, and in this respect they were unfortunate because the L.M.S. school system was beset by problems One of the problems of Tswana education during the nineteenth century was the conflict arising from the traditional modes of occupation on the one hand, and the equally persistent demands by L.M.S. agents that pupils should attend their schools regularly. In this connection hunting and cattle herding, which was observed to have been sanctified in the traditional education of Tswana boys (*see* chapter 2), accounted for their poor school attendance well into the twentieth century. Girls, on the other hand, were required to work in the fields and gardens, but because agriculture was a seasonal occupation, it did not take as much time as the perennial occupation of hunting and cattle herding, and for that reason the schools enrolled more girls than boys.[11] A Molepolole report of 1885 explains the problem of absenteeism:

> I have asked the reason why the boys do not come to school, and the men say that they [the boys] are away at the cattle posts in different parts of the country. If they, the boys, come to school, there will be no one to take care of the cattle.[12]

In 1885, one L.M.S. missionary (J. D. Hepburn) tried to improve school attendance by asking his adult church members to dig the gardens so that girls could attend school more regularly;[13] and since the same plan could not have been applied to the boys, Hepburn devised a programme for them whereby they were encouraged to take their books with them to the cattle posts so that they could teach each other how to read and write.[14] However, Hepburn's innovations achieved little success, for it was improbable for him to supervise his students at the cattle posts, while the task force he set up to relieve the girls from agricultural duties had to be abandoned since, for reasons that will be shown later, it impinged upon the chief's authority.

The school curricula, which were by no means uniform owing to the decentralized nature of school organization, included reading and writing, Scripture, arithmetic, and sewing; the Moffat Institution at Kuruman offered geography "of Bible lands" in addition to the above subjects. Until 1880 L.M.S. missionaries believed their school curriculum to be a flawless contrivance and the Tswana were repeatedly blamed for their failure to show sufficient interest in the L.M.S. schools.[15] However before the 1880s were over, some missionaries started questioning the usefulness of the type of education they were giving the Tswana. One reason for this reappraisal of their educational endeavors was sparked by Tswana preference—at least by the few parents who could afford it—of sending their sons to schools in Basutoland and the Cape Colony, a trend that missionaries belatedly construed to be a reflection of the poor quality of education in L.M.S. schools.

Even before L.M.S. missionaries themselves started reassessing the relevance of their education to Tswana conditions, the society's Foreign Secretary, the Rev. R. Wardlaw Thompson, conducted an inspection of Tswana schools in 1883 and made some useful suggestions on how they could be improved. He stressed the need to shift educational priorities from the largely religious and academic curriculum, which had hitherto dominated the L.M.S. schools, to one that would fulfill the economic needs of the Tswana.[16] While Thompson's recommendation was clearly a salutary departure from an educational philosophy that had long ignored Tswana economic needs, the Foreign Secretary's notion of an industrial education, like that of the B.D.C.'s on the issue, was too superficial and was probably influenced by the prevailing attitudes in England. To Thompson the harnessing of Bechuanaland's agricultural and pastoral potential did not lend itself to investigation, but instead he lamented over the fact that the country was a socioeconomic unit that appeared to be hopelessly beyond redemption. Hence, he could report:

> The greater part of the country is so far removed from markets, and conveyance is so serious a difficulty that it is not at present worth the people's while to attempt to grow corn enough for sale beyond their own borders. The only trade they have, which is worth anything, is in the produce of the chase, and that is becoming increasingly difficult every year. The hunting still claims the attention of a large number of the men, but it leads them farther and farther afield during several months of the year, and has not a healthy influence, either in relation to settled habits of life, or the development of moral [sic] principle.[17]

Among the people who joined in the reevaluation of the educational policy of the L.M.S. was J. S. Moffat, himself a former L.M.S. agent, who had left the society in 1879 to take up a government appointment in the Transvaal. Moffat could view the functioning of L.M.S. schools from a layman's point of view and, because of that measure of detachment, he was in a position to compare more perceptively the performance of Tswana school graduates with their counterparts in the Transvaal, the Free State, the Cape Colony, and Basutoland, having held government posts at various times in each respective area. One major weakness he noticed in the L.M.S. school system was the poor quality of its teachers and in March 1888 he wrote to the L.M.S. urging the directors to give more attention to the training of teachers than to that of evangelists.[18] The same view was expressed by Howard Williams at Molepolole in 1889.[19] By 1891 Moffat had become disillusioned by the society's slow progress in education and offered further suggestions on how Tswana schools could be improved generally; he thought the central school at Palapye should have a trained, white schoolmaster to relieve the missionary who was "so largely engaged in pastoral supervision that he cannot even supervise new schools adequately." He stated further:

> What is wanted is a man who would do this—and also carry such scholars as were worth it a step further. At present there is nothing progressive in your system of education. The Seminary at Kuruman does not meet the want and never will on its present footing.[20]

Nine months later Moffat repeated his criticism of L.M.S. schools, pointing out that the trend toward sending Tswana youths to schools in Basutoland and the Cape had increased:

> Two of Kgama's brothers have sent their sons to Lovedale and are paying for them there and it is said that more are going. This indicates an earnest longing for something more than what they have had supplied to them by us.[21]

The society's directors did not share the sense of urgency that Moffat and Williams tried to convey. In their reply to Moffat they regretted the fact that they were unable to muster a single Tswana man who had a passable command of the English language, even though they had had schools in Bechuanaland for over sixty years. They attributed their failure to lack of money, a dearth that they predicted would handicap their Tswana mission for a long time to come.[22]

II

L.M.S. agents had more problems to grapple with than just the quality and content of education, and foremost among them was the friction between chiefs and missionaries that seemed to increase in proportion to the converts each station mustered. Once a missionary had a sizable number of followers, he seemed inclined toward setting up a miniature theocracy within a chiefdom. Although the missionary's motive was ostensibly to counteract "backsliding" of converts, the scheme was clearly contentious, since the northern Tswana states were centralized polities in which the chiefs readily punished any persons—his subjects and aliens inclusive—who tried to usurp their authority. When, therefore, a missionary insisted that only church members could construct a school building, he unwittingly provoked the tribal chief, who took the traditional view that any public work should be done by a state regiment, regardless of the religious beliefs of its members,[23] and that the chief alone could sanction the erection of school buildings and assign work projects to the respective regiments. Whenever chiefs and missionaries refused to compromise over this issue, valuable time was lost before the buildings were erected.

Of all the Tswana chiefs, Sechele was the most rigid exponent of the supremacy of the chief over church and state. Part of Sechele's somewhat uncompromising attitude, no doubt, was inherited from the humiliation he suffered when he was suspended from church membership in 1848. Just as he had clashed with evangelist Sebobi over the issue in 1854, so did Sechele insist that he supervise all public works at Molepolole a quarter of a century later. And because the Rev. Roger Price was as obdurate as Sechele himself, their quarrels had the effect of crippling church and school work. In 1884 Price reported:

"To Make a Book Talk"

The church here is in a very important sense a state church; and it has been one constant struggle between myself and old Sechele as to who shall be supreme in the church fellowship. Still his influence over his sons and nephews, and other young headmen of the Bakwena, who are members of the church, is very great, and does not tend to promote their goodness and usefulness.[24]

Sechele coupled his assertion of unfettered sovereignty with a demand for reinstatement into the fellowship of the church, but, unhappily for the chief, his demands fell on deaf ears because of Victorian assumptions about the separation of church and state. It was similar assumptions that led Alfred Wookey, who had succeeded Price at Molepolole in 1884, to report a year later that he had rejected Sechele's application for reinstatement.[25] But old age seemed to have mellowed Sechele somewhat. Although he could occasionally defy both British administrators and missionaries late in the 1880s, reports from Molepolole suggest that the nagging preoccupation with the fate of his soul—for Sechele was very much a religious person—dictated that he should be more accommodating to his missionary than before, if his readmission was to be effected. Hence, in 1888, after he had demanded that Kwena regiments should build the Molepolole church, Sechele withdrew the order when Wookey insisted that only church members could build it. It is tempting to correlate Sechele's withdrawal with the religious literature he was then reading, for at that time he was reported to be reading Bunyan's *Pilgrim's Progress*.[26] In November 1888, Wookey reported that "Sechele has given in, and has left the work to the church people, including members, engineers, and attendants."[27] Sechele's conciliatory attitude paid off when in 1889 his church membership was reinstated after forty-one years' abeyance.[28]

The last three years of Sechele's life were bedridden, but even in his sickly condition he cooperated with the Molepolole missionary "in any good work for the benefit of his people, whether educational or religious." [29] After Sechele's death on 25 September 1892, L.M.S. missionaries who had worked in Kwenaland revealed some of Sechele's complex character in their eulogies to him. Howard Williams depicted him as an international figure: "With Sechele's death there disappears a prominent character, not only in the history of South African Missions, but [also] of South Africa itself." [30] Roger Price, who worked among the Kwena for over fifteen years, declared that "the church of the Bakwena will not be the same; it will seem strange without Sechele ... although he was never a member [during Price's time], he was always intensely interested in all that concerned the church," adding "Sechele's knowledge of the Bible was simply marvellous." [31]

Ngamiland also had its share of the problem of separating the church from state control. Although Khukwi had reported shortly after starting a school among the Tawana that his mainly adult pupils were making good progress in reading, he soon fell out with Chief Moremi over the question of church discipline. The occasion was a church meeting in 1880 when Khukwi insisted that the Chief behave himself by refraining from smoking tobacco. Moremi disobeyed Khukwi's order, whereupon the evangelist refused to preach "whilst the chief continued smoking and told him he was a man like other men." [32] Khukwi's equation of smoking with sin annoyed the Chief intensely and, according to his report to Hepburn, Moremi henceforth actively organized church members against Khukwi. As a result, the members were evenly divided in support of the two protagonists.[33] The dispute between Khukwi and Moremi was temporarily settled during Hepburn's visit to Ngamiland in 1881, but the Chief left the church permanently in 1886 when he refused to observe L.M.S. injunctions against polygamy and beer drinking.[34]

Moremi's neighbor to the northwest of Tawanaland,

Chief Ntare of the Yei (Koba), who no doubt like most Tswana chiefs of the time wanted a white missionary for security reasons, rejected Khukwi's offer to teach in his town on the superficial ground that "black men cannot teach," adding "and more than that I refuse to be taught or to allow my people to be taught."[35]

Ngwaketseland, unlike other Tswana chiefdoms, was not plagued by chief-missionary conflicts until the turn of the twentieth century. But in spite of this respite, it, too, had hurdles to overcome in its schools. While its central school was efficiently run, the outstations were neglected by the evangelist-teachers. In February 1886 Matsami was dismissed from his Pitsani post after the B.D.C. discovered that he had absented himself from his teaching job for a whole year without permission.[36] In 1890, Diphukwe Yakwe was expelled from his Moshupa job for drunkenness and negligence of duty, he himself reportedly confessing that he had been "destroying rather than building up the church under his care."[37]

In Ngwatoland Kgama's strained external relations with the Boers since 1876 augured well for a mutual understanding between the Chief and the Rev. J. D. Hepburn. Hepburn and some of the Shoshong traders assisted Kgama in his delicate negotiations with the emigrant Boers between 1876 and 1878 (see chapter 4); Hepburn again played a crucial role as interpreter when the British protectorate was declared in 1885 and when Kgama had his diplomatic and military problems with Boer freebooters between 1885 and 1890.[38] Another reason for the cordial relations between Kgama and Hepburn was the Chief's enduring desire to have his people evangelized, an attribute of Kgama's that is corroborated by missionaries and travelers alike.[39] And yet, paradoxically, the confidence that Kgama reposed in Hepburn, which the missionary took for granted in the course of time, was also the cause of the rupture between chief and missionary. As long as Hepburn could get Kgama's cooperation, all seemed well with him. But Hepburn failed to realize that Kgama, in addition to being a cooperative Christian ruler, was also very much a diplomat; so that as soon as the Boer threat to his chiefdom was removed by the presence of British officials late in the 1880s, there was a corresponding decline in Kgama's reliance on Hepburn and also a decline in the confidence he had traditionally reposed in his missionary.

The tragedy of this development was that Hepburn was unprepared for Kgama's change of attitude. In fact his report of 1887 shows that he had by then overestimated how much the Ngwato could respond to his missionary work:

> There is one thing about which I say nothing yet, but must wait to see how it shapes itself, and what progress it makes. I have not found it easy to practise patience, but it is most necessary to the growth of our work, if it is to be natural and not forced growth. . . . We are often greatly tempted to dig up the seed to see whether it has sprouted.[40]

Unfortunately for Hepburn, the turn of events did not allow him to test his own degree of toleration, for another problem superseded before Hepburn could even find out the depth of his tolerance. This was the age-old propensity of Tswana chiefs and their brothers to quarrel over the chieftainship.[41]

If Hepburn was impatient at the Ngwato response to his mission, as his candid confession suggests, he was psychologically ill prepared to direct the establishment of a new mission station when the Ngwato moved their town from Shoshong to Palapye in 1889.[42] And yet Hepburn conceived the erection of a new mission station on a grand scale, for the new Palapye church was designed to cost £3,000. In pursuance of his grand plan he required his church members to give large sums of money as church contributions (*phalalo*); according to some members of the Palapye church, he asked every church member to subscribe £200, while Kgama was required to contribute £10,000.[43] Kgama, on the other hand, was probably aware of his subjects' financial limitations and suggested that his regiments assist Hepburn in building the church, *gratis*. But Hepburn, in the tradition of Williams and Wookey in Kwenaland, rejected Kgama's offer and, according to some Ngwato church members, "in the middle of this work our teacher said that it ought to be built by the church members alone."[44] A stalemate had thus been reached in the struggle between church and state.

The tense situation that had built up at Palapye worsened when Hepburn sought to evangelize the Kalanga in the Shashi-Motlotsi area by sending Ngwato preachers there without Kgama's permission. Kgama opposed the move because he had not been consulted and also because he feared that the Ndebele, who claimed ownership of the same area as the Ngwato, might be provoked and retaliate by sending a punitive expedition against the Ngwato.[45] When Hepburn, who had taken offense at the Chief's veto of his Kalanga mission, charged Kgama with usurping his clerical authority, the rift between chief and missionary became open: Kgama transferred all church meetings from the temporary church building to his *kgotla* (court) because he had reason to believe that Hepburn was undermining his power.[46] An impasse was reached when the Chief and the missionary refused to discuss their differences. The breaking point was finally reached in December 1891 when Hepburn abruptly left for the Cape Colony.[47]

After Hepburn's departure, Chief Kgama, the Ngwato Church, Moffat, and Hepburn himself wrote to the L.M.S. trying to unravel what had happened. Even Kgama's brothers, who did not always agree with the Chief, supported him in assuring the society that the quarrel with Hepburn did not mean that they had broken their ties with the L.M.S. So, early in 1892 they jointly applied for two missionaries: "We write to our fathers, we are your children, we ask for two teachers so that one can be the teacher of the church the other one of the school, for this is a very large town." [48]

J. S. Moffat, who was Assistant Resident Commissioner for the northernmost part of the Protectorate, suggested that the L.M.S. investigate the Kgama-Hepburn dispute and the state of the society's schools before they should again send missionaries to the Ngwato. The society sent their Foreign Secretary to Palapye in August 1892. Thompson's investigations showed that Hepburn had acted peremptorily in the dispute with Kgama, but he exonerated the missionary's conduct on what he surmised to be medical grounds:

> He [Hepburn] was already overstrained by disease and long years of zealous labor when the task had to be undertaken. Neither the Bamangwato people nor the Directors will ever know fully what it cost him, not only in money but in mental anxiety and physical suffering, to carry out the task he conceived to be set him of erecting a place of worship worthy of the Christian aspirations of the people whom he loved as his own soul. . . . [49]

The Ngwato were advised by Thompson to dedicate themselves more fully to spiritual pursuits and to defy temporal power if it interfered with their religious conviction.[50]

Although Thompson's visit pacified the Ngwato and the society sent W. C. Willoughby to fill Hepburn's vacancy in 1893, the problem of delineating church affairs from state issues remained tenuous and periodically manifested itself in various guises well into the twentieth century. Nor indeed were Kgama's quarrels with his brothers healed by Thompson's visit. Instead, some of Thompson's remarks to the Ngwato provided material for Raditladi's group in their quarrels with Kgama.[51]

In May 1894 Raditladi and Tiro, together with Mphoeng and Gohakgosi, all of whom had in fact secretly supported

Hepburn against Kgama in 1891, wrote to the L.M.S. through Roger Price at Kuruman alleging that Kgama had again usurped the pastoral authority of the Palapye missionary and that he had embarked on a systematic persecution of Christians that the uninitiated Willoughby could hardly notice: "But it is certain that he, Monare [Sir] Mr. Willoughby will be deceived like the other one [Hepburn]: he is a white man . . . he does not understand the Se[Tswana] language."[52] Raditladi's group had thus found a convenient ground on which to continue the perennial fight with Kgama.

By 1895 the group had given Kgama so much trouble that the Chief wanted them removed from Palapye on the pretext that they violated his prohibition of the brewing and consumption of beer,[53] an allegation that impressed some government officials and led to the removal of the group from the Ngwato capital. But Raditladi's group wanted to justify themselves before the L.M.S. Thus, they highlighted Thompson's declaration of 1892 in which the L.M.S. Secretary had asserted that Christian duty ought to take precedence over secular demands,[54] and they used that cue to try to discredit Kgama. Hence, on 16 March 1895 the group told Thompson that Kgama had improperly exerted his authority in church affairs, alleging him to have said: "Let the church be in the chiefship, let it be ruled by the chief; but we [Raditladi's group] refused—we who were a part of the church; and so there were two churches: one of the chief—one of Jesus."[55] But the society had been forewarned of the faction's intrigues, thanks to Willoughby's reports,[56] and Thompson accordingly ignored their charges. Instead, he admonished them against initiating schism in the Ngwato tribe.[57] However, neither Thompson's counsel nor that of the Protectorate administration pacified Kgama and his brothers for any length of time; the rift between them widened until the British authorities intervened and moved the Raditladi group, first to a place bounded by the Motlotsi and Mpakwe Rivers, which was partly in the disputed

Tati area, and from there they moved to the Bulilima Mangwe district in Rhodesia in 1901.[58]

Meanwhile in Kwenaland, Sebele, who had succeeded his father (Sechele) in 1892, was periodically asserting his independence of British authority and jealously warding off missionary encroachment upon his sovereignty. But he, too, faced a serious challenge to his authority in 1896 when his brother, Kgari, and the latter's son, Baanami, hived off from the tribe with about 5,000 followers to set up an independant chiefdom east of Molepolole. The Kgari-Baanami faction, like that of Mphoeng-Raditladi in Ngwatoland, wished to involve the L.M.S. in their dynastic feud: their request for a missionary, if it had been granted, would have been construed to be a recognition of their independence. But the society foiled the Kgari faction's political stance by informing them "that until they [the faction] had a permanent location, and a permanent recognition as an independent tribe, it was scarcely possible that they should expect the Board to consider their claim to have a missionary to themselves." [59]

These disputes between chiefs and missionaries, and between chiefs and their brothers, had the unfortunate effect of braking progress in church and school life of the Tswana.

III

A special feature of Tswana education between 1880 and 1910 was the frequent inspection of L.M.S. schools. That the recommendations of these visitors—some of whom made very cogent observations—were largely ignored is one of the unhappy commentaries on the society's educational policy in Bechuanaland.

When he made a special trip to Bechuanaland to settle the Hepburn-Kgama conflict at Palapye in 1892, Thompson also inspected Tswana schools and was disappointed with the quality of education his society provided. He noted that school work might improve if the children could be disciplined; he recommended that the salaries of teachers be increased to attract an efficient teaching staff into the school system.⁶⁰ In contrast to Thompson's critical attitude, the majority of L.M.S. agents were apparently satisfied with their educational efforts but lamented what appeared to them to be the Tswana's congenital inability to make use of the educational facilities at their disposal. At their annual B.D.C. conference held at Kuruman in November 1892, they passed a resolution that amounted to a formal endorsement of their traditional attitude to Tswana education:

> The Committee regret[s] that the superior education offered by the Kuruman Boarding School for boys does not seem to be appreciated by the [Tswana] to anything like the extent they had hoped, and especially that up to the present time one of the, if not the, most important objects of the school, *viz* the providing of teachers for the elementary schools of the country, has remained unfulfilled—there is not an expupil of the school engaged in the work of teaching, or indeed in any work in which the education received in the school is of any special advantage, most of the boys having simply returned to the usual avocations of their countrymen—cattle herding, wagon driving, ...⁶¹

To combat this defection of trained teachers, the B.D.C. passed a supplementary resolution urging L.M.S. agents to be more judicious in their recommendation of prospective candidates so that only those students most likely to make teaching their career should be selected for training.⁶²

But some Tswana parents—especially chiefs and those commoners who could afford it—were not as complacent as the B.D.C. and continued to send their children to Lovedale (Cape) or Morija (Basutoland). As one newly arrived missionary reported, this Tswana gesture was a tacit disapproval of L.M.S. schools. Willoughby therefore refuted Thompson's rather simple analysis of Tswana parents' attitudes to education:

> I think the fact that many parents do this and pay £20 a year for their boys' education goes to disprove your statement that the [Tswana] do not care for education. . . . I look forward to the day when the white elephant at Kuruman [Boys' Boarding School] will make room for a more useful creature in some less remote part of the country.[63]

Part of the reason for Lovedale's and Morija's popularity was their renown—at least as far as the Tswana were concerned—in the teaching of English, whose mastery in the Protectorate enhanced one's social and economic status. In order to check this "drain" on their prospective students, some L.M.S. missionaries introduced a two-tier system of education at their stations whereby one stream of pupils paid a higher school fee than the other to enable them to take English lessons. Thus, in 1894 the newly arrived school mistress at Palapye, Miss Alice Young, divided the central school there into two streams: one group had 150 pupils who paid five shillings per year and had all their lessons in the vernacular, while the other stream of thirty-eight pupils paid two pounds each per year to get extra lessons in English.[64]

In Ngwaketseland Edwin Lloyd divided the Kanye school (1893) into two separate schools, one "Free-School" and the other "Fee-School." The "Free-School" did not charge fees and was under Mothowagae, an evangelist who later broke away from the L.M.S. and founded his own church. The "Fee-School" charged the pupils sixpence each per month and was under Lloyd's tutelage; it did not offer English lessons but was supposed to impart a superior kind of education to that provided at the "Free-School" by virtue of its schoolmaster's qualifications. However, by

October 1893, the "Fee-School" was in arrears: "At first the people entered into the idea of improving the school, and paying fees with heartiness, but, gradually, they wearied of paying for the school month by month, until by August scarcely anyone paid, though 50 or 60 children attended." [65] But at Moshupa, where the only school at the station charged fees, there were no arrears according to the evangelist there, John Kesieman.[66] Significantly, too, Mothowagae's school was better attended than Lloyd's and by the beginning of 1894 Lloyd predicted the demise of all "Fee-Schools" in northern Bechuanaland.[67] These predictions did not materialize, for it will be shown later some Tswana chiefs took the initiative in imposing an education levy on all taxpayers.

Meanwhile, the idea of building a trade school in some central part of the Protectorate, an idea that was gaining momentum, had been advocated by W. C. Willoughby and a few L.M.S. agents and J. S. Moffat at different times. The need for the school was even more acutely felt after the 1893 closure of the Moffat Institution at Kuruman, the sole supplier of indigenous teachers and evangelists.[68] In May 1896 the B.D.C. passed a resolution urging the directors to approve the construction of an industrial school at Mafeking in the Cape Colony. But the proposal was suspended when a rinderpest epidemic broke out late that year and the L.M.S., together with some British charitable organizations, channeled its funds to the relief of the impoverished Tswana.[69]

When the L.M.S. Foreign Secretary again visited Bechuanaland in 1898, he found that the suggestions he had submitted in 1892 regarding the improvement of L.M.S. schools had been very largely ignored. He noted, too, that the shortage of trained teaching-assistants had even become more acute since his last visit. Thompson again assertively recommended that the B.D.C. overhaul their educational system:

I ventured to tell the Committee that, after looking at the matter very seriously, I had come to the conclusion that the training of evangelists was a mistake, that what the people had needed for years past, and what they certainly needed very urgently now, was Christian men trained as teachers, who would in addition be prepared to carry on some measure of Christian work.The evangelist as he has been trained in the past has unfortunately been too much disposed to arrogate to himself the title and position of a missionary, and to regard school teaching as altogether beneath his dignity.[70]

Among some of Thompson's suggestions were an improved salary scale for assistant teachers and the recruitment of young European teachers into L.M.S. schools until such time as the proposed industrial school produced its own teachers.[71]

An important aspect of Thompson's recommendations was that, for the first time in the society's history in Bechuanaland, the principle of training students for careers in their own communities was clearly spelled out; the proposed trade school was designed to give "to all youths who leave school such a knowledge of tools as will enable them to be useful to themselves and to others. . . ."[72] However, for reasons connected with school administration and the society's financial limitations, Vryburg, a town in the Cape Colony, was selected as the home for the new school. Tswana communities, as shall be seen later in the chapter, deeply resented the location of the school.[73]

While Thompson's report covered the broad outlines of the contemporary state of Tswana education and projected what ought to have been its goals in the future, a more factual account of how L.M.S. schools were run was given by the Rev. James Richardson in his inspection report of 1899.[74] In the schools he visited, Richardson gave a reading test in the seTswana language to a sample of pupils. The position of Ngwato schools was as follows: at Sekao where there were 89 girls and 32 boys present, only five students passed the reading test; Boririma had 19 successful candidates out of its enrollment of 68 students (45 girls and 23 boys); the Khurutshe school had no successful candidate out of its student body of 61 students (40 girls and 21 boys); and equally poor results were obtained at the Talaote school, where only one student passed out of the school's 99 pupils (68 girls and 31 boys). The best results were obtained at the Palapye central school where 31 out of the 40 students passed the test; the school had an enrollment of 135 pupils. The Molepolole school, which had an enrollment of 173 (130 girls and 43 boys), had 15 successful candidates out of the 100 pupils tested, while only five out of 50 candidates at the Kanye central school passed the reading examination; the Kanye school had an enrollment of 260 pupils. Richardson's report showed that the majority of L.M.S. schools did not keep school registers. a practice that must have partly accounted for the poor attendance of students; it also must have been a factor in the children's poor achievement in reading, since school attendance and achievement are correlated. Richardson's concluding remarks, like those of Thompson's before him, exonerated L.M.S. missionaries but blamed the Tswana for what he judged to be a poor educational system.[75]

The financial limitation of Tswana schools, which most L.M.S. agents repeatedly reported to have curtailed progress in education over the years, was slightly improved in 1903 following negotiations that went on between the L.M.S. missionaries and the British Government between 1901 and 1903. In 1901 the B.D.C., supported by the Resident Commissioner, Surmon, applied to the High Commissioner in Cape Town for an educational grant-in-aid;[76] the application was given more weight by Reginald Balfour who, after his inspection of L.M.S. schools late in 1901, recommended that the B.D.C. be given some financial assistance.[77] The application was unsuccessful because of the expenses Britain was incurring in the Anglo-Boer War (1899-1902) that was in progress.[78] The first British contribution to Tswana education was not granted until 1903 when £600 was voted to the L.M.S.[79] Even so, Tswana education lagged behind Swaziland and Basutoland (the other British Protectorates in southern Africa) for many years thereafter.

IV

Perhaps the most important event to occur in the history of Tswana education was the opening of Tiger Kloof Industrial School in 1904. The idea of building an industrial school, as the above account shows, had been a lively issue during the last decade of the nineteenth century. Tiger Kloof's philosophy of education, which succeeding L.M.S. delegations and some B.D.C. members described in often garbled terms, was articulated by Reginald Balfour:

> The industrial school should begin with a definitely utilitarian aim. It should not be until comparatively late in school life that the [Tswana] mind should be trained to perceive that things may be attractive or beautiful apart from or beyond, the measure of their usefulness.[80]

That Tiger Kloof should have excluded girls is a reflection of the presuffragist, Victorian attitudes of L.M.S. teachers who attached more importance to a man's career than a woman's vocation. Balfour justified this policy when he commended the proposal for building an industrial school to the High Commissioner in 1901:

> But with regard to the men teachers, I may point out that there would be very little waste to the government, ...

because "those teachers who resigned their posts could always be employed as government clerks and court interpreters," a feedback that, in his view, could hardly be expected from women.[81]

"To Make a Book Talk" 181

But Tswana women were not entirely forgotten in the post-Balfour period, provision being made for them to improve their mastery of the courses that had always been offered in existing schools: they were taught to wash, starch, and iron clothes; also to make and mend them, and one L.M.S. agent was even more specific and recommended that Tswana girls be taught "to make and bake a decent loaf of bread in a three-legged pot." [82]

The Tswana yearning for a practical education was aptly summed up by Chief Sebele at the official opening of Tiger Kloof in 1905. Reinforcing Willoughby's opening speech, Sebele said:

> You speak words today that we have long had in our thoughts. Because you came and taught only from the books, we have had some doubt in our hearts; if we are taught only from books, and are not taught wisdom, how shall we live—how shall we get light if we are not taught the ways and means by which the white people live? . . . The book learning is no help to give to the people to live; the books told us some of the things which we may expect when we come to die. Today we have had words which I am very glad to hear. . . . Now we find what is to be done and what the books mean; a new prospect is now opened up before us.[83]

Nevertheless, some Tswana parents are reported to have withheld sending prospective students to Tiger Kloof presumably because the urban environment of the school might corrupt their children and also because it was situated far away from northern Tswana chiefdoms.[84]

The Ngwato opposed the location of Tiger Kloof because the L.M.S. had refused to locate the school at Palapye in spite of the tribe's offer to use the old church building and site free of charge.

Ngwato opposition to the location of Tiger Kloof was shown by what amounted to a virtual boycott of the school.

Some idea of their attitude is shown in Jennings's letter, where they are reported to have said:

> Monare [Sir] we tell you the wish of the tribe. The tribe wants to keep the church building at Palapye and make it into a school. Tiger Kloof is too far to send our children, and the tribe wants to get a teacher of its own to take charge of the school at Palapye.[85]

Before the emergency meeting at Serowe was convened in 1904, Ngwato resentment to the location of Tiger Kloof had been dramatized by the only Ngwato boy who tried to enroll as a student in it, Simon Ratshosa. Simon was expelled from Tiger Kloof on the same day he arrived there because he was not prepared to follow the rigid disciplinary code of the school:

> He swelled about [the school] in . . . master style all day, smoking cigarettes and patronizing the other boys; I [the principal] took careful notes of what was going on. . . . I was just sending for him when he appeared on the scene, and said he had come to tell me that he thought this place was scarcely ready for him yet; but that he might return later on. I soon corrected that notion, and sent him home.[86]

Students from Ngwaketseland and Kwenaland, though more restrained than Simon Ratshosa, showed a similar inclination to defy school regulations: of the five Ngwaketse boys who enrolled when the school started, two deserted before the end of the term; one of the two Kwena boys also left during the term because he did not like the food provided by the school nor Willoughby's stern discipline.[87]

The combined B.D.C.-Ngwato meeting held at Serowe in October 1904 pacified the Ngwato but only after a protracted discussion in which themes underlying the failure of L.M.S. schools and the conflict between the society's agents and the tribe had been fully discussed. Foremost among Ngwato grievances against the B.D.C. was the low quality of education provided in Ngwato schools, especially those situated in Serowe. The central school was heavily criticized and its headmistress, Miss Ella Sharp, was blamed for the school's lax discipline; they recommended that she be replaced by a man, for Ngwato boys tended to despise women generally. Thus, it would appear that, in spite of their criticism of Willoughby's stern discipline, the Ngwato appreciated some kind of order in the schools. Another grievance was the society's refusal to employ some of the Ngwato boys in their schools, in particular one, Tibe, whom the *pitso* felt was particularly suited to teach. The *pitso* further submitted that Ngwato boys could teach more effectively, because they were more fluent in the vernacular than Miss Sharp. The B.D.C. nevertheless opposed the Ngwato on this issue, maintaining that the majority of Lovedale graduates were notoriously immoral; that on that score only two out of about fifty former students of Lovedale (and Morija) in Bechuanaland were fit to teach in L.M.S. schools. The discussion on this issue was indecisive.

By the 24th of October, the Ngwato-B.D.C. meeting had reached an impasse. The Ngwato then relaxed their stand against the B.D.C. and made several concessions. Late on that same day Kgama sent his brother, Kebailele, to assure B.D.C. members that the Ngwato still had full confidence in the L.M.S.; they also withdrew their request to have Miss Sharp removed from the central school. But Ngwato retraction came at a time when the B.D.C. had already felt the impact of the *pitso's* criticisms, because he missionaries had in the meantime resolved to send a deputation to the British Administration urging them to take a more active role in Tswana education than previously; they also proposed that a schools' council be set up in each chiefdom to ensure full participation and cooperation of the Tswana in the education of their children. It was suggested that each school's council should be comprised of the local magistrate, the tribal chief, and a co-opted member. Finally, they recommended that there be an annual government inspection of schools, starting with James Burns's inspection late in 1904.[88]

The British Government did not participate in Tswana education as actively as the B.D.C. had anticipated, but, from 1904 on, voted an annual education grant to the L.M.S. The education votes from 1903 to 1910 were as follows: 1903–4, £600; 1904–5, £650; 1905–6, £822.19s.6d.; 1906–7, £650; 1907–8, £850; 1908–9, £1,000; and £999 for the financial year 1909–10.[89] Another major contribution made by the British Government to Tswana education was the appointment of E. B. Sargant as a school inspector for the High Commission territories (Bechuanaland, Basutoland, and Swaziland) in 1905.

Before he was appointed inspector of schools, Sargant, who was an education officer in the Transvaal, carried out another inspection of Tswana schools in 1905, the fifth independent inspection by an outsider in six years.[90] Some of Sargant's most important observations concerned educational priorities of African communities in the three territories and the methods used in the teaching of English and arithmetic. Sargant found that the prestige attached to the mastery of the English language had gravely undermined the vernacular:

> It should, however, be noticed that the first impulse of recently Christianised natives who send their children to school is the exact reverse of a desire for the more perfect command of their own language, whether spoken or written. The less the idiom is taught and the more rapidly English is introduced, the better they are pleased.[91]

But the mastery of English must have been difficult for the pupils, for as Sargant found out, the teachers concerned themselves more with pronunciation of words and less with the meaning of words and passages.

The teaching of arithmetic was found to be defective in the extreme: not only were some currency denominations (for example, farthings and half-pennies) not in use in the three territories included in the exercises assigned to the pupils, but the rules of working the problems were drilled mechanically.[92] The greater part of Sargant's report was devoted to aspects of Tswana education that had been covered by Richardson (1899), Balfour (1901), and Burns (1904). However, L.M.S. agents in Bechuanaland do not seem to have responded to the report with any seriousness. Their indifference to the report seems to have been caused by Sargant's critical strictures and the frequency with which their work had been unfavorably reviewed since 1898; the missionaries therefore became sensitive to what appeared to them to be unsympathetic observations by outside visitors. Haydon Lewis typified the casual manner in which missionaries reacted:

> From this visit we learnt a few things about ourselves, which tho not absolutely new to us were nevertheless clothed anew when touched upon from the point of view of an educational expert.[93]

Nevertheless, the post-Sargant era in Tswana education saw some marginal improvements in those aspects that Sargant and his predecessors had criticized. But some of these improvements, for example, the cooperation between chief and missionary, were erratic and were often effected independently of the missionary. In 1906 Bathoen donated £40 toward the education of the Ngwaketse.[94] In the same year Kgama contributed £120 toward the cost of a tower clock at Tiger Kloof and paid school fees for two Ngwato students there. Jennings, who had witnessed the Ngwato-B.D.C. discord of 1904, welcomed Kgama's gesture: "It is quite evident that Khama has still a very generous heart in all things connected with the L.M.S. and its work in this country."[95]

Among the Kwena, the rapport between the headmistress of the central school, Miss Partridge, and Sebele was conspicuous by its absence. Although he was interested in the education of the Kwena, Sebele seems to have been unimpressed with L.M.S. schools, which nevertheless plodded on without the cooperation of the tribe. By 1907 the enrollment at Miss Partridge's "fee-school" at Kanye was reported to have fallen from 119 in 1906 to 113 in 1907 because, "the sixpence fee is still a grievance and keeps a great number of children away." [96]

In 1908 Sebele opened a tribal school in his *kgotla* that, as Haydon Lewis's report shows, he ran independently of the L.M.S.: "[Sebele opened it] without referring to his missionary, and his reason was, that the schoolmaster who would be paid by the tribe, would be expected to do the chief's secretarial work, which would mean a saving of £8 per month to Sebele." [97] The opening of this school was another indication that the Tswana were dissatisfied with L.M.S. schools. In 1909 Sebele imposed an education fee of two shillings on every taxpayer; apparently he had by then patched up his differences with the L.M.S. that year, for he proposed to the Protectorate Administration that local schools in Bechuanaland be under the control of a committee comprising the Assistant Commissioner, the local missionary, and the tribal chief.[98] By 1910 school committees had been set up in all principal Tswana tribes; Miss Partridge abolished the school fee at the central school at Kanye and, significantly, enrollment at that school rose from 113 in 1907 to 342 in 1910.[99]

In Ngwatoland cooperation between chief and missionary seems to have been restored, for in 1909 the ageing chief was reported to have visited many villages, admonishing parents to send their children to school: "Why don't your children get taught? . . . You are not people to allow your children to grow up in such ignorance!" [100]

V

Meanwhile, Tiger Kloof was making steady progress. By

1908 its enrollment had risen from eleven students in 1904 to forty-nine. Although most missionaries had outgrown their nineteenth-century attitudes, this departure from conservatism seems to have eluded Willoughby. In 1908 he explained Tswana reluctance to send children to Tiger Kloof in superficial terms reminiscent of nineteenth-century attitudes: "We have of course to help the Bechuana [Tswana] in spite of their own foolishness, but it is unfortunate that the boys are not coming in faster than they are." [101]

Although Kgama's donation of 1906 suggested that he had accepted Tiger Kloof, Ngwato students do not seem to have emulated his example. Some of them failed to adjust to Willoughby's stern discipline and their resentment of school rules was tacitly encouraged by Jennings, who corresponded with them from Serowe. In 1908 Jennings received several letters from Ngwato boys in which they complained that life at Tiger Kloof was unbearable. One of the letters from Gaofhetoge Motiki (of 27 August 1908) discussed conditions at the school at great length:

> Here at school I am getting no advantage—I am sitting down merely. . . . I am not satisfied to stay here. . . . I inform you that if it depends upon me I shall not come back next year. I might return if Mr. Gillender [schoolmaster] were not here. . . . In this Institution I am afraid of the teacher and the principal.[102]

Another Ngwato student complained that "Mr. Willoughby says he is a chief and everything he says has to be done, has to be obeyed." [103] Gaofhetoge's father, himself an L.M.S. evangelist among the Kalanga at Letlakana in Ngwatoland, probably encouraged his son to disobey school rules, for on 22 July 1908, he complained to Jennings that the teaching staff at Tiger Kloof was needlessly severe on the students and that food at the school was bad; he urged the society to replace the entire teaching force by a more tolerant staff. But when Jennings subsequently laid charges of incompetence against Willoughby, the B.D.C. dismissed them as groundless.[104] When in 1909 Gaofhetoge and three Ngwato boys disobeyed Willoughby's order to transfer their course registration from carpentry to building, they were all summarily expelled.[105]

Between 1908 and 1910 Willoughby became a center of controversy because of his polemical statements on Tswana politics. In July 1908 he angered the Tswana when he informed a Cape Parliament Select Committee on Native Education that there was no need to teach agriculture in Tswana schools because the latter had "large stretches of land and esteem it their mission in life to put in crops in mealies, and waste a lot of time in gardening." [106] Willoughby, whose own school did not teach agriculture, even predicted that Europeans would in due course take whatever arable land the Tswana possessed; he further recommended the abolition of communal land tenure and its replacement by individual land tenure.[107]

Willoughby's views did not go unchallenged. They were disputed by delegates to the Bechuanaland Native Teachers' Association meeting at Mafeking on 29 September 1908. Delegates also took the occasion to review education in Bechuanaland and concluded that it lagged behind Basutoland; Chief Silas Molema, who was a guest speaker, ascribed it to the society's "primitive methods," which in his view did not match the "pushfulness" of the Paris Protestants in Basutoland.[108] Mr. Solomon Plaatje, editor of the weekly *Koranta ea Becoana,* criticized the society's virtual monopoly on Tswana education, which he thought ought to be removed if any progress was to be made.[109]

Chief Kgama, who was offended by Willoughby's testimony to the Select Committee, informed the Rev. Lloyd that the latter's views on land tenure were as unacceptable as Mackenzie's; and that in his view missionaries ought not to meddle in tribal politics. Also, by commenting on the sensitive issue of land tenure, Willoughby opened up old wounds

"To Make a Book Talk" 189

as Kgama recalled some of the conflicts he had had with him over the years:

> I went to England with him [1895]. There I was helped by Monare [Sir] Thompson and Mr. Albert Spicer. I do not reckon that Olloby [Willoughby] helped me at all. When in England, he kept me away from people to whom I wished to speak. After our business had been settled, I observed that a great change came over Olloby and I could not work with him any longer.[110]

Willoughby's unpopularity was reported to be widespread. An Ngwato church elder who attended a deacons' conference at Kuruman said: "Olloby batho ba mothsaba bothle," ["Willoughby: the people are all afraid of him."][111] As Kgama observed in his account, these grievances against Willoughby partly accounted for Tswana reticence to send their children to Tiger Kloof.

By 1910, when this study of Tswana education ends, Tiger Kloof was barely six years old. Although its theology department ordained the first Tswana ministers in 1910,[112] the fledgling school and other L.M.S. schools had as yet to wield greater influence on Tswana society.[113] In the course of time, the school created an elite that has had a great impact on contemporary affairs in Botswana. The Rev. A. E. Haile, who succeded Willoughby as principal of Tiger Kloof in 1914, writes:

> As for Tiger Kloof, it would be impossible to give you any comprehensive account of my experience over the years when I was principal from 1914–1945. I may say ... that 5 out of 6 African members of the present Botswana cabinet are old Tiger Kloof pupils, as well as the President, Sir Seretse Khama, and the Director of Education, Miss G. M. Chiepe.[114]

Even before L.M.S. agents had improved on their record of inept teaching, there is evidence to suggest that their efforts were not altogether in vain. Literacy among Tswana chiefs and commoners alike proved to be invaluable during the last quarter of the nineteenth century. Whenever chiefs corresponded with the British Government or with the L.M.S., they sometimes wrote the letters themselves or used their private secretaries to do so. Indeed literacy enabled them to keep abreast with events in southern Africa.

Reading vernacular papers from the Protectorate and from the Cape Colony kept them informed about events.[115] A case in point was the Ngwato reaction to a report in the January issue (1893) of *Mahoko a Becwana*. When they read about the B.S.A. Co.'s intention to annex Bechuanaland, the Ngwato were deeply concerned. Lloyd reported:

> I saw yesterday afternoon several leading men of the town sitting as solemn as a congregation of owls with this book [*Mahoko*] in their midst; so the thorn is in again which I extracted or tried to the other day.[116]

Nor was political consciousness the only advantage literacy enhanced; Willoughby's accounts show that he used pamphlets printed in the vernacular to teach hygiene and distributed thousands of them throughout Bechuanaland between 1904 and 1914.[117]

Thus, by 1910 Tswana education had undergone several transformations. Although L.M.S. agents for a greater part of the nineteenth century had been unable to correlate education to secular needs, they remedied that omission and made some improvements in the school system. The opening of Tiger Kloof in 1904 was a landmark in the evolution of Tswana education. Its importance lies not so much in the new educational experiences it offered Tswana youths as in the problems it posed in school organization, especially the relationship between parents, teachers, and L.M.S. agents. Attempts that were made by both missionaries and Tswana parents to solve these problems launched Tswana education into the modern era.[118] Regardless of its imperfections, education had thus been made more compatible with Tswana needs: it had become something much more than just "to make a book talk."

NOTES FOR CHAPTER FIVE

1. Alfred Wookey, "Literature for the Bechuana: Its Preparation and Influence," L.M.S. *Chronicle* (January 1902), p. 57; *also see* Richard Lovett, *The History of the London Missionary Society* 2 vols. (London: 1899), 1: Chapter 22, passim.
2. Minutes of the B.D.C., in Howard Williams and Albert E. Jennings to L.M.S. directors, 26 October 1904.
3. Report of Kuruman Institution, 14 December 1881, Box 2 (L.M.S.)
4. Lloyd to Thompson, 6 February 1885, Box 44, Jacket C, Folder 1 (L.M.S.).
5. Miss C. Wallace to Thompson, 15 May 1887, Box 44, Jacket C, Folder 5 (L.M.S.).
6. Howard Williams, Molepolole Report, 1891, Box 2 (L.M.S.).
7. James Good to Thompson, 2 April 1891, Box 48, Jacket C, Folder 1 (L.M.S.).
8. Minutes of the B.D.C., 3 June 1881, Box 41, Jacket C, Folder 5, (L.M.S.). For earlier reference to Mogodi *see* chapter 3.
9. Lloyd to Hhompson, 11 February 1887, Box 44, Jacket C, Folder 5 (L.M.S.).
10. Ralph Wardlaw Thompson to Whitehouse, 26 December 1883, Box 42, Jacket C, Folder 1 (L.M.S.). *See also* Bryden, *Gun and Camera*, pp. 274–75; Walter Montagu Kerr, *The Far Interior: A Narrative of Travel and Adventure from the Cape of Good Hope Across the Zambezi to the Lake Regions of Central Africa*, 2 vols. (London: 1886), 1: 27–28.
11. For boys' and girls' initiation ceremonies *see* chapter 3. The more profitable hunting season was roughly from April to September.
12. Wookey to Thompson, 7 September 1885, Box 43, Jacket A, Folder 2 (L.M.S.). In 1875 John Brown wrote: "The boys are sent to these posts and grow up there away from school, away from public worship . . . ," "The Bechuana Tribes," *Cape Monthly Magazine*, no. 5. 11 (July 1875): 2.
13. Shoshong Report in Hepburn to Thompson, 11 February 1887, Box 2 (L.M.S.).

14. Lloyd to Thompson, 13 January 1889, Box 46, Jacket A, Folder 1 (L.M.S.).

15. For example, *see* B.D.C. Minutes of 1892, in Ashton to Whitehouse, 19 November 1892, Box 49, Jacket B, Folder 2 (L.M.S.).

16. The Rev. R. Wardlaw Thompson, *Deputation to South Africa, September 4th, 1883 to April 9th, 1884,* printed for the use of the directors (L.M.S.), p. 30. *See also* Miss Wallace to Thompson, 15 May 1887, Box 44, Jacket C, Folder 5 (L.M.S.). Even at Molepolole, where the school was reported by Thompson to be satisfactory, Kwena parents (including Sechele) sent their children to Lovedale. Debate on education for Africans seems to have started earlier at the Cape than in Bechuanaland, for in 1875 a correspondent (in *Cape Monthly Magazine,* 10 [April 1875]: 210) advocated the opening of trade schools in African communities: "The crucial question is, what will the thousands of boys and girls do with their power[s] of reading, writing, and ciphering. . . , if they don't know how to use a plane or a saw, a needle or an awl, much less to cut out a coat or a gown. . . ?" Lovedale was a nondenominational, multiracial school that had been started by the Free Church of Scotland in 1841. By 1878 James Stewart, its principal, could write: "All colours, white and black, and brown and yellow are to be found among the pupils," in his *Lovedale Past and Present* (Cape Town: 1879), p. 9.

17. R. W. Thompson, *Report of the Deputation to South Africa (Confidential), January to March 1898* (L.M.S.), p. 21. For a survey of Victorian attitudes on education, *see* Brian Jackson, "100 Years of State Schools," and Sonia Jackson, "The Long Haul," *The Sunday Times Magazine* (London), 4 January 1970.

18. J. S. Moffat to Thompson, 21 March 1888, Box 45, Jacket C, Folder 3 (L.M.S.): "It seems to me that the preaching of the gospel in a broad sense includes this higher education. . . . These people [Tswana] will have to fight for their own lands some of these days; perhaps very soon, with the gold fever on in Southern Africa and reaching to the Zambezi; and if we don't give them something more in education than we have done, we don't give them a fair chance."

19. Howard Williams to Thompson, 13 May 1889, Box 46, Jacket D, Folder 1 (L.M.S.).

20. Moffat to Thompson, 13 September 1891, Box 49, Jacket C, Folder 1, (L.M.S.).

21. Moffat to Thompson, 3 May 1892, Box 49, Jacket C, Folder 1 (L.M.S.).

22. Thompson to Moffat, 24 May 1888, Box 21. The society received money from donations.

23. All L.M.S. agents reported the chiefs' opposition to this religious segregation.

24. Price to Thompson, 29 December 1884, Box 42, Jacket D, Folder 3 (L.M.S.). For Sechele's quarrels with British Officials, *see* chapter 4.

25. Wookey to Thompson, 4 August 1885, Box 43, Jacket A, Folder 2 (L.M.S.).

26. Wookey to Thompson, 27 April 1888, Box 45, Jacket B, Folder 3 (L.M.S.).
27. Wookey to Thompson, 15 December 1888, Box 43, Jacket E, Folder 3 (L.M.S.).
28. Howard Williams, Molepolole Report, 1889, Box 2 (L.M.S.).
29. Howard Williams, Molepolole Report, 1890, Box 2 (L.M.S.).
30. L.M.S. *Chronicle* (February 1893), pp. 39–40.
31. Ibid.
32. Hepburn to Whitehouse, 7 June 1880, Box 40, Jacket C, Folder 3 (L.M.S.).
33. Hepburn to Whitehouse, 7 June 1880, Box 40, Jacket C, Folder 3 (L.M.S.).
34. J. D. Hepburn, *Twenty Years in Khama's Country*, ed. G. H. Lyall (London, 1895), pp. 259–303.
35. Hepburn to Whitehouse, 7 June 1880, Box 40, Jacket C, Folder 3 (L.M.S.).
36. *See* Minutes of the B.D.C. meeting held at Kuruman, 9 February 1886, Box 44, Jacket B, Folder 1 (L.M.S.). The Rev. James Good had a good working relationship with Gaseitsiwe. But he, too, like the evangelists, was not hard working and often absented himself from Kanye. In 1897 (Thompson to Good 9, January 1897), Thompson wrote: "I suppose you are still the missionary of Kanye though I have had no reply from you to official letters of a serious character written a very long time ago." In 1901 (Thompson to Good, 26 January 1901, L.M.S.), he said: "[reports from Cape Town created an] impression in our committee that for some years past a very considerable portion of your time has been spent at Cape Town or in journeying to and fro."
37. James Good to Thompson, 8 January 1890, Box 47, Jacket A, Folder 1 (L.M.S.).
38. *See* chapter 4.
39. Frederick S. Arnot, *From Natal to the Upper Zambezi* (London: 1883), p. 26–27; J. Cooper-Chadwick, *Three Years with Lobengula and Experiences in South Africa* (London: 1894), p. 39; H. M. Hole, *The Passing of the Black Kings* (London: 1932), p. 269.
40. Shoshong Annual Report, in Hepburn to Thompson, 11 February 1887 (L.M.S.). The Ngwato remember him as a short-tempered person, *see* "Notes from the Bamangwato," in Wookey to Hawkins, 26 December 1914, Box 76 (L.M.S.).
41. For a discussion of this phenomenon *see* I. Schapera, "Kinship and Politics in Tswana History," *J.R.A.I.* 93 (July–December 1963): 159–73; *see also* Mackenzie's "Disputed Chieftainships," in Parliamentary Papers, 1885, C. 4588, 57: 66, when he noted the rivalry that existed between Tswana chiefs and their next of kin.
42. Scarcity of water supplies at Shoshong compelled the Ngwato to move their town to Palapye. See J. D. Hepburn, p. 305; Lloyd to Thompson, 27 May 1889, Box 46, Jacket D, Folder 1, and 1 July 1889, Box 46, Jacket A, Folder 2 (L.M.S.). This was confirmed by Mrs. Lucy Syson, Research Assistant, Surveys and Training for Development of Water Re-

sources and Agricultural Production, Botswana, personal communication, 10 October 1969.

43. Lloyd to Thompson, 13 January 1892, Box 49, Jacket A, Folder 1 (L.M.S.).

44. Church of Bamangwato to the L.M.S., 13 January 1892, Box 49, Jacket A, Folder 1 (L.M.S.).

45. Chief Kgama to the L.M.S., 10 November 1891, Box 48, Jacket D, Folder 1 (L.M.S.): "And I objected also during one Sunday Service Mr. Hepburn called for twenty members of the church to go out to teach the Makalaka who are under the rule of Lobengula . . . the proper way was to . . . write . . . to Lobengula."

46. Church of Bamangwato to L.M.S. directors, 13 January 1892, Box 49, Jacket A, Folder 1 (L.M.S.): in one church meeting Hepburn was asked by one, Mocwaedi, "Should the chief call out our regiment as usual, are we to obey the chief to go and do whatever he asks?", and Hepburn said, "No, and you must not obey the chief; you are the servants of Christ, and you must obey Christ alone." The Ndebele-based missionary, Cullen Rees, had had a severe reprimand from Kgama in 1890 when he meddled in Ngwato politics (see Kgama to the Rev. Mr. Rees, 4 August 1890, Chief's Papers, Selly Oak Library "Now I am chief of the country. You are a teacher. I cannot allow any teacher to act and speak as if he was a chief of my town."

47. Hepburn to Thompson, telegram, 4 November 1891, and Moffat to Thompson, 2 and 22 March 1892, Box 49, Jacket B, Folder 1 (L.M.S.); also Moffat to Thompson, 3 May 1892, Box 49, Jacket B, Folder 1 (L.M.S.).

48. Chief Kgama, Raditladi, and others to L.M.S. directors, 3 May 1892, enclosed in Moffat to Thompson, 3 May 1892, Box 4, Jacket C, Folder 1 (L.M.S.).

49. Moffat to Thompson, 22 March and 3 May 1892, Box 49, Jacket B, Folder 1 (L.M.S.).

50. R. W. Thompson, *Report of Special Visit to South Africa, during August, September, and October, 1892* (L.M.S.), pp. 3–4. See also Thompson to Kgama, 1 January, 1892.

51. Opponents of Kgama's were his half brothers, Mphoeng, Raditladi, and Seeletso, a cousin, Kuate, and a near-relative, Tiro. The group was occasionally joined by Kgama's full-brother, Kgamane. See A. Sillery, *Founding a Protectorate* (The Hague: 1965), p. 207. See also I. Schapera, "Kinship and Politics in Tswana History," *J.R.A.I.* 93 (1963): 159–73.

52. Raditladi and Tiro to Price, 4 May 1894, Box 51, Jacket C, Folder 1 (L.M.S.). Apparently the Ngwato wanted male missionaries, for the L.M.S. had sent them two lady missionaries (Ellen Hargreave and Alice Young) in February 1894; see Hargreave to Thompson, 18 March 1894, Box 51, Jacket B, Folder 1, and 20 August 1894, Box 51, Jacket B, Folder A (L.M.S.).

53. See Willoughby to Cousins, 23 February 1897, Box 54, Jacket A, Folder 1 (L.M.S.): ". . . when the chief and his younger brothers fell to quarrelling, both parties wanted to carry their quarrel into the church."

54. Thompson, *Report* (1892), p. 5: ". . . I reminded them that times

might come in the life of a man, or in the experience of the Christian community in Bechuanaland, when the law of God must be obeyed even though it might involve the penalty of disobedience to the law of the State. At once Raditladi, the chief's brother and a deacon of the church, responded to this that they were well aware that the church was not to be under the control of the State, and that if the chief, as chief, attempted to interfere with them in their Christian life and duty they would speedily let him know that he was interfering in matters beyond his province."

55. Palapye Church to Thompson, 16 March 1895, Box 52, Jacket A, Folder 1 (L.M.S.).

56. Willoughby to Thompson, 18 March 1895, Box 52, Jacket A, Folder 1 (L.M.S.).

57. Thompson to Tiro, 27 July 1895 (L.M.S.).

58. Willoughby to Cousins, 23 February 1897, Box 54, Jacket A, Folder 1 (L.M.S.), the faction had 100 adults, thirty of whom were Christians.

59. R. W. Thompson, *Report of the Deputation to South Africa (Confidential) January to March, 1898* (L.M.S.), p. 39.

60. Ibid., p. 17; salaries ranged from £10 to £24 according to the teachers' qualification; *see* Thompson to Gould 1 July 1899 (L.M.S.). Some schools engaged teachers without pay; *see* Willoughby to Thompson, 4 October 1900 (L.M.S.).

61. Minutes of the B.D.C. in William Ashton to Whitehouse, 19 November 1892, Box 49, Jacket B, Folder 2 (L.M.S.).

62. Ibid.

63. Willoughby to Thompson, 22 September 1894, Box 51, Jacket C, Folder 2 (L.M.S.). Not all Tswana students made full use of Lovedale facilities. Chief Kgama's son, Sekgoma, kept two thoroughbred horses at Lovedale and kept two servants, Baipedi and Kahiso; he was a frequent guest of G. M. Theal (Historiographer at Cape Town) and of Loch, the High Commissioner. According to Ratshosa, this soft life led to Sekgoma's failure at school; "My Book on Bechuanaland Protectorate . . . ," Rhodes House Library, p. 144.

64. Willoughby to Thompson, 19 November 1894, Box 51, Jacket C, Folder 2 (L.M.S.).

65. Edwin Lloyd to Thompson, 21 December 1893, Box 50, Jacket D, Folder 2 (L.M.S.).

66. Ibid. Edwin Lloyd to Thompson, 21 December 1893, Box 50, Jacket D, Folder 2 (L.M.S.).

67. Palapye Annual Report for 1893 in Lloyd to Thompson, 14 February 1894, Box 2 (L.M.S.).

68. The school was closed after the B.D.C. had failed to find a replacement for its principal, J. Tom Brown, who was going on furlough. *See* Minutes of the B.D.C., enclosed in J. T. Brown to Thompson, 20 November 1893, Box 50, Jacket D, Folder 3 (L.M.S.).

69. For the effect of rinderpest on the Tswana and their cattle, *see* Alfred Wookey to Thompson, 20 June 1896, Box 53, Jacket C, Folder 2, and 15 September 1896, Box 53, Jacket B, Folder 3, and 17 September

1897, Box 54, Jacket B, Folder 2 (L.M.S.); Willoughby to Cousins, 9 June 1897, Box 54, Jacket D, Folder 1, and 14 August 1897, Box 54, Jacket B, Folder 2 (L.M.S.). See also chapter 7.

70. Thompson, *Deputation 1898*, pp. 44–46. Before Thompson visited Tswana schools, the B.D.C. sent Willoughby on a tour of the following mission schools in Lesotho and the Cape Colony: Lovedale and Blythswood (Presbyterian); Morija (Paris Evangelical Society); Healdtown (Wesleyan), and several Anglican schools at Grahamstown, Keiskama, and Aliwal North. His conclusion was that missionaries at these schools were doing "very superior work. . . . At any rate I am bound to tell you that we are very far behind," in "Report of Visit to Certain Native Boarding Schools in South Africa," 1 February 1898, Box 55, Jacket E, Folder 1 (L.M.S.).

71. Thompson, *Deputation, 1898*, pp. 44–45. In July 1899 (*see* Thompson to Gould, 1 July 1899 [L.M.S.]), Khukwe and Shomolakae had their salaries raised from £24 to £36 per annum.

72. Thompson, *Deputation*, p. 47.

73. Ibid., p. 51: "One important consideration which reconciled me to placing the school within the colony was that it would thus come within the range of Government inspection, and that the Society might reasonably hope to obtain Government grants for the Normal School and for the Industrial Department."

74. James Richardson, "Report of an Examination of the Chief Schools in Bechuanaland, July–September, 1899," Box 56, Jacket B, Folder 3 (L.M.S.). Richardson's report does not seem to have been uniform, for example, he did not show the number of students he tested at the Khurutshe school.

75. Ibid. "I sympathize very much with the missionaries in Bechuanaland, battling against such enormous inertia among the people, and the great irregularities in the attendance of the scholars makes a teacher almost despair."

76. C. O. 879/76, African (South), No. 694, p. 113, Surmon to Kitchener, June 1901, enclosed in Kitchener to Chamberlain, 87 of 16 August 1901. Part of the grant was given to a Palapye European school of twenty-four pupils run by a Boer teacher, J. B. Oelrich (pp. 37–38).

77. C. O. 879/78, African (South), No. 702, pp. 90–94, Reginald Balfour's Report, 11 November 1901, enclosed in Milner to Chamberlain, 88 of 14 February 1902. Balfour, like Thompson in 1898, emphasized the need for industrial training. Kgama, who had sold lots of cattle to the British during the Anglo-Boer War (1899–1902), donated £1,760 toward Ngwato education, Howard Williams to Thompson, 25 April 1901.

78. Willoughby Papers, Folder 778, 25 May 1900, "Notes of Conversation with Chamberlain," Willoughby's informal request for an educational grant-in-aid was approved with a proviso, Chamberlain replying, "Yes, I don't see why you should not . . . just now we cannot think of anything else; but after the war is over"; *see also* Folder 376, "The Contribution of Protestant Missions to the Life of the World," by Willoughby.

79. *Annual Report of the Bechuanaland Protectorate* (1904–5), No. 73, Cd. 2684–25, pp. 10–13.
80. Balfour's Report, C. O. 879/78, p. 93.
81. Ibid., p. 91. For a background of the school systems that influenced missionary attitudes to education, see P. W. Musgrave, *Society and Education in England Since 1800* (London: 1968), passim; S. J. Curtis, *History of Education in Great Britain* (London: 1967), p. 140, passim.
82. Willoughby to Ralph Williams, 13 August 1903, C. O. 879/79, p. 662, enclosed in Lawley to Lyttleton, 426 of 16 November 1903. Balfour, who was a Transvaaler, did not approve of multiracial schools: "Their [three white children] presence in a school [at Palapye] where the medium of instruction is Sechwana, and where only the headmistress is of European race [sic] is, I am informed, bad for them and for the native children with whom they associate."
83. W. C. Willoughby, "Historic Gathering at Tiger Kloof," L.M.S. *Chronicle* (January 1905), pp. 312–13.
84. Willoughby, "Historic Gathering at Tiger Kloof," L.M.S. *Chronicle* (January 1905), pp. 312–13. With the exception of Jennings, all missionaries did not accept criticism for having built Tiger Kloof outside the Protectorate proper. Hence, the Ngwato complaint against the location of Tiger Kloof was dismissed very lightly: "They evidently wish to have control of the missionaries and their work, even the deacons striving to make church polity subservient to tribal policy"; B.D.C. Minutes, 26 October 1904 (L.M.S.). *See also* Norman Goodall, *A History of the London Missionary Society, 1895–1945* (London: 1954), pp. 245–46.
85. Jennings to Thompson, 3 May 1904 (L.M.S.).
86. Willoughby to Thompson, 15 January 1904. Ratshosa does not deal with this aspect of his early life in his manuscript.
87. Willoughby to Thompson, 15 January 1904 (L.M.S.). Simon Ratshosa was Kgama's grandson and is the author of the manuscript "My Book on Bechuanaland Protectorate Native Custom," (1931), kept at Rhodes House, Oxford. Willoughby enforced strict discipline from the beginning, as is shown in his account 8 March 1904 (L.M.S.): "Within a few weeks of our arrival we had between thirty and forty native lads who wanted to learn the building trade . . . of these lads some soon tired of industry, and others we weeded out as being unlikely to learn. . . ."
88. Minutes of the B.D.C., 26 October 1904 (L.M.S.), James Burns, Report on the L.M.S. schools in the Bechuanaland Protectorate, Tiger Kloof, 14 December 1904 (L.M.S.).
89. C. O. 879/84, Africa (South), no. 746, pp. 249–50, Milner to Lyttleton, 148 of 25 April, 1904; *Annual Reports of the Bechuanaland Protectorate:* (1905), 73, Cd. 2684–25: 9–13; (1905–6), 53: 5; (1906), 68: 6; (1907–8), 57: 5; (1908–9), 57: 5–7; (1910), 64: 4–5.
90. E. B. Sargant, no. 52, *Report on Native Education in South Africa, Part III, Education in the Protectorates* (Headley, Surrey, England: 1908).
91. Ibid., p. 4. This was criticized by Solomon T. Plaatje, who, reminiscing on his school days (*see* his book, *Sechuana Proverbs with Literal Translations and Their European Equivalents* [London: 1916], pp.

15–16) observed: "The head teacher is usually the white missionary, who, even if a good linguist must, except in rare cases, has the accent and uses the idiom of a foreigner, the pupils invariably drop their mothers' accent and speak . . . 'as teacher speaks it' . . . a kind of 'school Sechuana.'"

92. Sargant, *Report*, p. 20.

93. Haydon Lewis, Molepolole Report, 1905, Box 3 (L.M.S.); Edwin Lloyd, Serowe Annual Report, 1908, Box 4 (L.M.S.), had objections to the report: "For the educational work of Serowe Mr. Sargant has no word of praise, but only severe words of criticism. But it is not clear whom he blames, whether the chief or the missionary, or both."

94. Howard Williams, Kanye Report, 1906, Box 4 (L.M.S.).

95. Jennings, Serowe Report, 1906, Box 4 (L.M.S.).

96. Miss Partridge, Report for Molepolole School, 1907, Box 4 (L.M.S.). In 1909 the Ngwaketse complained against school fees.

97. Haydon Lewis, Molepolole Report, 1908, Box 4 (L.M.S.).

98. Lewis, Molepolole Report, 1909, Box 4 (L.M.S.). It appears that the Committee that was reported to have been set up in 1904 from the Burns *Report* had not functioned. See Minutes of the B.D.C., 26 October 1904 (L.M.S.).

99. Mary Partridge to Thompson, 16 June 1910 (L.M.S.).

100. Lloyd, Shoshong Report, 1909–10, Box 4 (L.M.S.).

101. Willoughby, Report of Tiger Kloof Institution for 1908 (L.M.S.).

Analysis of Pupils for 1908

	Apprentices	Boarding School	Working Pupils	Bible Students	Total
Present at end of 1907	33	27	6	–	66
Failed to return in 1908	1	14	–	–	15
Returned in 1908	32	13	6	–	51
Admitted during 1908	14	1	1	2	18
Left during 1908	16	3	1	–	20
Transferred during 1908	–	3	1	–	4
Transferred to Tiger Kloof in 1908	1	–	1	2	4
Present at end of 1908	31	8	6	4	49

102. Jennings to Thompson, 31 July 1909, Box 71 (L.M.S.).

103. Letter of 24 July 1909, in Jennings to Thompson, ibid.

104. Jennings to Thompson, 31 July 1906 (L.M.S.).

105. Jennings to Thompson, 31 July 1909, Box 71 (L.M.S.). His criticism of Tiger Kloof and its principal was rejected by the B.D.C. in May 1909, when the latter cabled their society: "The B.D.C. have unanimous and complete confidence in Tiger Kloof and Willoughby," in Minutes of the B.D.C., 1–11 May 1909, Box 71 (L.M.S.). For Tswana-missionary conflicts over land, see chapter 4.

106. Ibid.

107. Ibid.

108. "Bechuanaland Education, Meeting at Mafeking—Attack on London Missionary Society," *Diamond Field Advertiser,* 19 October 1908.
109. *Diamond Field Advertiser,* 19 October 1908.
110. Chief Kgama's statement of 29 July 1909, in Jennings to Thompson, 31 July 1909, Box 71 (L.M.S.).
111. Lloyd to Thompson, 20 August 1909, Kgama suggests (in "Notes on the Remarks of the Chief Khama and the Serowe Deacons, 1909," that his private secretary, Seiso, and Willoughby swindled some of his money during the Chief's visit to England in 1895: "I took £600 to England. Seiso . . . stole some of this money. I told Olloby [Willoughby] to buy something for Mrs. Willoughby . . . he bought her a saddle . . . when we returned to Palapye, Olloby gave me £60, which was the amount remaining over from £600 . . . my people complained of him," ibid.
112. Minutes of the B.D.C. Annual Meeting held at Kuruman, 1 May to 11 May 1909; Minutes of B.D.C. meeting, 18 April to 30 April 1910 (L.M.S.).
113. For which the Hon. B. C. Thema, Minister of Education in the Republic of Botswana was grateful in 1969: "Their [L.M.S.] educational philosophy was simply that man did not only have a soul to nourish, but he also had reason to develop and skills to cultivate, and on this basis they provided Botswana with education of the heart, the head, and the hand," in *Kutlwano* 8, no. 12 (December 1969). However, this could hardly be an accurate assessment of their nineteenth-century schools.
114. Rev. A. E. Haile, Sussex, in letter communication of 12 December 1968 to the author.
115. The B.D.C. published newspapers mainly for their church members; beginning in 1856, the following papers have been in circulation during the specified times: *Molekudi ua Bechuana,* monthly, 1856–7; *Mokaeri oa Bechuana,* monthly, 1857–9; *Mahoko oa Becwana,* monthly, 1883–98; *Koranta ea Becoana,* weekly, 1901–8; and *Tsala ea Batho,* weekly, 1909–10. Except for the last paper that was printed at Tiger Kloof, all were printed at Kuruman. While most of the stories in these papers were of a religious nature, some reports were exposés of what the missionaries thought to be social injustices; for example, in 1890, when *Mahoko oa Becwana* published a story alleging that Kgama had killed a woman, Kgama wrote to Thompson (11 April 1890, Box 47, Jacket C, Folder 1) complaining that ". . . Mr. Wookey has put a letter in the paper. The letter is by one of Sechele's people. It has been done to help Khari Macheng [Kgama's rival]. Why does it tell old words of long ago?" The Rolong chief, Montshiwa (Lloyd to Thompson, 14 June 1893, Box 50, Jacket A, Folder 2, L.M.S.) was reported to have written to the same paper in defense of "payment of cattle for wives. He has three wives himself." The Hermannsburgs published *Moshupa-tsela.* For the history of the Tswana press, see Plaatje, *Sechuana Proverbs,* pp. 4–5; I. Schapera, *The Tswana* (London: 1952), p. 18. See also C. O. 879/37, Africa (South), no. 441, p. 55, Chief Kgama to the Editor of *Cape Argus,* 3 December 1892, enclosed in Loch to Ripon, 49 of 19 December 1892.
116. Lloyd to Thompson, January 1893. For more examples, *see* Kanye

Church to Thompson, 3 November 1902, (trans. Kgosikobo Chilongona), Chief Bathoen to Thompson, 19 February 1903, Box 50, Jacket A, Folder D (L.M.S.) (trans. Chilongona), Chief Kgama to L.M.S. directors, 3 May 1892, Palapye Church members to Thompson, 16 March 1895, Bathoen to Thompson, 21 May 1903.

117. Willoughby Papers, Folder 376, Selly Oak Colleges. Between 1904 and 1914 Willoughby distributed about 80,000 pamphlets in the Tswana language dealing with syphilis, chest trouble, wounds, and some infectious diseases.

118. By 1907 a "Native Advisory Council" had been set up that was comprised of missionaries and representatives from the principal tribes. At its meeting held at Kanye in January 1907, Chief Bathoen was reported to have "delivered an able address on the questions before the meeting." For an assessment of the effectiveness of Tswana education during the first half of this century, *see* G. Chiepe, "An Investigation of Problems of Popular Education in the B.P." (Masters thesis, University of Bristol, 1957).

6
Boikgololo: Millenarians and Church Secessionists in Northern Bechuanaland, 1898-1910

THE TURN OF THE TWENTIETH CENTURY SAW NORTHERN TSWANA chiefdoms embroiled in a movement that was in many respects complementary to the efforts the Tswana were making to improve the prevailing system of education. Church schism, which had its beginnings in Basutoland and the Cape during the last quarter of the nineteenth century, spread to northern Tswana chiefdoms in earnest in 1898. Led by disgruntled L.M.S. evangelists, "Ethiopians" or separatists were spurred on by secessionists from neighboring territories; and in Ngwaketseland there is evidence to suggest that legal counsel discouraged the breakaway group from reconciling with the L.M.S. church at Kanye.

Yet throughout the nineteenth century, L.M.S. missionaries relied on teacher-evangelists (or "native agency") for the proselytization of the Tswana especially in the outlying "bush" schools. Some of the society's evangelists were Paul Mebalwe,[1] Khukwi Mogodi, Diphukwe Yakwe, and Shomoloekae Sebolai.[2] Missionary reports suggest that Tswana evangelists rendered faithful service, although the quality of their work was often judged to be poor. Even so, this incompetence was explained away in oversimplified terms, the Tswana being thought to be naturally incapable of performing good work. Missionaries influenced L.M.S. directors who, like their agents in Bechuanaland, readily concluded that African evangelists were less resilient workers than their white counterparts. Thus, when Khukwi Mogodi fled from Ngamiland in 1885 after his house had twice been ransacked by the Ndebele, the L.M.S. Foreign Secretary wrote:

> I am not greatly surprised that Khukwi should have come to the conclusion not to return to the Lake after all he has endured. Had he been a European missionary we might have expected a little more resoluteness, and the manifestation of a determination to persevere in spite of all obstacles.[3]

If missionary views on the Tswana capacity to work were inaccurate, they nevertheless influenced them in determining the rank of evangelists in the pastoral leadership of the church. Thus, although missionaries readily conceded that the services of Tswana evangelists were invaluable to evangelization, it never occurred to them that native evangelists should be elevated to the Congregational ministry. Also, remuneration was meager, and irregular, a condition that compelled some evangelists to trade in ivory to augment their salary.[4] Yet when in 1881 the B.D.C. discovered that Khukwi had engaged in small-scale trade in ivory, they recalled him from Ngamiland and reprimanded him before they transferred him to Moshupa in Ngwaketseland.[5]

Relations between Tswana rulers and teacher-evangelists were by no means cordial either. The misunderstanding between chiefs and evangelists was partly inherited from the beginnings of the L.M.S. mission when, for strategic and military reasons, chiefs preferred European missionaries to African evangelists.[6] Another factor that militated against cordial relations between chiefs and evangelists was that pastoral leadership too often conflicted with the secular authority of the chiefs.[7] Thus, for a greater part of the nineteenth century, African evangelists occupied an ambivalent position in Tswana society: on the one hand, the L.M.S. judged them to be inefficient agents, on the other, Tswana chiefs were continually irritated by the evangelists' assertiveness in church affairs, while the majority of the Tswana were indifferent to the Christian message of salvation. However much Tswana evangelists might have felt the need to improve their conditions of service, the social and political milieu in which they worked condemned them to menial, pastoral positions. In due course L.M.S. missionaries came to believe that their mission to the Tswana was beyond reproach. This attitude influenced them to impose a system of education that easily lent itself to criticism toward the end of the nineteenth century. And just as the high quality of education at Morija (Basutoland) and Lovedale (Cape) spurred the Tswana to agitate for better schools,[8] so were members of the Boikgololo movement inspired by secessionists from neighboring territories.[9]

The Transvaal, which wielded considerable influence on the Boikgololo movement in Bechuanaland, experienced the first African secession from a white church in 1892, when for reasons stemming from racial discrimination, the Rev. Mangena Mokone broke away from the Methodist Church. Mokone consequently formed a church of his own, which was recognized by the Transvaal Government in August 1896.[10] The new church assumed a universal character, for its members called it the *Ethiopian Church,* a name that purported to embrace all blacks in the world.[11]

The universal claims of the Ethiopian Church were given more weight in 1896 when that church affiliated itself to the African Methodist Episcopal Church in America. Contact between the two churches was initiated by Charlotte Manye, a niece of Mokone's, who had traveled to America with a church choir in about 1893 and subsequently enrolled as a student at Wilberforce University in Ohio. Charlotte informed Mokone of the existence of the African Methodist Episcopal Church with headquarters in Atlanta, Georgia. At their third annual conference held in Pretoria in March 1896, Ethiopian delegates resolved to join the A.M.E. Church. The preamble to the resolution had Pan-African overtones: "This conference is strongly of the opinion that a union with the African Methodist Episcopal Church will not only be hailed by our people, but would [also] be the means of evangelising numerous tribes of this vast continent." [12] The conference appointed the Rev. James Dwane and the Rev. Jacobus G. Xaba to go to the United States to negotiate the affiliation of their church to the A.M.E. Church. However, only Dwane was able to go to America and late that year the Ethiopian Church was affiliated to the A.M.E. Church.[13]

Meanwhile, the Ethiopian Church seems to have stepped up its organization in the Transvaal; its recruitment of disaffected members of established churches into its fold seemed unorthodox to white ministers of religion. The Rev. George Weavind must have captured the mood of the clergy when he complained that

> this independent church has already created many difficulties in the country. The leaders have laid hands upon any native, without respect to character, who had some little education, and in some cases ordained him and in others placed him in positions of responsibility. These men . . . have . . . caused trouble and the governments are beginning to see that Native churches without a

European head, will set the country in a flame if they are not suppressed.[14]

But Transvaal officials did not consider the Ethiopian movement sufficiently dangerous to be outlawed.[15]

Meanwhile in Bechuanaland proper, no significant indigenous church had thus far emerged to challenge L.M.S. dominance. Although there had been some schism in the south at the Taung church between 1886 and 1890 and at Manthe in 1893, the Tswana region north of the Molopo River remained essentially unaffected until the end of the 1890s. In 1898 two Ethiopian representatives from Khunwana in Rolongland, Seile and Mareko, visited Chief Bathoen at Kanye. They assured the Rev. James Good that they had no intention to interfere with his work, as such, but that "their presence would be valuable to the tribe affording them variety in teaching." [16] To L.M.S. agents, who no doubt remembered with anguish their encounter with Matsame at Taung in 1886 and must have also known the activities of the Ethiopian Church in south Africa,[17] the Ethiopian overture was intolerable. But in spite of the visitors' offer to improve the quality of education with which the Ngwaketse were slowly becoming disenchanted, Chief Bathoen was not enthused either. After Seile and Mareko had stated the object of their visit in the *kgotla,* the *pitso* urged them to renounce Ethiopianism and to come back to the L.M.S. fold. Bathoen seems to have been largely responsible for the rejection of this incipient Ethiopianism. In his summation of the *pitso* proceedings, Bathoen reminded the Ngwaketse that they owed literacy and some measure of political independence to the L.M.S. (or "The London"). In Bathoen's view, the Ethiopians could never hope to match the impressive record of the L.M.S. and, under the circumstances, he saw no need for another church. Hence, he could declare: "No, Hear me! I am a London, I have always been a London, and if you wish for change here, you must wait till I have gone, and my son Seapapitso is ruling in my stead." [18] When the B.D.C. met at Kuruman in March 1899, they resolved not to recognize the Ethiopian Church and to punish any evangelists or church members who might join it.[19] Nor did that measure stop the spread of Ethiopianism in Bechuanaland.

In 1901 five Ethiopians appeared in Ngwatoland under the guise of being "prophets"; they claimed to possess the power to solve all social and political disabilities of the tribe. Although their message appealed to some Ngwato in and around Palapye, Kgama apprehended them swiftly. He convened a *phuthego* on 15 April 1901, at which the "prophets" were tried on charges of false pretences. At that trial one of the prophets was reported to have "confessed that he had commanded the people to worship him." [20] The *phuthego* found them guilty and ordered that their houses be burned down; the court also ruled that persons who had given the prophets some presents be fined twice the value of the goods they had given away.

Meanwhile, Afro-Americans had become more active in south Africa since the affiliation of the Ethiopian Church to the A.M.E. Church in 1896. As a consequence, two years after the affiliation, A.M.E. Church membership in south Africa rose from 2,000 to 12,000,[21] a trend that must have encouraged American Blacks to send a free-lance representative to south Africa in 1899. Even before that delegate arrived, northern Tswana chiefdoms had attracted the attention of the A.M.E. Church for in 1898 it sent a representative to start a church at Palapye. However, that mission was nipped in the bud because Chief Kgama III, who had by then been a staunch supporter of the L.M.S. for thirty-six years, summarily expelled the Ethiopian from Ngwatoland.[22] In 1899 C. A. A. Rideout, a free-lance missionary, went to south Africa to organize the A.M.E. Church. A former District Judge in the U.S.A., his legal training seems to have fired the imagination of Ethiopians in southern

Africa. The Rev. Mangena Mokone's welcoming speech, which was subsequently published in the A.M.E. Church paper, *Voice of Missions,* was clearly laudatory:

> Praise God! such a man as Rideout [is] on our shores. He is the first man of this kind in these parts of South Africa. We never saw a black judge in our lives, only Rideout . . . we want a man of some qualifications, and who will stand [against] . . . prejudice, one who will fight for equal rights for the [black] race on the face of the globe. The men of honorary M.D. and M.A. won't do much here. We want the men who passed their degrees who can face an opposer with great power; we want the engineers.[23]

Mokone concluded his eulogy by appealing to American Blacks to come and live in south Africa.

There is no evidence to suggest that Mokone's appeal was taken seriously by American blacks; it appears that the few American blacks the A.M.E. Church sent to south Africa merely filled administrative posts in the church hierarchy. Nevertheless, A.M.E. Church officials had some impact on the spiritual and secular life of blacks in southern Africa. Hence, soon after Rideout's arrival in south Africa, Gordon Sprigg, the premier of the Cape Colony, reported that the American visited Pondoland and freely dabbled in the internal politics of that chiefdom:

> The influence Rideout endeavoured to exert amongst the Pondos was not exercised in a right direction, the tendency of his teaching being to set native against European.[24]

This allegation was later denied by some Ethiopians, who pointed out that the A.M.E. Church in the Cape had a white minister.[25] Nevertheless, by 1902 the activities of the A.M.E. Church (or the Ethiopian Church) were considered by some observers of the geopolitics of southern Africa to be a serious threat to European hegemony in that region.[26]

Yet in spite of this Ethiopian onslaught in south Africa proper, northern Tswana chiefdoms remained largely impregnable to church separatists. One reason for this quiescence was that the frontier politics on the high veld during the second half of the nineteenth century had fostered mutual interdependence between L.M.S. missionaries and Tswana chiefs.[27] However, two factors seem to have favored the penetration of the Ethiopian spirit in northern Bechuanaland: first, the poor quality of education, which easily lent itself to criticism by outsiders and by the Tswana themselves;[28] second, the overly paternalistic L.M.S. policy toward teacher-evangelists,[29] which led missionaries to believe that no Tswana evangelist was good enough to be promoted to the clergy. Thus, when a persistent Ethiopian sect appeared in any chiefdom in northern Bechuanaland, missionaries were ill prepared to deal with it; their leverage lay in Tswana chiefs, who appear to have suppressed Boikgololo incursions more for political reasons than for religious ones.

In Ngwaketseland the Kanye church and Chief Bathoen were embroiled in a church schism at the turn of the century when an L.M.S. evangelist asserted his right to lead the church. The leader of the dissident group was Mothowagae Mohlogeboa, himself a member of the Ngwaketse tribe. Mothowagae's early life is obscure, but it is known that from 1874 to 1880 he was an assistant teacher at Kanye under the Rev. James Good. Between 1880 and 1884 he was a student in the Bible school at Kuruman, returning at the end of 1884 to become an evangelist at Kanye.[30] By 1893 he had enhanced his popularity by conducting a nonfee-paying school while the Rev. Lloyd witnessed a decline in attendance in his fee-paying school.[31] Mothowagae's own testimony suggests that by 1900 he believed himself to be a minister of religion and a co-equal of the Rev. Edwin Lloyd.[32]

The B.D.C. precipitated Mothowagae into belligerent

Ethiopianism when, in 1901, they transferred him to Lehututu in the Kgalagadi Desert. According to Chief Bathoen, Mothowagae was willing to go but could not do so because of his wife's illness.[33] Mothowagae's own account asserts that Chief Bathoen and the church at Kanye wanted him to stay,[34] while the Rev. Lloyd reported that he was dismissed in July 1901 for refusing to go to Lehututu. The dismissal was condemned by the church at Kanye and the church members took the occasion to criticize the L.M.S. over a number of issues. According to Lloyd, "those who were inquirers were dissatisfied because they were not admitted into [the] church at once. . . . The dissatisfied headmen joined the now dissatisfied evangelist." [35] The dissident group demanded that Mothowagae be ordained as a minister of the L.M.S. and that he should take charge of the Kanye church. The group included Bathoen's brother, Kwenaetsile, the Chief's brother-in-law, Tsime, the latter having accompanied Bathoen to England in 1895.

Early in 1902 the B.D.C., no doubt shaken by Mothowagae's support, summoned Mothowagae to a meeting at Palapye even though the evangelist was no longer an officer of the L.M.S. There the B.D.C. conducted a test to find out if Mothowagae could be considered for ordination. He was reported to have failed the test.[36] Although missionaries did not state what type of test they gave him, Mothowagae maintained that he was given a Latin test:

> I attended in 1902 at Palapye at the conference held there and on my presenting myself for ordination I was given a Latin Book and asked to read same. I informed them that they had not taught me this Language in their schools and they refused to ordain me.[37]

That failure notwithstanding, there was now popular support for Mothowagae's leadership. On 12 June 1902 Bathoen wrote to the Protectorate administration saying he had refused demands from the secessionists to authorize Mothowagae to baptize children.³⁸ Bathoen again wrote to Assistant Acting Commissioner Jules Ellenberger on 27 June 1902 asking if Mothowagae could marry and baptize members of his congregation.³⁹ But Ellenberger was in the meantime corresponding with L.M.S. missionaries,⁴⁰ who in turn, tried to present their protagonist in a bad light.

Lloyd wrote to Ellenberger on 27 June 1902 acquainting him with the church dispute at Kanye and suggesting that the government had no business to meddle in church affairs.⁴¹ The Rev. James Good, who had retired to the Cape in 1900, wrote to Ellenberger on 30 June 1902 recounting what he surmised to be the underlying principles of Mothowagae's sect and other Ethiopians generally. To Good, Tswana Ethiopianism was part of a southern African movement whose desire was "to cast off the tutelage in which [the Tswana] have lived up to the present." ⁴² Good ascribed Kanye Ethiopianism to the influence wielded by Tswana migrant workers returning from the Johannesburg and Kimberley mines and also to Tswana students at Lovedale, both bringing back "the most wonderful stories about the churches and their methods in the colony—the Ethiopians in particular." ⁴³ The Resident Commissioner subsequently informed the B.D.C. that the church dispute at Kanye was not within the purview of the government but, as will be shown later, the political overtones of the dispute entailed government intervention not only at Kanye but also at all other Tswana centers as well.⁴⁴

Meanwhile, L.M.S. directors thought they could pacify the Mothowagae group by transferring the Rev. Lloyd to a station in the Cape Province. But the transfer was opposed by a section of the Kanye church. On 3 November 1902 twelve members purporting to represent five-hundred L.M.S. church members at Kanye wrote to the L.M.S. directors urging them not to transfer Lloyd.⁴⁵ A month later forty-six church members wrote to the directors demanding that Lloyd be reinstated to his Kanye post; they regretted the fact that Mothowagae was administering the sacrament and that he allowed his followers to drink *khadi*.[46] This permissive attitude seems to have attracted an impressive following. In January 1902 Mothowagae's followers were estimated at forty-four,[47] in January 1903 Lloyd reported that eighty-eight members had left his Kanye church to join Mothowagae's group,[48] and by February that year the number had risen to ninety-five, which was about one-third of the 266 church members at Kanye,[49] while in October 1903 Mothowagae himself declared that his followers at Kanye, Moshupa, and Moshaneng amounted to 700 souls all told.[50]

The Bechuanaland District Committee took some steps to try to bring the Mothowagae faction back to the L.M.S. fold. Early in January 1903 they set up a commission of two missionaries to inquire into the dispute and to initiate reconciliation. However, when Willoughby and John Brown went to Kanye in February 1903, they were unable to meet Mothowagae owing to their impatience to negotiate with a man they considered to be a misguided rebel.[51] Yet, in spite of their failure to hear Mothowagae's version of the dispute, the two missionaries reported that Lloyd was not to blame for the religious schism at Kanye.[52] When Bathoen complained about the irregular manner in which Brown and Willoughby had conducted the inquiry and recommended that Lloyd be removed,[53] the directors of the L.M.S. informed the Chief that he was needlessly meddling in church affairs and that neither Bathoen nor the British Government, for that matter, had the right to expel a missionary.[54] In May 1903 Bathoen again wrote to the directors bemoaning the fact that the church schism at Kanye was so deep that reconciliation was not longer possible,[55] and about the middle of 1903 Bathoen allowed the Mothowagae faction to build their own church at Kanye;[56] he then retracted his earlier request to have Lloyd removed from Kanye.[57]

In the meantime, Mothowagae was alienating Bathoen's sympathy and even drawing the attention of the Ngwato church. Some of the points of conflict between the Chief and the evangelist were political, while others were slightly religious. Bathoen's main complaint was that Mothowagae flouted his authority.[58] This allegation impressed Ralph Williams who, although he had said in 1902 that his Administration did not wish to interfere in church affairs,[59] declared:

> I don't care if a man is a fire worshipper, a Mohometan, or a Christian, he is entitled to his own views—but if he uses the fact of his religious beliefs to create disturbance in the tribe . . . it cannot be tolerated.[60]

Williams said that if Mothowagae's insubordination could be established, Bathoen would be justified in punishing the Ethiopian.[61]

But before he was banished, Mothowagae petitioned the Resident Commissioner, Ralph Williams, on 19 October 1903 to be allowed to solemnize marriages, under the provisions of what he said was an English law of 1838. Mothowagae had also by this time named his group 'King Edward Bangwaketse Mission Church," [62] a name that seems to have been chosen in order to flatter British officials, for the then reigning monarch in Britain was King Edward VII. But events were moving swiftly against the King Edward church. On 26 October 1903 Bathoen convened a *pitso* in which he announced the banishment of Mothowagae from Kanye for reasons stemming more from the evangelist's political activities than from religious ones.[63] Failing that, on 10 and 11 November 1903 Bathoen cited instances in which Mothowagae had clashed with him. These ranged from Mothowagae's refusal to allow Mabe, a member of the Ngwaketse tribe, to teach Scripture, his refusal to appear before Bathoen on four occasions in 1897, his refusal to pay taxes, and to Mothowagae's failure to return some money he had borrowed from the Chief. Perhaps the last straw in a series of acts of insubordination occurred on 7 September 1903 when, during an interrogation, Mothowagae answered back

Boikgololo

to Bathoen, which in Tswana protocol is a gesture of extreme insolence. Thus, Bathoen could maintain:

> According to our laws, only a chief may speak to another chief in this way, the word "kabomo" [purposely] may only be used by one chief talking to another: a member of the tribe, addressing his chief in that way, brings himself to the same level as his chief. The people all blamed him for thus addressing me.[64]

These indiscretions notwithstanding, the Ngwaketse did not approve of the banishment and, according to the chief's testimony, a large section of Kanye residents became so hostile to Bathoen that he had to be guarded.

On 30 October 1903 Seametso, one of Bathoen's messengers, took Mothowagae to Ellenberger to report the evangelist's refusal to leave Kanye. In his defense, Mothowagae said banishment was too severe a punishment and that it deprived his followers of a teacher. When Ellenberger suggested that he join the L.M.S., Mothowagae refused, saying his group was hurt by "certain proceedings of the L.M.S.," but did not elaborate. He then pleaded: "We want to have our own church under the protection of the Government as other churches are." [65] He alleged that Bathoen was thrashing his followers and that the Chief's hostility toward him had more to do with a quarrel Mothowagae had had with Bathoen in 1884 than with his religious activities.[66] Ellenberger did not take sides on the issue.

When Mothowagae returned to Kanye, he seems to have again irritated the Chief by his refusal to leave Kanye. On 4 November 1903 Bathoen wrote to Ellenberger alleging that Mothowagae did not give him due respect and asked the official to intervene; the Chief reported that Mothowagae had since sought refuge with Makabe, one of Bathoen's brothers, where he commanded more support from Kanye residents, while the Chief was virtually deserted.[67] Ellenberger investigated the cause of the quarrel between chief and evangelist at Kanye on 10 and 11 November 1903. At that inquiry Bathoen maintained that Mothowagae was undermining his authority, while the evangelist pleaded that the Chief had been too severe on him. Bathoen then displayed typical ambivalence when he regretted that his people had "gone astray" in accepting Mothowagae's Ethiopianism, while in the next breath he asserted that religion had no bearing on Mothowagae's banishment. Ellenberger refused to sanction banishment on the grounds that it would be too severe a form of punishment.[68]

In the meantime Mothowagae, who displayed considerable inclination to rely on tribal and English legal remedies to support himself well into the 1920s,[69] sought refuge in the "belly" of Bathoen's deceased father Gaseitsiwe, a desperate step that brought his pardon. As Ralph Williams reported, "Mothowagae, in seeking the protection of the late Chief Gaseitsiwe, took a most serious step. He invoked the ancient customs of the Bangwaketse. Then Chief Bathoen carried out those customs and pardoned Mothowagae." [70] Bathoen's withdrawal of the banishment certainly played into the hands of Mothowagae, and he seems to have become even more determined to sustain his sect. But the Ngwato were alarmed by Mothowagae's activities and Bathoen's apparent leniency on him. On 25 November 1903 an article purporting to give an Ngwato view appeared in a Tswana paper suggesting that if Mothowagae had in fact stopped rain,[71] as had been rumored, then he was a witch and by that act forfeited his claims to Christianity. The article warned that Mothowagae was using his sect as a guise to usurp the Ngwaketse chieftainship; the Ngwaketse were urged to be more vigilant in their dealings with Mothowagae.[72] In another article Mothowagae was declared to be a false prophet who was indeed seeking the chiefship; "Pray, we assure you that it is not a church, but deceit with a view to seeking the chieftainship only, it is nothing else." [73] The Ngwaketse were informed that the Ngwato punished false prophets more resolutely than Bathoen's indecisive strictures.

Elsewhere the Boikgololo movement was making some headway. Among the Khurutshe, the Ngwato neighbors at Selepeng in the Tati concessions area, the evangelist Tumedi successfully led a revolt against the L.M.S., and the secret of his success seems to have been his ability to get the support of Rauwe Sekoko, Chief of that Khurutshe community. The Khurutshe leader, like his southern neighbors, seems to have been encouraged to secede from the L.M.S. by Ethiopian representatives from south Africa and some Ngwato youths living in Rhodesia. In 1904 the Rev. Gould observed:

> Some years ago an Ethiopian protégé came to visit Tumedi and he evidently sowed his seed there and then and it has been slowly maturing ever since. He told Tumedi that the missionaries of the L.M.S. did not allow such men as he the rightful privileges, such as baptising, giving the communion, marrying and such like duties. . . . That they should have the same status as any European missionary.[74]

When the unnamed Ethiopian visited Selepeng for the second time, he is reported to have converted Tumedi, who was the L.M.S. teacher-evangelist at that station. Tumedi in turn mustered the support of Chief Rauwe Sekoko, the Chief's son-in-law, Molefhi, and some headmen.[75] Tumedi tried to spread Ethiopianism to Serowe but was expelled by Kgama;[76] he was reported to have been expelled also from the Ngwato exiles in Rhodesia, but that measure seems to have been ineffectual, for Raditladi's sons, who were educated at Lovedale, displayed strong Ethiopian tendencies. By 1904 Raditladi's sons, who freely drank beer in defiance of their father's orders,[77] had made the L.M.S. evangelist Moyahi's work so difficult that he wanted to resign from his post.[78]

Once the Tumedi group had decided to assume full control of the Selepeng church, they avoided a direct confrontation with the L.M.S., but instead found a pretext to justify the removal of the Rev. Gould. In 1903 they demanded Gould's removal on the grounds that he was inefficient.[79] Whatever truth there was in the charge, it is noteworthy that six out of eight deacons supported Tumedi.[80] In September 1904, the Rev. Gould reported to the Protectorate administration that Ethiopianism had taken root in Tati and that the government ought to suppress it while he was away on furlough.[81] The Administration agreed to watch Ethiopianism closely but cautioned against any hasty action against its leaders.[82] The Tati concessions company promised to cooperate with the missionaries.[83] In the meantime secessionists were making themselves felt at the Selepeng church. By June 1904 the L.M.S. church attendance on Sundays had fallen from fifty to fifteen,[84] and in September that year Tumedi was reported to have attracted sixteen members from Gould's church.[85]

When Gould went on furlough in November 1904, the Tumedi group had ample time to organize. Evangelist Moyahi, who remained acting in Gould's place, appears to have been ineffectual as opposition to Gould's tenure mounted in his absence. In March 1905 the M.D.C. was informed that Mpotokwani and Modisane, the only deacons who had hitherto supported Gould, had now joined the Boikgololo faction. The Rev. Cullen Rees, who investigated Khurutshe attitudes to Gould, concluded that "Gould was personally hated by the Bakhurutshe as a church and people." [86] Rees's report must have influenced L.M.S. missionaries in Matebeleland, for the M.D.C. did not reinstate Gould to the Selepeng post. Khurutshe opposition to the L.M.S. coupled with the Tati Concessions Company's refusal to issue long-term leases forced the L.M.S. to close its Tati station in 1908.[87]

Leadership within the Boikgololo sect at Selepeng passed

from Tumedi to one Lobang some time after 1905, when Tumedi fades away from missionary correspondence. By 1908 Lobang, who had previously been a schoolteacher in the Transvaal, was reported to be running a school of three hundred pupils and that he had the support of Rauwe Sekoko and his subjects. Lobang's relationship with Moyahi (L.M.S. evangelist) must have been a strained one because in his letter of 1908 to his society, the Rev. Carleton used highly pejorative terms to discredit the new Boikgololo leader.[88] The year 1908 also saw the emergence of an Ethiopian church in the Tati area when the Rev. Marcus Gabatshwane started an A.M.E. Church among an emigrant Rolong group under Chief Moroka at Francis Town.[89]

In Ngwaketseland Mothowagae put his pardon of 1903 to some good use and he set up what appears to have been a network of organizers. In 1904 it was reported that Setlagole, an outstation of Kanye, had been taken over by Ethiopians.[90] In the same year Mothowagae demonstrated the influence he wielded at Kanye following the death of Kwenaetsile, one of Bathoen's brothers who was an Ethiopian. At Kwenaetsile's funeral Mothowagae demanded and obtained the right to conduct the services together with the Rev. Lloyd of the L.M.S.[91] Elsewhere in Ngwaketseland the Ethiopians continued to make some progress. In 1905 Moshupa, an L.M.S. outstation, was reported to have been converted to Ethiopianism en masse, the local headman being one of the converts.[92]

Whatever setbacks Ethiopians had elsewhere in Bechuanaland, it was their good fortune that Ngwaketseland had a vacillating chief. Thus, although Bathoen pleaded with L.M.S. directors not to repost Lloyd in 1903, he changed his mind three years later and asked for a new missionary.[93] The directors referred the issue to the B.D.C., who in turn sent Williams and Willoughby to Kanye in July 1906 to find out why Bathoen desired to have a different missionary. The delegation was informed by Bathoen and other church members that they wanted Lloyd removed because he was lazy.[94] Lloyd was replaced by Williams late in 1906, but his removal did not curb Ethiopianism in Ngwaketseland.

The Ngwato, too, had their share of Ethiopian spasms in spite of Kgama's opposition. When he was asked by a member of the South African Native Affairs Commission in September 1904 if Ethiopians had reached his chiefdom, Kgama said, "I have heard the name, but so far there are no Ethiopians in my country."[95] Yet hardly four years later Kgama, like other Tswana chiefs, had to deal with prophetism, which was a variant of Ethiopianism. According to the Rev. Williams, the Ethiopians called themselves "prophets" in order "to cover a propaganda calculated to stir up bad feeling in the . . . native mind towards the whites."[96] Like their predecessors in Ngwatoland in 1901, the 1908 prophets claimed to possess supernatural powers to solve the social and economic problems of the Tswana. In 1908 a traveling prophet, Sencho Legong, appeared on the borders of Bathoen's territory and "proclaimed himself an 'angel' of God, a prophet, the Lord Jesus himself, and this was the burden of his message: rain which should cover hill tops, three harvests a year, absolute freedom from the white man's control, and a return to all the old heathen customs of the past."[97] Some Ngwaketse responded to Sencho's promise of a millennium by burning their Bibles and church hymn books; others offered the "prophet" some gifts. Sencho is reported to have "reluctantly" accepted 30 heifers, 129 sheep and goats, a gun, a span of 14 oxen, 1 wagon, several fowls and some corn.[98]

However, what appeared to be the triumph of Ethiopianism in northern Bechuanaland was soon reversed by Tswana chiefs. At Kanye Sencho's followers were whipped in the *kgotla*. White traders, who no doubt feared that their stores might be boycotted in anticipation of a millennium of bliss, persuaded the Resident Magistrate to prosecute Sencho. He was subsequently tried at the Magistrate's

Court—presumably charged with false pretences—but was declared insane and ordered to live under the custody of his parents.[99] But no sooner was Sencho sent to his parents in 1908, than he escaped and went to Sebele's chiefdom, where he burned down an L.M.S. church at Mokhibidu. At Molepolole Chief Sebele welcomed a prophet with presents of several herd of cattle, some sheep, and a bride. But the fortunes of that prophet were reversed at Serowe, where Kgama typically had him arrested and tried in his court. The *phuthego* sentenced him to caning and ordered that all his "gifts" be confiscated; the bride was sent back to her parents in Kwenaland.[100] In 1908 Serowe became a target for Ethiopianism originating from Matebeleland, where the Rev. Maghato's activities were causing concern to Rhodesian authorities.[101] In that year a man from Matebeleland was sentenced by a Serowe magistrate to three months imprisonment for his Ethiopian activities.[102]

Thus, the Boikgololo movement, which reached the apogee of its impact on Tswana chiefdoms in 1908, had its momentum braked that year. Harried by chiefs,[103] government officials and missionaries from all sides, the Ethiopians were unable to make further progress. The only smoldering embers of that movement remained in Ngwaketseland, where Mothowagae and Sencho displayed some measure of resilience. Mothowagae, in addition to his Ethiopian activities, continued to commit acts of insubordination, which subsequently led to his banishment. Even before his banishment, Mothowagae and his followers had shown their determination to stick to Ethiopianism. Minutes of the Ngwaketse tribal assemblies (*lechulo*) show that the Ethiopians continued to meet between 1908 and 1910 in spite of Bathoen's disapproval.[104] Thus, on 22 February 1910 Bathoen summoned a *lechulo* to discuss the Ethiopian movement in the presence of the Resident Commissioner, Ellenberger. At that meeting the Ethiopians "stated that they refuse[d] to abandon their faith."[105] Soon after Bathoen's death on

1 July 1910, the new chief, Seapapitso, informed the Ngwaketse about his attitude to Ethiopianism: "Bangwaketse, I tell you that I do not want two religions here, even if they are practised [privately] in your homes." He reaffirmed his father's decree that had banned Ethiopianism in 1908.[106] When the Ethiopians did not yield, Seapapitso banished Mothowagae in July 1910; the Chief gave him the option to go to either Potsane or to Lekgolobotlo.[107] But Mothowagae refused to comply, saying both places were not suitable for farming.[108] Seapapitso asked for government intervention, which he obtained, and on 11 August 1910 Mothowagae was reported to have left for Lekgolobotlo.[109]

Banishment does not seem to have mellowed Mothowagae, for in 1911 he was reported to be in touch with Ethiopians at Taung and Moshupa and, on the advice of Malolo of Taung, he was also bringing a legal suit against the Ngwaketse chief, restraining the chief against interfering with his church.[110]

Sencho's Ethiopian activities seem to have gone unabated in spite of legal restraints placed against him in 1908. His influence at Kgoro, a village thirty-two miles south of Kanye, and also in Ngwaketseland generally seems to have disturbed Chief Seapapitso so much that in January 1913 the Chief had him sent to a prison in Gaborone. But a medical officer again ordered him to be looked after by his relatives. Sencho subsequently went to work in the mines in the Transvaal and returned shortly afterwards to lead what appears to have been a quiet life in Ngwaketseland.[111] If the Boikgololo movement was weakened largely by Tswana chiefs, the A.M.E. Church representatives were unable to make much headway either. Like its Boikgololo counterpart, the A.M.E. Church found it difficult to penetrate northern Tswana chiefdoms.

Yet in spite of the obstacles they had to face, Ethiopians achieved some of their objectives. One of their major victories was the marked change of missionary attitudes toward the Tswana and the former's reexamination of the effectiveness of their educational system. Whereas previously the B.D.C. did not bother to consult the Tswana on religious as well as educational issues, Ethiopianism compelled L.M.S. missionaries to share the leadership of the church and the schools with the Tswana more than they had hitherto done. Missionaries began to criticize themselves more openly than they had done in the past. For example, in 1907 the Rev. Alfred Wookey wrote an introspective account that was revealing. He conceded that Ethiopianism was a Tswana

> effort to regain some of their former liberty. Perhaps, too, we have been repressing them too much in religious and church as well as political life. . . . We are too apt to think that if they do not agree with us they are immoral, or not fit to be church members; or if they want to have more liberty in the management of their affairs they must be wicked; but unless we are prepared to meet them as far as possible in their requests they will leave us, or we shall have to leave them.[112]

The Rev. Wookey's article suggests that secessionists were justified in calling themselves *Boikgololo*. Significantly, too, the first two Tswana ministers were ordained in 1910.[113]

Students of Ethiopian movements have often been baffled by what appears to be an absence of doctrinal differences between the seceding African sect and the parent European church.[114] Some observers of these essentially religious schisms have tended to impute all Ethiopian leaders with political motives, while others have suggested that economic self-aggrandizement alone inspired the leaders of these secessions. One reason for this lopsided view of Ethiopianism is that most of the observers in question have been missionaries who, being protagonists themselves, seem to have been unable to give balanced accounts of Ethiopians who challenged their competence. The other reason lies in the fact that far too few Ethiopians have presented their own case in person or in writing, with the result that many scholars have had to rely on secondary sources for the study of these movements The evidence from a few Ethiopians who have provided reasons for seceding from parent churches suggests that religious motives far outweighed political considerations. For example, the Rev. Mangena Mokone's declaration of secession in 1892 shows that what compelled him to break away from the Methodist Church was the failure of white ministers to foster Christian brotherhood.[115] Significantly the South African Native Affairs Commission, which collected evidence on the "Separatist Movement" from eighty-three persons including some blacks between 1903 and 1905, was persuaded to resolve that Ethiopianism was "the outcome of a desire of part of the natives for ecclesiastical self-support and self-control," which in the commission's view was not in itself a political act.[116] In 1905 a French missionary in Basutoland justified Ethiopianism on the grounds that it was the only effective way to make Christianity indigenous to Africa.[117] In Bechuanaland proper, Mothowagae repeatedly asserted the right of his sect to pray according to their conscience and, apart from his quarrels with Ngwaketse rulers, there is no evidence to suggest that he amassed wealth for himself. Even the traveling prophets who accepted some gifts seem to have accepted them more in deference to Tswana custom than from any greed for wealth. The important point to note is that Ethiopians dramatized the plight of the Tswana before a missionary society that did not pay nearly enough attention to the material well-being of its pastorate. Thus, whatever political overtones Tswana Ethiopians might have engendered, the Boikgololo movement was essentially a religious organization that challenged Christianity to be compatible with the religious as well as the economic life of the Tswana.[118]

NOTES FOR CHAPTER 6

1. David Livingstone, *Livingstone's Missionary Correspondence, 1841–1856*, ed. I. Schapera (London: 1961), pp. 49, 102.

2. J. Tom Brown, *The Apostle of the Marshes: The Story of Shomolekae* (London: 1925); Willoughby Papers, "Shomolekae," Folder 807, Selly Oak Colleges Library.

3. Thompson to Hepburn, 17 June 1886, Box 19 ,L.M.S.). Mogodi was again posted to Ngamiland in 1886. See also Thompson to Lloyd, 22 December 1887, Box 21 (L.M.S.), in which he advised Lloyd to be patient (*festina lente*) when dealing with Tswana evangelists. Methodist missionaries seem to have shared the same view on African evangelists; see, for example, H. Wainman to Hartley, December 1891, M.M.S., Box Transvaal, 1891–96, in which he reported that teacher-evangelists required the constant supervision of European missionaries.

4. Alfred Wookey to Thompson, 14 October 1902 (L.M.S.), who said the salaries varied from £6 to £12 a year.

5. Minutes of the B.D.C. meeting held at Kuruman, in Ashton to Whitehouse, 3 June 1881, Box 41, Jacket C, Folder 5 (L.M.S.). Khukwe Mogodi returned to Ngamiland in 1883.

6. See, for example, Chief Ntare et al., in chapters 3 and 5.

7. See, for example, Sechele's response to Mebalwe's pastoral leadership in chapter 1.

8. See, for example, an editorial in *Koranta ea Becoana*, 2 November 1904, cutting enclosed in Jennings to Thompson, 31 July 1909, Box 71 (L.M.S.), in which Lovedale and Morija were reported to be like "what Oxford and Cambridge had been to the Englishman"; that they were "two pioneer civilizing agencies" without which Africans in southern Africa would be the poorer.

9. For an assessment of the effectiveness of Tswana schools see chapter 5. For the origin and meaning of Boikgololo, see Williams, Report of the Kanye Mission, 31 December 1908, Box 4 (L.M.S.), where he said of the secessionists, also called *Ethiopians:* "The people who belong to this say, 'No we are not Ethiopians but Boikgololo' . . . it means 'the free,' i.e., free from the control of the white missionary." See also John Brown, *Secwana Dictionary* (London: 1895), p. 102, where *golola* is rendered as "to set free, or deliver." I am grateful to Miss Leloba Molema (of Royal Holloway College) for confirming the meaning of Boikgololo. See also, B. N. A., the Rev. James Robb, Port Elizabeth, to Milner, 18 September 1902, no. 2384, S.0178/1, who said separatists were called *Ethiopians*.

10. Josephus R. Coan, "The Expansion of Missions of the African Methodist Episcopal Church in South Africa, 1896–1908" (Ph.D. dissertation, 1961, Hartford Seminary Foundation) (University Microfilm, Ann Arbor, Michigan), Appendix 111, p. 443; R. R. Wright, et al., *The Encyclopedia of the African Methodist Episcopal Church* (Philadelphia: 1947), p. 318.

11. Wright, p. 318; B.N.A., no. 2384, S. 178/1, Athlone, High Commissioner, to Resident Commissioner, 15 August 1924; L. L. Berry, A

Century of Missions of the A.M.E. Church, 1840–1940 (New York: 1940), p. 74; Coan, p. 425. In the southern African context (*see* J. D. Taylor, ed., *Christianity and the Natives of South Africa* [Lovedale, South Africa, 1925], pp. 75, 86, "Ethiopian" and "Separatist" are used interchangeably to describe black secessions from Christian churches led by whites.

12. Berry, p. 75.

13. Ibid., pp. 76–78; Wright, pp. 318–19; E. Roux, *Time Longer than Rope* (London: 1948; reprinted Madison, Wisconsin: 1966), pp. 81–83.

14. M.M.S., Transvaal Box, 1886–96, George Weavind to Marshall Hartley, 29 August 1896, *see also*, Weavind to Hartley, 25 September 1896 (same source).

15. The Ethiopian Church was in fact recognized on 12 August 1896 (*see* sources in footnote 10).

16. Good to Thompson, 11 November 1898, Box 55, Jacket D, Folder 2 (L.M.S.). For the schism at Taung, see Neil Q. Parsons, "Independency and Ethiopianism among the Tswana in the Late 19th and Early 20th Centuries," (Seminar paper, The Societies of Southern Africa in the 19th and 20th Centuries, Institute of Commonwealth Studies, University of London, 29 January 1970). *See also* Bengt G. M. Sundkler, *Bantu Prophets in South Africa* (London: 1948), pp. 38–39.

17. For the growth of a viable separatist movement, *see* C. C. Saunders, "Tile and the Thembu Church," *Journal of African History* 11, no. 4 (1970): 553–70.

18. Good to Thompson, 11 November 1898, Box 55, Jacket D, Folder 2 (L.M.S.).

19. Minutes of the B.D.C., 14 March 1899, Box 56, Jacket B, Folder 1 (L.M.S.).

20. Willoughby Papers, "Worshipping the Daft," Folder 770, Selly Oak Colleges. This was not unprecedented, for in 1864 (*see* same source), a "prophetess" called *Mmaborola* is said to have arisen among the Ngwato; she claimed to possess supernatural powers, but Willoughby does not say what she was supposedly capable of doing.

21. Coan, *Expansion of A.M.E. Missions*, pp. 426–27.

22. Howard Williams to Thompson, Palapye Report, 1898, Box 3 (L.M.S.). For Kgama's observance of Christian teaching, *see* chapter 3, footnote 58.

23. B.N.A., no. 2384, S. 178/1, "Ethiopianism at Kama's" Gordon Sprigg to Milner, 9 December 1902, enclosed in Milner to Chamberlain, 12 of 29 December 1902.

24. Ibid.; *see also* Harry Dean (with S. North), *Umbala* (London: 1929), pp. 243–47, where they noted that the first A.M.E. Church resident Bishop to south Africa, the Rev. J. Coppin, urged eighteen African chiefs who had come to see the Prince of Wales in Cape Town in 1901 to befriend one another and also taught them the Ethiopian song: "Ethiopia, stretch forth thy Hands. . . ."

25. *See*, *South African Native Affairs Commission, 1903–5, Minutes of Evidence Taken in the Cape Colony*, Vol. 4 (Cape Town: 1904), p. 474, hereafter cited as S.A.N.A.C.

Boikgololo

26. R. Wardlaw Thompson to Willoughby, 20 September 1902 (L.M.S.). But the S.A.N.A.C. report advised against "any measure of legislative repression" against the Ethiopian movement. See *Report of the South African Native Affairs Commission*, 55, Cd. 2399 (Cape Town: 1905): 64.

27. *See*, for example, Tswana chiefs' reliance on missionaries as interpreters and advisors in chapter 4 supra.

28. *See* chapter 5.

29. *See*, for example, M.M.S., Rev. H. Waiman to Marshall Hartley, December 1891; Thompson to J. D. Hepburn at Shoshong, 17 June 1886, Box 19 (L.M.S.).

30. B.N.A., no. 715, R. C. 10/11, Mothowagae, B. C. Koko, Tsime, et al., Petition of King Edward Bangwaketse Mission Church to Resident Commissioner, 19 October 1903, Chief Bathoen to Acting Assistant Commissioner, 27 June 1902.

31. Lloyd to Thompson, 14 June 1893, Box 50, Jacket A, Folder 2, 21 December 1893, Box 50, Jacket D, Folder 2 (L.M.S.). *See also* chapter 5.

32. B.N.A., Petition of King Edward Bangwaketse Mission Church.

33. B.N.A., Bathoen to Acting Assistant Commissioner, 27 June 1902.

34. Petition of King Edward Bangwaketse Mission Church.

35. Lloyd to Thompson, 9 May 1902 (L.M.S.).

36. Willoughby to Thompson, 17 December 1902 (L.M.S.), who described Mothowagae as "an ignorant fellow"; B.N.A., 410, R. C. 7/8, Bathoen to Acting Assistant Commissioner, 13 June 1902, who said Mothowagae failed in every subject.

37. B.N.A., no. 715, R. C. 10/11, "Mothowagae's Declaration," in Petition.

38. B.N.A., 410, R. C. 7/8, Bathoen to Assistant Acting Commissioner, 12 June 1902.

39. B.N.A., 410, R. C. 7/8 Bathoen to Ellenberger, 27 June 1902.

40. B.N.A., 410, R. C. 7/8, Jules Ellenberger to Lloyd, 17 June 1902.

41. B.N.A., 410, R. C. 7/8, Lloyd to Assistant Acting Commissioner, 27 June 1902.

42. B.N.A., 410, R. C. 7/8, James Good, Kenilworth, Cape, to Ellenberger, 30 June 1902.

43. Ibid.

44. B.N.A., 410, R. C. 7/8, Ralph Williams to B.D.C., 18 August 1902.

45. Kanye church members to Thompson, 16 December 1902 (L.M.S.). However, there were less than 400 church members at Kanye, *see* John Brown and Willoughby in "Report of a Visit to Kanye," 14 February 1903, Box 3 (L.M.S.).

46. Kanye church members to L.M.S. directors, 16 December 1902 (L.M.S.). *Khadi* was an intoxicating drink, *see* chapter 7.

47. B.N.A., 410, R. C. 7/8, Lloyd to Assistant Acting Commissioner, 27 June 1902.

48. Kanye Annual Report, in Lloyd to Thompson, 28 January 1903, Box 3 (L.M.S.).

49. Brown and Willoughby, "Report of a Visit to Kanye," 14 February 1903, Box 3 (L.M.S.).
50. B.N.A., 410, R. C. 7/8, Petition, 19 October 1903.
51. Willoughby to Thompson, 5 March 1903 (L.M.S.), in which he conceded that they had felt insulted by Mothowagae and his followers.
52. Brown and Willoughby, "Report of a Visit to Kanye," 14 February 1903, Box 3 (L.M.S.).
53. Bathoen to Thompson, 19 February 1903 (L.M.S.).
54. Thompson to Bathoen, 28 March 1903 (L.M.S.). Cf. Thompson's view on church and state, chapter 5, fn 52.
55. Bathoen to Thompson, 21 May 1903 (L.M.S.).
56. Bathoen to Thompson, 27 August 1903 (L.M.S.).
57. Bathoen to Thompson, 23 October 1903 (L.M.S.); for Bathoen's earlier stand *see* fn 53.
58. B.N.A., no. 715, R. C. 10/11, Ralph Williams to Assistant Commissioner Ellenberger, 2 November 1903, Bathoen to Ramaeba, undated.
59. B.N.A., 715, R. C. 10/11, Williams to B.D.C., 18 August 1903.
60. B.N.A., 715, R. C. 10/11, Williams to Ellenberger, 2 November 1903.
61. Ibid.
62. B.N.A., 715, R. C. 10/11, Petition of 19 October 1903; I. Schapera, *A Short History of the Bakgatla-baga Kgafela* (Communications from the School of African Studies, University of Cape Town, 1942), p. 20.
63. B.N.A., no. 715, R. C. 10/11, Minutes of Inquiry by Ellenberger at Police Quarters at Kanye, 10 November 1903, in which Bathoen observed that a chief could summarily banish a subversive person without the *pitso*'s approval.
64. Ibid. See also I. Schapera, "Tswana Legal Maxims," *Africa* 36, no. 2 (April 1966): 122.
65. B.N.A., 715, R. C. 10/11, statements taken at Gaborone on 30 October 1903.
66. Ibid.
67. B.N.A., 715, R. C. 10/11, Bathoen to Ellenberger, 4 November 1903.
68. B.N.A., 715, R. C. 10/11, Minutes of Inquiry at Kanye, 11 November 1903.
69. *See*, for example, B.N.A., 715, R. C. 10/11, Messrs. Minchin and Kelly, Mafeking, to Resident Magistrate, Kanye, 10 June 1927, through whom Mothowagae sought an injunction against Chieftainess Ntebogan for interfering with his faith.
70. B. N. A., 715, R. C. 10/11, Ralph Williams to Ellenberger, 20 November 1903. According to Bathoen (*see* B.N.A., 715, R. C. 10/11, Bathoen to Assistant Commissioner, 14 November 1903), murder was an exception to this kind of pardon.
71. B.N.A., 715, R. C. 10/11, Bathoen to Ramoeba, undated, in which the chief alleged Mothowagae to have said: "I, Mothowagae stopped the rain last year; recently I have bewitched your work."
72. "Khane ea Bangwato," in *Koranta ea Becoana*, 25 November 1903.

Boikgololo

73. "Bangwaketse," in *Koranta ea Becoana*, 2 December 1903.
74. The Rev. Gould to Tiddie, 16 September 1904 (L.M.S.).
75. Ibid.
76. Gould to Thompson, 19 June 1903 (L.M.S.).
77. Gould to Tiddie, 16 September 1904. In 1892 it was reported that two of Kgama's brothers had sent their sons to Lovedale; *see* J. S. Moffat to Thompson, 3 May 1892, Box 49, Jacket C, Folder 1 (L.M.S.).
78. C. D. Helm, in Minutes of the M.D.C. held at Bulawayo, Rhodesia, 11 November 1904 (L.M.S.).
79. Gould to Thompson, 19 June 1903 (L.M.S.).
80. Ibid.
81. B.N.A., no. J. 1288, S. 41/2, Gould to Panzera, Confidential, 13 September 1904.
82. Gould to Thompson, 23 November 1904 (L.M.S.).
83. Ibid. *See also* G. C. H. Reed to Thompson, 17 September 1903 (L.M.S.).
84. Gould to Thompson, 16 June 1904 (L.M.S.).
85. Gould to Tiddie, 16 September 1904 (L.M.S.).
86. Minutes of M.D.C., 11 November 1904.
87. William M. Carleton to Thompson, 15 July 1908 (L.M.S.).
88. Carleton to Thompson, 15 July 1908 (L.M.S.).
89. Coan, "The Expansion of A.M.E. Church in South Africa," p. 474.
90. Lloyd to Thompson, 23 January 1904 (L.M.S.).
91. Lloyd to Thompson, 24 June 1904 (L.M.S.).
92. Lloyd to Thompson, 30 March 1905 (L.M.S.).
93. Chief Bathoen to Thompson, 8 February 1906 (L.M.S.).
94. Report of a Deputation to Kanye, July 1906 (L.M.S.).
95. S.A.N.A.C., Vol. 4, p. 252.
96. Williams to Thompson, 25 March 1908 (L.M.S.).
97. Williams, in Kanye Annual Report, 31 December 1908, Box 4 (L.M.S.).
98. Ibid.
99. Ibid.
100. R. H. Lewis, in Molepolole Annual Report, 1908, Box 4 (L.M.S.).
101. *See*, for example, "Report of the Chief Native Commissioner, Southern Rhodesia, Matebeleland, for the year ending 31 March 1906," p. 1, 31 March 1907, pp. 4, 16, Royal Commonwealth Society, London. For Rev. Maghato's break with the Dutch Reformed Church, *see* S.A.N.A.C., 4: 199–204; T. Ranger, "The Early History of Independency in Southern Rhodesia, "*Religion in Africa* (Centre of African Studies, University of Edinburgh: 1964), pp. 58–59.
102. Shoshong Annual Report, 1908, Box 4 (L.M.S.). For church schism in northern Rhodesia, *see* T. Ranger, "The 'Ethiopian' Episode in Barotseland, 1900–1905," *The Rhodes-Livingstone Journal* 37 (June 1965): 26–41.
103. *See*, for example, Williams, in Kanye Annual Report, 1909, Box 4 (L.M.S.).
104. I. Schapera, ed., *The Political Annals of a Tswana Tribe: Minutes*

of *Ngwaketse Public Assemblies, 1910–1917* (Communications from the School of African Studies, University of Cape Town, 1947), pp. 20–21.

105. Ibid.

106. Ibid., p. 25, being part of minutes of *lechulo* held on 31 August 1910. By two religions he meant Ethiopianism and the L.M.S. church.

107. Ibid.; B.N.A., no. 968/10, Seapapitso to Resident Commissioner, 20 July 1910.

108. B.N.A., no. 968/10, Seapapitso to Resident Commissioner, 20 July 1910. Interview between Resident Commissioner and Mothowagae, 9 August 1910.

109. B.N.A., ibid., E. Joyce to Resident Commissioner, 11 August 1910.

110. B.N.A., ibid., Clark Nettelton to Hodson, 28 June 1911, Chief Seapapitso B. Gaseitsiwe to Resident Commissioner, 23 June 1911.

111. Schapera, *Minutes of Ngwaketse Public Assembly*, pp. 26–27.

112. A. J. Wookey, "Missionary Work in Bechuanaland," *Diamond Field Advertiser*, 11 February 1907. See also W. C. Willoughby, "Notes on the Relation of the Black and White Races in the Civilization of the World," in British Museum, *Tracts on Natural History* (Cape Town: 1913), p. 16, in which he asserts that "the destiny of all the varieties of humanity is that of complementary helpfulness" and he implies that whites ought to emulate the patience of blacks.

113. Minutes of the U.D.C. Meetings at Inyati, 18 April to 30 April 1910 (L.M.S.).

114. See, for example, W. C. Willoughby, *The Soul of the Bantu: A Sympathetic Study of the Magico-Religious Practices and Beliefs of the Bantu Tribes of Africa* (New York: 1928), p. 131, passim, W. C. Willoughby, "African Thought and Custom in Relation to Christianity," MS (L.M.S.). P. H. J. Lerigo, "Prophet Movement in the Congo," *International Review of Missions* (April 1922), pp. 270–77; C. T. Loram, "The Separatist Church Movement," *International Review of Missions* (July 1926), pp. 476–82; H. R. Fox-Bourne, et al.' eds., *The South African Natives: Their Progress and Present Condition* (London: 1908), p. 20: "Apparently none of these secessions have been due to doctrinal differences."

115. "Founders Declaration of Independence," Appendix 1, in Coan, "The Expansion of the A.M.E. Church," p. 440.

116. S.A.N.A.C. Report, p. 64. See also L. N. Mzimba, "The African Church," in *Christianity and the Natives of South Africa*, ed. J. D. Taylor (Lovedale, South Africa: 1928), pp. 86–95.

117. E. Jacottet, *The Native Churches and Their Organization* (Morija, Basutoland: 1905), pp. 4–6, 8.

118. Here the observation of Rev. L. N. Mzimba, who preferred to substitute African for Ethiopian, is instructive (ibid., p. 91): "The African church is not a political organization. Neither was it planned to be a national church. She has however succeeded in awakening the Bantu to the full understanding of the text 'God helps those that help themselves.'"

7
More Aspects of Tswana Transformations

I

IN THIS CHAPTER AN ATTEMPT IS MADE TO EXAMINE THE IMPACT of Europeans on some of the institutions of the Tswana. An important feature of the interaction was that European enthusiasm to bring about cultural changes was matched by Tswana reluctance to alter their mode of living, the latter phenomenon manifesting itself in various guises way into the twentieth century.

Yet missionaries and laymen alike remained undaunted and persistently introduced measures to try to transform Tswana chiefdoms into polities that would resemble as closely as possible metropolitan notions of an ideal Christian community. Among the institutions that L.M.S. agents tried to change or abolish were the initiation ceremonies *(bog-*

wera and *bojale*),[1] and the drinking habits of Tswana. In spite of concerted efforts to stamp out these practices, the society achieved limited results.

Some chiefdoms—notably the Ngwato under Kgama III—responded to missionary endeavors a little more readily than others, and by 1890 some elements of their ritual and social life had been changed.[2] Part of the reason for this marginal success was that, after the establishment of the Protectorate in 1885, the British administration supported the L.M.S., especially in suppressing initiation ceremonies. In doing so it appears that the British officials were impelled more by medical considerations than by religious motives. For example, the flogging administered in the course of initiation ceremonies, especially the wounds sustained during the *bogwera* rites, could be fatal. The Rev. Wookey's report of 1888 gives an indication of the physical hardships experienced by novices (*bagwera*) and of the pressure missionaries were exerting upon the new administration:

> A short time ago the *bogwera* circumcision rites were held for the boys of this place. According to the usual custom, as many boys as possible were brought together. . . . Two or three of the boys died almost as soon as they entered. Their arms and legs were cut off and the flesh made into medicine and mixed with the food of the rest of the boys and given to them to eat. Shortly after, an epidemic broke out amongst them and over fifty of them died. The cruelties . . . are very great and under the British Protectorate should be brought to an end.[3]

The British administration had, in fact, been informed about the health hazards of circumcision in July 1886, when J. S. Moffat, resident magistrate in British Bechuanaland, wrote:

> It is a well-known fact that a certain percentage of the boys who go through this [circumcision] ceremony succumbs, either as a consequence of severe floggings to which they are subjected or of the inflamation following

on the operation from its being performed in a clumsy manner, or from the undue exposure to the weather in a state of nakedness, [adding] the deaths are carefully hushed up, though there is an allusion to them in the songs connected with the ceremonies.[4]

After he had received this report, Shippard instructed Moffat to prevent the forcible abduction of boys and girls for initiation, but as Moffat's account suggests, the secrecy that surrounded *bogwera* and *bojale* precluded close observation from outsiders.[5]

The reports of missionaries on the ceremonial and ritual life of the Tswana show that they too often underestimated the depth of these practises. Hence, in 1890 the Rev. Williams reported that observance of initiation ceremonies at Molepolole was declining, and yet hardly five years later he suspended several church members who defied his injunctions and participated in them.[6] The Kwena proved to be the most persistent observers of traditional ceremonies partly because of Sechele's tacit support for these institutions, but largely because Kgosidintsi, a most influential councillor and a brother of Sechele's, encouraged them to do so.[7]

Witchcraft (*boloi*), too, appears to have flourished side by side with Tswana ceremonial rites, and until the turn of the twentieth century the British administration was unable to intervene largely because the cases escaped their attention. When in 1888 two Kwena women were charged with witchcraft in Sechele's *kgotla* and condemned to death, the sentences were commuted when the Rev. Williams pleaded to Sechele for clenmency.[8] The Ngwato, too, appear to have practiced witchcraft in spite of their chief's ascetic character. This is suggested in Hepburn's report of 1885 when he observed that the non-Christian inhabitants of Shoshong had revived "immoral customs and baldly in the face of open day." [9] Among the Ngwaketse, Bathoen's efforts to abolish initiation ceremonies were not very successful, as is indicated in his address to the Native Advisory Council in 1907, when he admitted that *bogwera* and *bojale* were some of the obstacles to progress. Nor was the Protectorate administration doing much to stop them. Hence, the Native Advisory Council, which seems to have been dominated by Christian delegates, could complain that their children were "morally destroyed by these ceremonies and that the Government [was] more careful for the preservation of game in their reserves, than for the welfare of their children." [10]

If Christian members of Tswana society were concerned about the prevalence of heathen practices, the non-Christians were equally determined to preserve their traditional ceremonials and institutions. Among the Tawana and the Ngwato members of the ruling families, the observance of traditional ceremonies was regarded as a punishable offence.[11]

In spite of the persistence of some customs, Tswana interaction with missionaries produced some changes. By 1898 the Ngwato observance of *molomo* (i.e., tasting the first fruits of the harvest) had been adapted to conform to Christian notions of Thanksgiving. In this respect the combined efforts of the missionary and the chief seem to have minimized resistance to change.[12] An 1896 report gives an idea of Ngwato adoption of Christian elements in the *molomo*:

> Every year on the appointed day, just before sunrise the whole of the natives assemble at the [*kgotla*], not only the Christians, but heathens as well, and it is curious to note that this is the one ceremony in which the two opposite creeds assemble for the same purpose. As the sun slowly appears . . . the chief or his representative, rises, uncovers his head, and announces, "We come to bite the year." [13]

In Ngwaketseland Bathoen banned initiation ceremonies in 1896, while in Kwenaland Sebele proscribed them late in

1904, four years after he had been, in fact, actively promoting them. Legislation against initiation ceremonies by both chiefs was reported to have been influenced by the chiefs' visit to Britain in 1895. Nevertheless, traditional ceremonies—especially *bogwera* and *bojale*—persisted even when Tswana chiefs had legislated against them.[14] In 1906 the B.D.C., some of whose members had hitherto underestimated the depth of Tswana customs, conceded that large numbers of Christians along with the non-Christian members of Tswana society observed *bogwera* and *bojale*.[15] In 1907 The Rev. Wookey reinforced the B.D.C. in an article to a Kimberley newspaper in which he asserted that initiation and rainmaking ceremonies were an essential part of Tswana life:

> *Bogwera* and *bojale* still remain, for they seem to contain the rites and ceremonies connected with them all that really pertains to Secwana religion, and to tribal or national life. . . .[16]

II

Marriage was another institution that missionaries and government officials sought to transform, particularly those aspects pertaining to *bogadi* (bride wealth or bride price), *beelelwa* (betrothal), *lehuha* (polygamy), and *tlhalano* (divorce). Although payment of *bogadi* was the most contentious issue, observers of Tswana institutions were not agreed on its significance. Some thought *bogadi* was a form of purchase;[17] others maintained that it was merely a token to strengthen bonds of union between the families of the bride and the bridegroom,[18] a view that has gained current support.[19]

Because of the missionaries' strong objections to the notion of bride purchase (however mistaken such a notion might have been), one of the earliest church laws (*melao yaphuthego*) passed by the B.D.C. was directed against payment of *bogadi*. In 1875 the B.D.C. conceded that payment of *bogadi* was widespread but nevertheless condemned it as "being evil," and resolved to discourage its payment by refusing to solemnize any marriage in which *bogadi* had been paid.[20] Betrothal of girls was condemned by missionaries from the very beginning of their Tswana mission, the majority of missionaries actually equating it with domestic slavery.[21]

Polygamy was another controversial marriage practice. So widespread was the custom that the Tlhaping chief, Molehabangwe, was surprised that none of the members in Lichtenstein's embassy of 1805 was a polygamist.[22] Traditionally polygamy was associated with wealth because only a rich man could afford to marry more than one wife; it thus understandably enhanced one's prestige. But in 1801 Molehabangwe's wife, Makaiitschoah, suggested that the population ratio between men and women in Tlhapingland induced polygamy, for she pointed out that monogamy "would not suit the [Tswana], because there were so great a number of women, and male population suffered such diminution from the wars." [23] Owing to a paucity of statistical data for the Tswana region, it is not possible to test Makaiitschoah's observation. However, in 1849 John Freeman, who recorded figures of a census taken by David Livingstone at Kolobeng, showed that there were over 20% more females in that town than males.[24]

One of the greatest handicaps to the substitution of Christian for traditional marriage customs was that the chiefs and church deacons themselves invariably abrogated marriage laws, which must have encouraged commoners and church members alike to follow suit.[25] In this connection the L.M.S. had enormous problems to contend with in all the major chiefdoms. Among the Tshidi-Rolong the most formidable opponent to their mission was Chief Montshiwa, who was himself a polygamist and a staunch supporter of the payment of *bogadi*. In 1893 he expelled the L.M.S. evangelist at Disaneng, Motlanke, and contributed an article to an L.M.S. monthly (*Mahoko oa Becwana*) in which he supported payment of *bogadi*.[26] A 1904 report concerning the Khurutshe enclave in the Tati Concessions showed that the L.M.S. evangelist there, Tumedi, and Chief Rauwe Sekoko were both polygamists, although the former had assisted the Rev. Gould in founding the mission station there hardly six years previously.[27]

Nor was the Ngwato church a model of the "City of God" as travelers' accounts suggest. In this regard Theodore Bent's praise of Kgama typified the prevailing attitudes of whites toward Kgama:

> Somehow one's spirit of scepticism is on the *qui vive* on such occasions, especially when a Negro is in question; and I candidly admit that I advanced towards Palapye fully prepared to find the chief of the Bamangwato a rascal and a hypocrite, and that I left his capital, after a week's stay there, one of his most fervent admirers.[28]

However, the state of the Ngwato church was more complex than Bent's simplistic view suggests. In 1898 Willoughby reported a return to traditional custom that must have been extant when Bent prepared his glowing report on that station. One of the cases Willoughby reported concerned an elderly church deacon. Although the deacon in question had strenuously opposed the abduction of a certain girl from Palapye, for religious reasons, he also had personal reasons for doing so, as Willoughby's report suggests:

> It has transpired that the Deacon in question has been carrying on immoral intercourse with the girl's mother, who is also a member of the Church. They had kept their secret well, but at last it could no longer be hid. Then the woman told all about it. We have . . . expelled them from the church; but it has done us much harm. They

had both been members of the Church for 20 or 30 years; and were counted as our most reliable people. . . . He confessed it at last, so there was no doubt about it.[29]

Part of the reason for what the missionaries called *backsliding* among the Ngwato might have been influenced by Kgama's marital life. Mma-Bessie, his first wife, died in 1889. Kgama married Bathoen's sister the following year but she died shortly after her marriage.[30] In 1895 Kgama married Sefakwana, a commoner and a non-Christian and, for that reason, "the match was not very popular in the tribe." [31] The marriage was dissolved in 1899 and later that year Kgama married Semane, who survived him when he died in 1923.

Whatever justification Kgama might have had for divorcing Sefakwana, it is quite clear that his disaffected brothers and some Christians used the Chief's divorce to justify their political demands and to divorce their own wives. And of more significance than the fodder it provided Kgama's opponents at Palapye, Kgama's divorce revealed the lack of consistency in the society's marriage laws. In 1899, the Rev. Howard Williams wrote sympathetically about Kgama's divorce:

> If you have any recollections of the "lady" you will probably have concluded that she was not fitted to be the wife of a man like Khama.[32]

The L.M.S. Foreign Secretary seemed equally sympathetic:

> The news of Khama's marriage was a surprise, though not so great a surprise as if he had been a European. I am glad he has got so suitable a wife this time. Please give him my warm greetings.[33]

If Kgama considered himself compelled by circumstances beyond his control to divorce his wife in 1899, Chief Sebele irritated missionaries and government officials alike when he decided to take a second wife. Although he had tried unsuccessfully to assert his chiefdom's political autonomy in the 1890s, Sebele's quarrel with Protectorate officials in the marriage issue seemed to have the sanction of Tswana custom. Hence, he maintained that, so long as he conformed to Tswana marriage customs, his disgruntled first wife could not sustain her grounds for complaining against him. What turned out to be Sebele's time of troubles started in 1900 when he disregarded a Tswana custom that required him to sleep with his wife during the *molomo* (tasting the first fruits of the harvest) ceremony. Sebele's breach of this custom was indefensible, as was his cohabitation with the wife of one Mhiko.[34] However, when the Kwena capital was moved to Borakalalo in 1901, Sebele remained at the old capital, Molepolole, with the woman, Bautlwe (also called Matadi), whom he wanted to marry. The L.M.S. agent opposed it because it was apparently being used by the Kwena as justification for polygamy. In 1902 the Rev. Haydon Lewis observed:

> Polygamy still holds the people in its grip and has the chief as its prime advocate. The actions of Sebele [have] shaken the Christian community profoundly, and have disturbed many a man's faith who regarded the chief's marriage as sealed by the irrevocable law of Christ, ... On the contrary I believe it to be but an excuse, eagerly seized by some members of the Christian community as a pretext for similar conduct.[35]

The Protectorate administration started playing a more definite part in Sebele's marital affairs in 1900 when Assistant Commissioner Surmon convened a *pitso* at Molepolole to settle what was supposed to be Sebele's estrangement from his first wife, Macholohelo.[36] Once Surmon had started investigating the issue, the delicate balance so common to members of Tswana ruling families in the nineteenth century was upset, and the Kwena polarized into two factions:

one faction supporting Macholohelo (this included her sons, Kealeboga and Kebohula, and Sebele's cousin, Baruti Kgosidintsi); the other faction supporting Sebele. At the end of the *pitso* proceedings, Surmon ordered the chief to take back Macholohelo, but this Sebele did not do. On 18 April 1901 Macholohelo wrote to Surmon complaining that Sebele had not taken her back but instead was living with Bautlwe at Molepolole; she urged Surmon to use his influence to stop Sebele's impending marriage to Bautlwe.[37]

When Surmon subsequently contacted Sebele on the issue, the Chief gave a candid account of his determination to marry Bautlwe and commented freely on what appears to have been a series of sex scandals among the Kwena ruling elite.[38] Sebele stated, *inter alia*, that he had lived with Bautlwe for twenty-one years and had had six children by her. In his view opposition to his impending marriage did not come from the Kwena as such, but was engineered by people who were jealously in love with Bautlwe, that one of these people, Baruti Kgosidintsi, had in fact had sexual relations with Bautlwe on several occasions. Sebele observed that all Tswana men (heathen and Christian alike) maintained several mistresses: "All Christians [have] sweet hearts, and you only speak about me because I do all things in plain. If you speak about Bechuana's marriage, you will be tired."[39] Sebele complained that Surmon was trying to judge him according to English law, which the chief said was not binding on him; as far as he was aware, Tswana customary law vindicated him, as had been demonstrated by the Kwena's approval of his impending marriage to Bautlwe. Sebele further submitted that he was not in any way being cruel to Macholohelo, for he was not divorcing her; above all, some of his sons approved of the marriage.[40] Sebele married Bautlwe early in 1901.

In May 1901 the Rev. Wookey wrote to Surmon asserting that Sebele's marriage to Bautlwe in defiance of the Assistant Commissioner's disapproval warranted the Chief's instant dismissal from office.⁴¹ On 11 May that year Surmon informed Sebele of his disappointment at the Chief's marriage to Bautlwe in accordance with Tswana custom; he warned Sebele that he would hold him responsible for any political disturbance that might break out in Kwenaland.⁴² Macholohelo continued to campaign for a reconciliation with Sebele. In July she wrote to Assistant Commissioner Jules Ellenberger complaining that her estranged husband was still irreconcilable.⁴³ Macholohelo's letter appeared to have had serious political consequences, for it led to a direct statement by the Administration on measures they would take to punish Sebele. Ellenberger recommended that Sebele be deposed from the chieftainship,⁴⁴ and further showed what little regard he had toward Sebele when the Duke and Duchess of Cornwall and York visited south Africa in 1901. He humiliated the chief by inviting his son, Kealeboga, and Baruti Kgosidintsi to go to Cape Town to meet the Royal visitors, a diplomatic move that was clearly at variance with Tswana protocol. But official snubs did not weaken Sebele's love for Bautlwe.

In August 1901 Sebele restated his determination to live with Bautlwe as his second wife and rejected Ellenberger's allegation that Bautlwe interfered with his official duties:

> But with regard to the woman, I really do not see how she could prevent a chief from ruling his people justly or interfere with him in the ruling of his people, because a woman remains in the yard whilst her husband is at the Kgotla, and that is why I say I shall not abandon Matadi.⁴⁵

Although the arguments advanced in the missionary and government correspondence on the Sebele-Bautlwe issue clearly uphold Sebele's right to marry according to Tswana custom, the political overtones of the case were less apparent but were quickly detected by the newly appointed Resident Commissioner, Ralph Williams, who complained that the issue had got out of all proportion:

The correspondence which I find with regard to Matadi appears to me to be merely what is known as tittle-tattle, and I don't think the consideration of it by the Assistant Commissioner has had a good effect on the tribe.[46]

Missionary reports show that, on various occasions toward the end of the nineteenth century and early in the twentieth century, L.M.S. agents required that their church members who married according to Tswana custom before they joined the church be married according to Christian rites in L.M.S. churches. Thus, in 1904 the Rev. Jennings reported that he had solemnized sixty such marriages at Serowe and forty in Ngamiland.[47] The British administration also passed legislation governing Tswana marriages, although it was often framed in legal language that missionaries and officials themselves—let alone the Tswana—found difficult to understand.[48]

III

If L.M.S. missionaries and British officials had persuasive moral and medical grounds for wanting to abolish payment of *bogadi* and the traditional initiation ceremonies among the Tswana, the grounds for wanting to abolish the consumption of European liquor and the Tswana brew (*khadi*) were as slender as they were dubious. And yet correspondence on prohibition in both the L.M.S. archives and the Public Record Office is disproportionately heavy. The reason for this anomaly is that the archprohibitionists (government officials, missionaries, and to some extent Tswana chiefs) failed to appreciate the importance of beer drinking in Tswana social life. To the Tswana and their neighbors beer drinking was one of the highest forms of enjoying their leisure and of extending hospitality to strangers and friends alike. In 1903 a missionary observed:

The idea of a mo[Tswana] is to make a big brew, and

invite his friends to a . . . beer-drink, which will begin in the morning and last till beer is consumed, perhaps in the courtyard till the afternoon. There they sit soaking around these beer pots for the greater part of the day. . . . Then in a day or two another of the clique will have his brew ready, and the process is repeated in his courtyard. Sunday is the favourite day.[49]

According to Kgalagadi tradition, beer drinking has always been a favorite pastime. In 1938 an informant said:

As far as I know, we always drank *Kgadi*. It is something known for a long time. It is very popular with us.[50]

Another fallacy that persisted at the end of the nineteenth century was that European liquor had only been recently introduced to the Tswana.[51] On the contrary, travelers' accounts suggest that brandy might have been introduced in the eighteenth century. Dr. Henry Lichtenstein's account shows that the Tlhaping and their neighbors had by 1805 acquired a pronounced fondness for European liquor and menacingly demanded to buy some brandy.[52] By 1873 brandy had become such an important item of consumption that Dr. Holub's party was mobbed at Taung by crowds

shouting eagerly towards [them]. They were nearly all provided with bottles, or pots, or cans, and cried out for brandy, "suppy, suppy, bas, verkup Brandwen" they repeated impatiently.[53]

Accounts by traders show that northern Tswana communities were also amply supplied with liquor between 1850 and 1875.[54]

While it is often difficult to determine drunkenness or addiction to alcohol, accounts left by government officials and missionaries suggest that some African communities in

Bechuanaland were drinking excessively. By 1877 the drinking habits of tribes around Kuruman seem to have reached alarming proportions and prompted the B.D.C. to send a resolution to the Colonial Office urging them to close all beer-selling canteens in southern Bechuanaland.[55] In August 1877 the Rev. Wookey reported that Griquas were selling their farms to Europeans to enable themselves to buy liquor.[56] And when the Tlhaping and their neighbors rose in insurrection against the British in 1878, some missionaries ascribed the rebellion to drunkenness.[57] By 1879 the B.D.C. were so flabbergasted by what they believed to be the demoralizing influence of liquor that they again urged Governor Frere of the Cape Colony to close all beer-selling canteens in southern Bechuanaland, pointing out that they were "unmitigated curses to all connected with them." [58]

Northern Tswana communities seem to have had liquor supplied to them throughout the second half of the nineteenth century, as is suggested in the journals of Mrs. Price.[59] The Ngwaketse likewise had access to liquor because in 1877 Alexander Bailie reported that Chief Gaseitsiwe and his subjects were being demoralized by it.[60] By the 1870s the Kwena could still get ample supplies of liquor; Sechele himself was a regular drinker, obtaining it from his close acquaintance, Henry Boyne. In 1881 Mrs. Price observed that the Kwena residents at Molepolole were "fast impoverising themselves by [buying expensive clothes] and by brandy drinking." [61] In the same year she noted that Sebele drank brandy when he could get it and *khadi* when European liquor was not available. The effects of that admixture seem to have been disastrous:

> There is constantly a disturbance arising in the town, thro [ugh] his drunkenness and passion. . . . One cannot fancy his ever becoming chief in his father's place. Certainly as he is now he cannot be.[62]

More Aspects of Tswana Transformation 243

The Ngwato seem to have had sufficient supplies of liquor in spite of their chief's puritannical stand against it. In 1876, hardly a year after he had usurped the Ngwato chieftancy, Kgama III wrote to Queen Victoria asking for a protective alliance so that he could enforce, among other measures, the prohibition of the sale and consumption of liquor.[63] His views on prohibition were not initially influenced by Christianity. The Rev. Willoughby, who worked among the Ngwato from 1893 to 1904, was informed by Kgama on several occasions that the Chief's views on prohibition were formed in his youth, independent of religious influence, following an incident in which his drunken father would have been swindled of valuable tusks of ivory, but for Kgama's decisive intervention.[64] Soon after he became Chief, he banned the sale and consumption of all alcoholic beverages and seems to have enforced the law resolutely until he suspended it in 1895.[65] By 1880 Kgama's views on prohibition had gained him international repute. In October that year the directors of the Scottish Temperance League wrote to Kgama commending him for the

> noble stand which you have made against the traffic in intoxicating liquors, introduced and carried on by white men in your town of Shoshong.[66]

Among the Kwena, liquor traffic went on unabated because Sechele did not cooperate with the Rev. Wookey in enforcing prohibition. Hence, by 1888 Wookey could report that Henry Boyne was selling liquor to whites and blacks and even organizing drinking parties for white policemen and laymen alike, with impunity:

> I went to Sechele yesterday and tried to get him to put an end to the sale of drink on the station, but I fear it is not much use going to him.[67]

In Ngamiland Chief Moremi, who obtained liquor from traders there, was a confirmed drinker and could advance physiological reasons to justify his liking for brandy and *khadi*. When he visited Shoshong in 1880 he paid lip service to Kgama's injunction against liquor, but, in fact, secretly asked one of Kgama's brothers to supply him with some beer, a breach for which the latter was punished by Kgama.[68] In 1885 Moremi was reported to have become a moderate drinker after Hepburn had reprimanded him.[69] However, a year later he renounced all pretensions to Christianity and henceforth drank liquor and *khadi* unfettered.

Kgama's lonesome fight against alcoholism received a boost in 1888 when Bathoen became an abstainer,[70] a move that the L.M.S. Directors praised highly.[71] In 1890 Bathoen prohibited the sale of liquor in Ngwaketseland.[72]

In the meantime some charitable organizations in Britain and elsewhere were building up pressure upon imperial powers of Europe to enact antiliquor laws in their colonies. In 1890 several European countries, Britain included, passed the Brussels Act, which bound signatories to prohibit the consumption of European liquor ("fire water") in their respective colonies. Hence, in 1891 the Native Races and Liquor Traffic United Committee (N.R.L.T.U.C.) could write to the Colonial Office drawing their government's attention to a report that purported Cecil Rhodes to have said the B.S.A. Company might abrogate antiliquor laws in those areas falling under the Company's sphere of influence.[73] Although Britain did not enforce the Brussels Act immediately, the campaign for prohibition was strengthened by reports that alleged Tswana communities to have become addicted to liquor.[74] Hence, in February 1892 the High Commissioner issued a proclamation that controlled the distribution and consumption of liquor in Bechuanaland.[75]

However, liquor laws and regulations were passed at a time when public opinion regarding prohibition lacked a consensus among Africans and Europeans. Opposition to prohibition seems to have centered round two main schools of thought: the first school of thought was derived from a pseudoscientific notion that alcoholic beverages, especially the local brews variously called *secwana boyalwe, khadi,* or *kaffir* beer, were a veritable source of energy and made Africans who drank them more productive workers than abstainers;[76] the second school of thought was inspired by economic considerations and was ably enunciated by an editorial in the *Bechuanaland News*. In a rebuttal to Advocate Molteno, who had supported prohibition in an address to the Church Temperance Society at Cape Town, the editor dissented:

> I do not believe in it [prohibition], I do not think it possible. Such a gospel in an avowedly wine-producing country is unwise, and productive of bitter opposition, as instanced by the formation of an anti-teetotal League at the Paarl and Wellington. Let us be moderate, temperate in the true sense of the word.[77]

Under these circumstances, traders were apt to infringe liquor laws by carrying on a clandestine traffic. The number of offenders who escaped punishment must have been considerable.[78] Nonetheless, some were apprehended and punished. In April 1895 a Vryburg magistrate fined a Mr. M. W. Theal £2.10s shillings for supplying a bottle of brandy to an African, Dirk Mentor.[79] In November that year two African transport riders—a driver and a conductor—who broached a case of whiskey at Palapye, were arrested and sentenced to two months' imprisonment each.[80] But at Molepolole Chief Sebele obtained regular supplies of liquor from traders in spite of the Protectorate laws on prohibition, as, for example, in December 1894 when he obtained ample supplies of liquor after he had persuaded an army doctor to prescribe brandy for him.[81] Later that year the veteran trader, Henry Boyne, was convicted on a charge arising from his illicit supply of liquor to Sebele; he was fined £10 and forfeited his liquor licence. Significantly Sebele successfully pleaded to the British Administration for clemency and Boyne's licence was restored.[82]

Among the Ngwato prohibition heightened tensions between Chief Kgama and his brothers. In 1895 Kgama accused one section of the Ngwato church of drunkenness, the faction included his perennial opponents, Raditladi, Mphoeng, and Tiro.[83] His puritanical views on liquor not withstanding, Kgama rescinded his rigid liquor laws in 1895 to forestall a major split in his chiefdom;[84] later that year the Chief attributed all the political bickering at Palapye to liquor.[85]

Once prohibition had been lifted, it appears that liquor consumption increased in Ngwatoland and had deleterious effects on the inhabitants. A report from Palapye in 1896 said:

> A transport rider informs us that carriers have great difficulty in getting away from Palapye; their boys [drivers] go on the spree as soon as they get there and openly defy their masters when it is time to trek on, telling them to go and inspan [harness] themselves. Last month [December 1895] as many as 100 wagons were standing in the town.[86]

This account was confirmed by Assistant Commissioner Ashburnham in May 1896.[87]

While press reports tended to lament losses sustained by European traders through alcoholism, there are some accounts that assessed the ill effects alcoholism had on the Tswana. One side effect was that the Tswana brewed beer at the expense of their food supplies. In 1896, a British official observed:

> Large stocks of grain, which in former years would have been held in reserve or bartered away for other supplies, have this year been consumed in the beer making. . . .[88]

As a consequence, Kgama again imposed (1896) prohibition partly to ward off starvation but largely because he no longer feared the effect it might have on tribal unity, for Raditladi's group attracted few followers.[89]

Meanwhile at Molepolole, Chief Sebele epitomized Tswana defiance to government and church law. But in this respect his reliance on Tswana custom was more suspect than his carefully reasoned rejection of Christian marriage laws at the turn of the twentieth century. He consistently exercised his right to drink beer and liquor until his death in 1911. Soon after his return from England in 1896, Sebele broke his pledge to abstain from alcohol and drank large quantities of brandy.[90] In June 1896 he was reported to have been intoxicated on the two bottles of brandy that he had obtained from the trader, Van Zyl;[91] later that year Sebele obtained eighteen bottles of brandy and avoided meeting the Rev. Williams for six weeks.[92] By November 1896 Sebele's drinking habits had become so bad that Chief Kgama and Chief Bathoen went to Molepolole to counsel him against excessive drinking. They warned Sebele that if he did not take heed of their advice, they might be compelled to regard him as a hostile neighbor.[93] Sebele is reported to have exercised restraint after Kgama and Bathoen's departure. In April 1898 Henry Boyne, who was perhaps the trader closest to the Kwena ruling family, died in Molepolole.[94] Still, the Chief and his subjects were able to obtain liquor from other sources.

In Ngwatoland Chief Kgama's laws on prohibition do not seem to have been observed by the majority of his subjects. In 1896 Kgama informed the N.R.L.T.U.C. that his efforts to outlaw the consumption of liquor had yielded minimal results: "And concerning liquor I am still trying, but I do not think that I can succeed." [95]

If Kgama's apprehension was premature, his observation was perceptive on at least one issue: the traders' calculated contravention of liquor laws.[96] Although the Assistant Commissioner at Palapye had assured the Resident Commissioner in 1896 that the Protectorate's liquor laws were rigidly enforced, there is reason to believe that liquor licences were issued indiscriminately and in contravention of the pledges Chamberlain gave to the chiefs in 1895. In 1897 the question of licenses was raised in the House of Commons when Sir Mark Stewart asked for assurances that railway canteens along the railway line linking Bechuanaland and Rhodesia, would not be granted licenses against Kgama's wishes. In reply Chamberlain, the Colonial Secretary, said that Kgama's views on the issue and British pledges to uphold prohibition enunciated since 1895 would be respected.

If Chamberlain's assurances were given in good faith, or just because he wouldn't be bothered or just was not interested, officers of the Protectorate administration do not seem to have had strong convictions on prohibition. Their attitude might have been influenced by white opinion in south Africa, which was generally against prohibition; hence, the laxity with which liquor laws were enforced.[97] Nor were missionaries themselves agreed as to the ethical validity of total abstinence. When Rev. John Brown complained that James Richardson had inspected L.M.S. schools in 1899 (*see* chapter 5) while he was under the influence of alcohol, the B.D.C. absolved Richardson on 25 October 1900, adding:

> Even if the words in Mr. Brown's letter regarding Mr. Richardson not being a total abstainer are strictly true, the committee is unable to regard that statement as being a reflection on Christian character.[98]

On that occasion the B.D.C. resolved that Tswana church members abstain from drinking all intoxicating beverages except the *secwana boyalwe,* which they deemed mild enough for consumption.[99]

Even when the B.D.C. had passed regulations upholding

More Aspects of Tswana Transformation 249

prohibition, there is evidence to suggest that individual missionaries either forgot about these rules or enforced them only haphazardly. Thus, in 1902 the Rev. Willoughby reported that the Ngwato were drinking excessively and suggested:

> We must either take a resolute stand against it in church membership, or it will wipe us out. I wish you were here to see and discuss things.[100]

In 1904 the Rev. Jennings reported (apparently unaware of the B.D.C. resolution of 1900) that he had banned beer drinking among Church members at Serowe.[101] In Kwenaland the Rev. Haydon Lewis reported in 1907 that he had enforced "the total prohibition of beer at Christian marriage feasts."[102] What emerges from the above account on liquor is that missionaries, British officials, and Tswana chiefs were lax in their enforcement of liquor laws and that as a result Tswana communities—both Christian and non-Christian—did not observe prohibition with any seriousness.

In 1904 some Khurutshe church members informed the Rev. Gould about their views on beer drinking:

> We drink beer very much and so long as our hearts wish to drink it, we will continue to drink it.[103]

In Ngamiland the church deacon at Tsau and several church members there confessed to Jennings in 1905 that they had always drunk brandy and *khadi*;[104] in 1908 Motlapise, a Mongwato who had been a celebrated preacher between 1871 and 1891, was reported to have lapsed as a Christian, the Rev. Lloyd adding: "Strong drink has been his downfall."[105]

By 1900, of the four principal Chiefs in northern Bechuanaland, Bathoen, Sekgoma (Chief of the Tawana), and Kgama observed total abstinence, but Mathiba, the heir apparent in Tawanaland, and Sebele were confirmed drinkers.[106] In May 1901 Sebele was reported to be failing to fulfill his duties as chief because of drunkenness, a misdemeanor for which he was severely reprimanded by the Resident Commissioner. By August that year Sebele accepted the principle of moderate drinking but maintained that *khadi* was a kind of food:

> I have also heard with regard to Khadi and I shall leave it alone, as you have advised me to do, although I merely look upon it as food, for we all drink it, but, if a person drinks much of it, such persons might get under the influence thereof. That is the fault I find in it. So far as I am concerned, I have not seen myself under the influence thereof. . . .[107]

Sebele's pledge to stop drinking *khadi* was clearly never honored. In 1908 the Rev. Lewis reported: "It is a fact that during 1908 Chief Sebele has seldom been sober."[108] Nor was Kgama's fight against the consumption of *khadi* and liquor wholly successful either. When the Rev. Jennings tightened church laws on prohibition in 1901, many people resigned their church membership while some professed Christians drank beer secretly.[109]

Thus it would appear that attempts to transform initiation ceremonies, marriage customs, and the drinking habits of the Tswana met with little success. Viewed in the context of the Tswana social milieu and also in the light of parallel experiences elsewhere in Africa, attempts made by Europeans to transform African social institutions met strong resistance largely because they sought to change a people's personality in the shortest possible time, and the Tswana, like other Africans, were not so susceptible.[110]

IV

Of all the spheres in which Europeans tried to influence and, on their town terms, improve Tswana life, the economic realm seems to have been most beset by vicissitudes way into the twentieth century. A pattern of unrelieved economic hardship set in after the heyday of the ivory trade in the 1850s that had declined so sharply by the 1880s it was no longer a profitable enterprise. It has also been observed that, partly as a result of these diminishing game resources, Tswana rulers compromised the traditional systems of land tenure and issued land concessions in order to replenish the revenues of their chiefdoms.[111] It is also tempting to correlate economic hardship with the readiness with which the Tswana accepted innovations to some of their farming practices. The introduction of the plow in the 1870s had important social and economic consequences.[112] By the 1880s —thanks to the white traders—the use of plows seems to have been widespread,[113] as is suggested by a visitor to Bechuanaland who observed:

> The number of wagons and ploughs in the country is very considerable. They use hardly anything but American and Swedish ploughs, which are much lighter than the English make.[114]

Even the Tawana, who did not have as many white traders as their southern kinsmen, were reported to be in possession of eight plows in 1894;[115] a year later it was estimated that the Ngwato had 1,500 plows.[116] Nevertheless, the introduction of plows coincided with persistent droughts, with the result that there was little real progress in agriculture. Even the few wells that the British administration sank along the main routes barely sufficed for Tswana household consumption.[117] In the absence of a regular water supply, crop failures remained endemic, the dearth of corn invariably inducing price fluctuations of great magnitude. For example, in 1890 a 205 pound bag of maize that previously cost ten shillings rose to thirty-six shillings a bag.[118] The outbreak of rinderpest in March 1896 caused a sharp increase in the price of maize owing to the shortage of draft animals normally used for transporting grain to the Protectorate. Hence, between March and October 1896 the price of maize rose from £2, ten shillings[119] to £20 a bag.[120] Another factor that caused price fluctuations was the ephemeral nature of the demands for Tswana produce. One such demand was created in 1890 when the Chartered Expeditionary Force (the so-called "Pioneer" Column) passed through the eastern portion of Bechuanaland on its way to Mashonaland. The Tswana suddenly found a ready market for their cattle, goats, and labor.[121] On another occasion the Ngwato found a market for their labor when in 1893 hostilities broke out between the Ndebele and white settlers in Matebeleland. Chief Kgama sent a force of 1,900 men to assist the white settlers and was paid £1,100 in return.[122]

If the Ngwato benefited most from the war of 1893, the Anglo-Boer war (1899–1902) provided a market for all principal Tswana tribes. British demand for livestock for slaughter,[123] timber,[124] water,[125] and auxiliary laborers brought substantial cash to Tswana chiefdoms.[126] By May 1900 the Rev. Williams estimated that British forces had purchased livestock worth £65,000, adding—no doubt with some exaggeration—that the Tswana had become the "chancellor of the Government exchequer . . . all the ready cash is in the hands of the natives." [127] It was the Tswana's misfortune that these spells of economic opportunities were punctuated by droughts and epidemics, which in turn affected the pace at which the chiefdoms could be transformed.

What perhaps was the greatest catastrophe to strike Tswana communities during the last quarter of the nineteenth century was the rinderpest (*bolowane*) epidemic of 1896–7. Although European observers tended to exaggerate the number of cattle that the Tswana lost, there is no doubt that rinderpest killed large numbers of cattle. In its wake missionaries and government officials tried to check its spread by persuading the Tswana to destroy all infected cattle and by restricting the movement of live ones, but they failed to get the cooperation of some Tswana communities. In Kwenaland the destruction of cattle was opposed by a faction led by Kgosidintsi, who asserted that the *dingaka* (witch doctors) alone were capable of curing rinderpest. Kgosidintsi is reported to have lost all his cattle; Chief Sebele lost all except seventy-seven of the 10,000 head herd he possessed.[128] The Ngwaketse, too, sustained heavy losses,[129] while the Ngwato lost over ninety percent of their cattle in spite of the combined efforts of the chief, the veterinary officer, and a large section of the tribe to check the spread of rinderpest.[130]

In a region that had always been plagued by droughts, the outbreak of rinderpest deprived the Tswana of one of their most valuable forms of wealth and it brought in its train great hunger. In the wake of the epidemic chiefs, missionaries, and government officials set up some relief projects. Initially chiefs, for various reasons, resented European participation on the grounds that the chief alone had the prerogative to distribute food.[131] On the other hand, Chief Kgama objected to the free distribution of food, especially to those members of his tribe who were still able to do some manual work: "I am averse to the maintenance of my people by the charity of the government or of the English people. . . . I desire that my people may be allowed to earn their living."[132] Chief Bathoen was also desperate to save his people. To him expediency transcended all questions of protocol, hence, he pleaded: "We have no money, but we want food."[133] The chiefs' varying reactions notwithstanding, relief projects were launched and in due course many Tswana communities received food rations consisting mostly of corn and sorghum. In Ngwaketseland the Rev. Lloyd reported that between November 1896 and September 1897, 1,868 people received food rations,[134] that by September 1898, 400 pounds of grain were being distributed each morning to 10 men, 410 women, and 81 children.[135] Relief schemes seem to have succeeded in Kwenaland, too, once Sebele had agreed to work with missionaries and government officials. In August 1898 Wookey reported that about 500 people received food rations every morning.[136] By December that year, over 1,400 people—mostly women and children—were on relief.[137]

When Kgama requested that his people be provided with jobs in order to earn their living, he had in fact anticipated the Colonial Secretary's views on the issue, for in April 1896 Chamberlain instructed Robinson to encourage all able-bodied Tswana men to go and work in the goldfields in south Africa, and that only needy women and children could be supplied with food.[138] A month later he instructed that some men be employed as laborers on the railway line that was being built between Gaborone and Bulawayo.[139] While some men worked on the railway line, others were employed to fence it on the Protectorate side of the railway strip, an engagement that entailed the supply of timber by Tswana communities living along the railway line. Thus in one report, a government official estimated that the Tswana would be paid £765 to supply poles for fencing the line between Mochudi and Ramakgwebana.[140]

At first many Tswana men were reluctant to work as laborers because their families tried to eke out an existence on carcasses of cattle. However, once the meat of these rinderpest victims was known to be contaminated,[141] Tswana men were compelled to seek employment so that they could earn money with which to buy food for their families. Tswana participation in the work projects within the Protectorate was commended by the High Commissioner in 1897; Robinson was so impressed with their work that he introduced another scheme whereby Tswana communities could earn money by selling brushwood and timber to the Kimberly diamond mines.[142] This scheme was facilitated by the completion of the railway line linking the Protectorate with the Cape in 1897, for the wood and timber could now be carried by trains more expeditiously and at a cheaper rate than by road transportation.[143] The railways also made it cheaper to transport grain to Bechuanaland. In 1897 a government official reported that, because of cheap transportation, maize was being sold at £1 7 shillings 6d a bag, which was less than half what it would have cost if there had been no railway line.[144] Railways again played an important role in restocking Bechuanaland because cattle, sheep, and goats were conveyed from the Cape to the Protectorate at rates that were one-third of the normal cost.[145] Before the advent of the railways cattle had had to be moved on the hoof.[146]

In the aftermath of the rinderpest the Tswana appear to have accepted European veterinary measures, such as dipping cattle and killing infected ones to check and prevent the spread of diseases. The Protectorate administration, which had had little to do with veterinary measures since 1885, stepped up its efforts to check cattle diseases after 1900. In 1904, a veterinary officer, Mr. G. W. Lee, was brought to the Protectorate on a temporary basis to help prevent the spread of a cattle disease called the East Coast fever. In 1905, Mr. W. H. Chase was appointed a permanent veterinary officer for the whole Protectorate.[147] Mr. Chase's work seems to have been effective, helped no doubt by fears of a repeat performance of the disease of 1896–7; for example, when he asked the Ngwato to destroy their infected cattle in 1908, all those who attended the *pitso* except for six men voted to destroy all infected cattle. Other Tswana chiefdoms must have cooperated with the veterinary officer, for in his annual report for the period 1908–9, Mr. Chase commended the Tswana for agreeing to have their cattle inoculated:

> So far, not a hitch has occurred; thousands of head of cattle have been successfully inoculated; many outbreaks

of the disease [rinderpest] have been smothered by the prompt destruction of affected cattle; and throughout the country the people are awakening to the fact that the disease, from the devastation of which they have suffered so long, can be stamped out, and are clamouring for assistance.[148]

The move to improve pastoral farming tapped the Protectorate's most viable industry and after 1900 the Tswana relied more on cattle and products derived from cattle, such as hides and skins, for trade than they had done in the past. However, Ngamiland was an exception, because the Tawana and their neighbors had, in addition to cattle, ample hunting grounds that abounded with a variety of game. The Tawana hunted in the Mababe-Chobe forests, the Luiana River, and the Tsodilo hills areas; some hunted on horseback. Their produce consisted of cattle, skins of various animals, horns, tails, ostrich feathers, and hides of hippos, out of which white south African farmers made canes for driving cattle (*sjamboks* in Afrikaans);[149] they marketed part of their produce through the five white traders in Ngamiland. Some Tawana engaged in transport riding and carried part of the produce to south Africa in their wagons. A trip from Ngamiland to south Africa earned a Tawana operator £80–£100.[150] However, transport riding was gradually made obsolete, especially among the Ngwato, Kwena, and Ngwaketse, by railway trains that from 1897 onward conveyed goods to and from south Africa more expeditiously. Not that agricultural produce was altogether wanting. During the infrequent seasons when rainfall was good, the Tswana grew maize and sorghum, which some of the farmers sold and used the money they obtained from the sales to buy cattle; others do not appear to have handled their produce wisely because they are reported to have been in the habit of selling their grain at harvest time, only to find themselves in need of buying it back from the same traders for their own consumption later in the year and at much higher prices than they had sold it.[151]

The settlement of Europeans along the eastern strip of Bechuanaland after 1903—known as *Tuli block farms, Lobatsi block farms,* and *Gaberone block farms*—opened few opportunities for employment. Nor did the stores and hotels in the Protectorate employ many Tswana workers either; in 1903 they employed 600 men all told, a figure that represented a very small fraction of the population.[152] Nevertheless, the settlement strip was used as permanent refuge on at least two occasions by whites who Kgama did not want to remain in his chiefdom: the Rev. Edwin Lloyd in 1914,[153] and Paul Jousse of the Bechuanaland Trading Association in 1916.[154]

The preceding account has shown that economic opportunities and natural resources within the Protectorate were scanty. It is against this background of scarcity that the Tswana were lured to the mining and other labor markets of south Africa. The Tswana had been going to work in the diamond fields since the 1870s. By 1880 there were 2,135 Tswana workers at Kimberley; in 1881 the number had increased to 2,571, the majority of them being Kwena, Ngwato, and Kgatla. The discovery of gold on the Witwatersrand in 1886 led to more demand for laborers. Thus, the precedent set by Alexander Bailie in 1876 was repeated by even more aggressive labor-recruiting agents who frequented the Protectorate. By 1898 the conduct of some of these agents was causing concern to British officials in Bechuanaland. In that year the assistant Resident Commissioner pointed out some of their improper practices:

> The natives are persuaded to leave their homes under promises of high wages ... which are seldom paid, or if presumably paid there are so many reductions made that the native seldom gets what he was led to expect.[155]

As a consequence, the High Commissioner introduced measures in 1899 to protect Tswana migrant workers. One of the measures required that every labor-recruiting agent obtain an annual license from the Resident Commissioner for Bechuanaland at a cost of £5; each agent had to deposit £100 as a guarantee against abusing recruits.[156]

Migrant workers seem to have fended for their families if only after spells of absence. In 1897 the High Commissioner observed: "During their absence it is probable that many of their wives and children are being left with but scanty provision, but the men as a rule return in due time to their own country to spend their earnings." [157] However, in 1904 Ellenberger, a Protectorate official, informed a government commission that Tswana migrant workers were apt to spend all their money in south Africa and returned home only with some goods.[158] This suggests that many of the workers did not have sufficient cash with them on their return, a practice that must have limited their purchasing power within the Protectorate. In another vein Ellenberger's testimony suggests that Tswana men were beginning to pay little attention to their families, owing probably to the detractions caused by living in mining compounds in which they were unable to lead normal married life.[159]

If migrant labor was not the ideal way of salvaging the economic life of the Tswana, there was at least one chief who was resourceful enough to try one of the white man's methods of making a living. Although he had previously opposed the sale or purchase of business premises,[160] Kgama decided to purchase the ailing Serowe retail stores of Reginald P. Garrett and Adolph G. Smith, but retained the former owners as his managers.[161] Kgama, who obtained permission from the government to enter into retail business, maintained that at the time he purchased the stores in 1909 he had become a poor man, adding, no doubt with some exaggeration, that the declining revenue of the chief's coffers had reduced him "practically on the same footing as any individual member of the tribe." [162]

By 1916 the business had expanded, with branches at Tsau, Mopepe, Karoube, and Bobonon; it was reported to represent a capital investment of £20,000 and yielded the chief an annual income of £800.[163] However, Kgama's venture was short-lived, for in 1916 the government ordered him to withdraw from the business following repeated allegations by the management of the Bechuanaland Trading Association Company that the Chief was influencing the Ngwato to boycott their stores and to patronize his own business.[164] Nor does Kgama seem to have received any compensation from Garrett and Smith, who continued to operate the business after his withdrawal; the only consolation appears to have come from the Protectorate administration in the form of an annual grant worth £500.[165] It is doubtful indeed if this grant was adequate to cover Kgama's household needs and to fulfill his obligations as cheif. The important point to note is that 1916 marks the year in which Kgama joined the list of colonial chiefs receiving some stipend from a British administration. And since the allowance was clearly not a tribute to Kgama in the traditional sense, it marks a turning point in the life history of a chief who had always encouraged his subjects to earn their living and whose own position as chief did not entitle him to remuneration.

V

One of the ironies of the advent of Europeans in Bechuanaland is that, while their presence tended to circumscribe the political autonomy of Tswana chiefdoms, Europeans were largely responsible for the amelioration of the civil and economic conditions of the Sarwa and the Kgalagadi. Hitherto, Tswana masters held the Sarwa and the Kglagadi in an abject form of servitude.[166] This system of servitude was probably started at the time (*c.* 1720–1800) that Tswana groups settled in the regions that were to come under Tswana control. They found the Sarwa and the Kgalagadi occupying most of the region and sought to make them into serfs.[167] Initially the process of enticing serfs seems to have been a peaceful one, consisting mostly of placing some cattle under the care of a band or group of the Kgalagadi;[168] in the case of the Sarwa, early contacts with the Ngwato were established during hunting trips, when the latter befriended them with presents of meat.[169] This was probably the method adopted by other Tswana groups in bringing serfs under their control. On the other hand, the Tawana claim to have used witchcraft to bring serfs under their control.[170] In all Tswana chiefdoms, overseers (*mong*) of serfs collected produce from them as tribute (*lekgetho*). This consisted of ivory, ostrich feathers, hides, and skins and as a reward for their service the Tswana master supplied them (through the overseer) with hunting dogs, allowed them to retain the meat of the animals they killed, and they were also free to milk the cows for their own consumption.[171] Serfs remained attached to their master's family for the rest of their lives and they were inherited by his children and could be captured in war as booty. Serfs had no access to tribal courts.[172]

Whatever amicable conditions surrounded the initial contacts between the Tswana and the Sarwa and the Kgalagadi, there is little doubt that by the turn of the nineteenth century Tswana dominance over their serfs had become absolute, some Tswana masters actually offering serfs for sale. In 1806 a Tlhaping man offered to sell to Dr. Lichtenstein's party two boys aged eight and ten years. The prospective seller is reported to have informed the white visitors that the boys had been captured by him in war and were his forever. He demanded a sheep for each but the visitors refused to buy human commodity.[173] In 1824 Robert Moffat

More Aspects of Tswana Transformation   261

saw two elderly persons (who were probably Tlhaping) who offered to sell their children to him in vain.[174] In 1859 William Baldwin, who was in Ngamiland, was given a present of a Sarwa man by a Tawana man and in turn bought a Sarwa companion for him with beads.[175] While recorded instances of traffic in humans are few, there are ample accounts that suggest that Tswana masters illtreated their serfs.[176] In 1843 Livingstone reported the relationship between the Tswana and their serfs in unfavorable terms, alleging the Kgalagadi to have been "enslaved" by Tswana masters.[177] J. D. Hepburn, who visited Ngamiland in 1877 and 1881, described the condition of the serfs there in the same vein.[178] And John Mackenzie observed that Tswana masters treated their serfs with contempt, the Kgalagadi being held in a little more esteem than the Sarwa. He said: "Bushmen [Sarwa] seldom secure much liking or consideration from their Bechwana masters. 'Masarwa a bolotsana thata' ('Bushmen are perfect rascals'), 'Masarwa Ki linoga hela' ('Bushmen are perfect snakes'), are remarks often heard among the Bechwanas." [179] This suggests that by 1884, when Mackenzie's book was published, Tswana attitudes toward their serfs had not changed much.

Yet, since their arrival in northern Bechuanaland, missionaries had preached against serfdom. In Ngamiland, where serfdom seems to have been more prevalent than in other chiefdoms, Hepburn and evangelist Khukwi Mogodi preached against serfdom. Thus, between 1877 and 1881 Hepburn reported that Chief Moremi of the Tawana promised him to stop serfdom and the traffic in human beings and that some Tawana masters had freed their serfs.[180] However, reports from Ngamiland show that between 1881 and 1895 the Tawana retained some serfs.[181] In 1895, the Rev. Wookey, who was stationed in Ngamiland, reported that Chief Sekgoma Lecholathebe was opposed to the presence of the L.M.S. there because he feared missionaries might influence the serfs not to pay tribute to him.[182]

The advent of white traders enhanced the economic status of serfs. Although Tswana masters forbade the serfs to barter with whites, the vastness of the Tswana region made it difficult to enforce the ban, with the result that the serfs were able to sell some of their produce. In this connection Mackenzie observed:

> It is not difficult to account for the well-known reluctance of Bechwana chiefs to allow traders to pass through their country, as it is well known that the [serfs] do not hesitate to keep back part of the produce from their masters, and barter with themselves as soon as a European wagon makes its appearance.[183]

In an attempt to discourage clandestine barter, the masters found themselves offering more presents to their serfs. In economic terms, this was certainly a boon to the serfs.

Of the four principal northern Tswana chiefs, Kgama relaxed the restrictions placed against serfs soon after he became chief.[184] In 1916 Kgama said he removed the restrictions because he

> considered it as interfering with the freedom of the people. [That] the tribes became in the first instance apprehensive of the declaration so that at least I had to ask European traders to travel amongst them and sell goods . . . and eventually I asked these Europeans to establish trading stores amongst them.[185]

Kgama coupled this ruling with the prohibition of the sale of Sarwa children and the transfer of serfs from one master to another; by 1890 he had allowed serfs to acquire and keep livestock and he encouraged masters to reward their services by gifts of stock. Among the Ngwaketse, Gaseitsiwe forbade his people to arrogate for themselves the goods of Kgalagadi serfs or to enter their villages without his permission.[186] Although it is difficult to attribute these measures entirely to European influences, Kgama seems to have emulated the British for their abolition of slavery, as is suggested in his letter to emigrant Boers in 1877, when he said: "I love the nation which tries to stop wicked men from buying and selling black people . . . and treat them worse than their dogs."[187]

The advent of British rule reinforced missionaries, whose efforts to stamp out servitude had met with little success. In 1896 the Rev. Lloyd assured Chamberlain that there was no servitude in the chiefdoms of Bathoen, Sebele, and Kgama, pointing out that the Kgalagadi owned cattle, sheep, goats, horses, plows, and wagons, which they had previously been denied; he also observed that Kgalagadi youths were now free to take up jobs in the mines of south Africa.[188] Bathoen also wrote to Chamberlain asserting that serfdom was no longer in vogue. The chief gave an account of a master-servant relationship in which the Sarwa and Kgalagadi were free to own property and to work for rewards.[189]

However, eye-witness accounts by Protectorate officials suggest that the status of serfs had not improved to the extent that Tswana chiefs claimed. It appears that the chiefs, in an attempt to present themselves in favorable light before British officials, exaggerated the extent to which serfs enjoyed economic and civil rights in their respective chiefdoms. Thus, hardly a week after Bathoen had written to Chamberlain on Ngwaketse relations with serfs, Goold-Adams sent an eye-witness account to a colonial official at the Cape that portrayed the serfs as having a more circumscribed status than Bathoen and Wookey had asserted. He said:

> Whatever may now be said by the missionaries as to the Bakalahari being part of the tribe, I am convinced that if the Bakalahari were allowed to choose freely for themselves whether to live separately or not from the Bangwaketse, they would gladly accept the former; at the

present moment, writing as I am amongst the Kraals of the Bakalahari, I can safely say that they are a subject race, kept in their present position by force, obliged to give their labour for nothing, and only allowed, except in a few instances, to be the possessors of a few sheep and goats.[190]

Writing from Ngamiland in 1897 Lieutenant Scholefield described the conditions of the Sarwa and the Kgalagadi under the Tawana to be similar to those reported by Goold-Adams a year earlier.[191]

Among the Ngwato, Kgama's quarrel with his son, Sekgoma, at the turn of the century revealed that the Sarwa and the Kgalagadi were still held in servitude. In 1898 Goold-Adams reported that Kgama did not allow some Sarwa to join the seceding Sekgoma faction because the chief required them to herd his cattle and to collect ostrich feathers for him.[192] In 1899 Goold-Adams took up the question of servitude with Kgama and urged him to stop it among his subjects. Kgama is reported to have said that he would put more efforts to stamp out servitude but is said to have conceded that the "servitude of the Bakalahari and Masarwa was an old tribal custom which would take some years to entirely overcome." [193] This was certainly a more candid observation than Bathoen's account of 1896, for the question of servitude was destined to simmer unresolved way into the twentieth century, as the L.M.S. found out to their dismay in 1905 when a Ngamiland evangelist admitted that he kept a serf who rendered him service without pay.[194]

Yet in spite of Tswana reluctance to accept the Sarwa and the Kgalagadi as their equals, the serfs achieved a measure of economic and civic freedom that had hitherto been denied them. This stemmed largely from the fact that government officials and missionaries insisted that serfs and their Tswana masters be treated as equals in secular as well as in religious affairs.

NOTES FOR CHAPTER 7

1. For a discussion of initiation ceremonies, *see* chapter 3.
2. For example, in 1890 Chief Gaseitsiwe of the Ngwaketse was buried in accordance with Christian rites; *see* Kanye Report, in Rev. Good to Thompson, 6 April 1890, Box 2 (L.M.S.).
3. *See* Wookey in Molepolole Report, 1888, Box 2 (L.M.S.). *See also* Wookey to Thompson, 3 October 1888, in which he reported that fifty boys died during a *bogwera* ceremony.
4. Parliamentary Papers, 1887, C. 4890, 59: 2, Moffat to Shippard 6 July 1886.
5. Ibid., but Edward Mohr (*see* chapter 3) seems to have been able to observe the rites more closely than Moffat.
6. Williams in Molepolole Report, 1890, Box 2, Williams to Thompson, 6 August 1894 (L.M.S.).
7. Most visitors to Kwenaland reported Kgosidintsi to be a most consistent traditionalist. *See,* for example, Williams to Thompson, 6 March 1901 (L.M.S.).
8. Williams, Molepolole Reports, 1888, Box 2 (L.M.S.).
9. Hepburn to Thompson, 6 November 1885, Box 43, Jacket B, Folder 2 (L.M.S.).
10. Minutes of the B.D.C., 1 February 1907 (L.M.S.).
11. Jennings, Serowe Report, 1904, Box 3 (L.M.S.).
12. Willoughby to Thompson, 28 May 1898, Box 55, Jacket C, Folder 1 (L.M.S.). *See also Bechuanaland News*, 25 July 1896.
13. "To Bite the Year, a Native Ceremony," *Bechuanaland News*, 25 July 1896. Willoughby to Thompson, 30 March 1896, Box 53, Jacket C, Folder 1 (L.M.S.).
14. C. O. 879/69, Africa (South), no. 659, pp. 374, 378; Wookey to Commissioner Surmon, 3 May 1909, who reported that early that year *bogwera* ceremonies were "begun in the *Kgotla* and the religious services which had been conducted in the *Kgotla* had to be discontinued and have since been conducted at a Mopipe tree near the town as there is not a church there yet." *See also* I. Schapera, "Uniformity and Variation in Chief-made Law: A Tswana Case Study," Burg Wartenstein Symposium, 1966.
15. Jennings, Serowe Report, 1906, Box (L.M.S.). For a change of missionary attitudes toward some Tswana instutions, *see* chapter 5.
16. Alfred Wookey, "Missionary Work in Bechuanaland: Interesting Historical Reminiscence," *The Diamond Field Advertiser*, 11 February 1907.
17. *See*, for example, W. J. Burchell, *Travels in the Interior of South Africa*, 2 vols. (London: 1822), I, p. 393; Ratshosa, "My Book. . . ," p. 86; C. O. 879/52, Africa (South), no. 552, p. 197, where M. W. Searle advised a commissioner" . . . these so-called native marriages . . . are in the nature of a 'sale' of the woman by her father, and are in their essence repugnant to civilized laws." For a more perceptive comment, *see* Ellenberger's testimony in S.A.N.A.C. 4: 243; "[bogadi is] simply a gift to the

father. A man does not purchase his wife."

18. J. J. Freeman, *A Tour in South Africa* (London: 1851), p. 270; A. E. Jennings, *Bogadi: A Study of the Marriage Laws and Customs of the Bechuana Tribes of South Africa* (Tiger Kloof, South Africa: 1931), p. 20.

19. I. Schapera, *A Handbook of Tswana Law and Custom* (London: 1938; reprinted 1959, 1970), p. 125. It appears that, although *bogadi* was considered to be a bond of union between two families, it had by 1931 become commercialized as is suggested by Ratshosa and Raditladi in "My Book...," p. 86.

20. Minutes of the B.D.C., in Ashton to Mullens, 27 October 1875, Box 38, Jacket B, Folder 1 (L.M.S.).

21. Minutes of the B.D.C. meeting held at Kuruman, October 1875, Box 38, Jacket C, Folder 1 (L.M.S.).

22. Henry Lichtenstein, *Travels in Southern Africa in the Years 1803, 1804, 1805, and 1806*, 2 vols., trans. Anne Plumptre (London: 1815), 2: 386.

23. Ibid., p. 396.

24. Freeman, *A Tour of South Africa*, p. 280.

25. Perhaps conveniently observed by commoners in deference to an old Tswana custom (*see* Dr. Livingstone, *Private Journals* [London: 1960], p. 299): "Sechele says the immemorial custom of the people in this country has been to imitate their chiefs. If he is fond of oxen all the men live at the cattle posts, if fond of hunting all rear dogs and hunt with them."

26. Lloyd to Thompson, 14 June 1893, Box 50, Jacket A, Folder 2 (L.M.S.).

27. Gould to Thompson, 16 June 1904 (L.M.S.).

28. J. Theodore Bent, "Among the Chiefs of Bechuanaland," *British Museum Pamphlets* 121 (1892): 651. See also, N. Q. Parsons, "The 'Image' of Khama the Great—1868–1970," *Botswana Notes and Records* 3 (1971): 41–58.

29. Willoughby to Thompson, 22 April 1898, Box 55, Jacket B, Folder 1 (L.M.S.).

30. L.M.S. *Chronicle*, January 1891.

31. Willoughby to Thompson, 29 June 1896, Box 53, Jacket C, Folder 2 (L.M.S.). Simon Ratshosa, who was Kgama's grandson, probably gave a biased account about Sefakwana's character, for he described her as a "very wicked woman, who caused the Chief many troubles, having allied herself with worthless men...." See, Ratshosa, "My Book...," p. 136. *See also*, "Inquisitor" [pseudo], "Khama, the King: Truth about the Bechuanas," Central News Agency, being a compilation of articles that appeared in *The Sunday Times* (Johannesburg), on 4 January, 8 February, 15 February, 1 March, and 22 March 1914, in *Botswana Pamphlets*, Center of African Studies, University of Edinburgh.

32. Williams to Thompson, 21 July 1899, Box 56, Jacket B, Folder 2 (L.M.S.).

33. Thompson to Willoughby, 29 December 1900 (L.M.S.).

More Aspects of Tswana Transformation

34. C. O. 879/69 pp. 5–6, War Office to C. O. 5 of 27 December 1900, enclosure 5, Surmon to Milner, 13 December 1900.

35. Lewis, Molepolole and District Report for 1902, Box 3 (L.M.S.).

36. C. O 879/69, Africa (Souht), no. 659, p. 374, Acting Resident Commissioner Surmon to Kitchener, 13 May 1901, enclosed in Kitchener to Chamberlain, 260 of 7 June 1901.

37. Ibid., Macholohelo to Surmon, 18 April 1901; she asked Surmon to send his reply through B. J. Vickerman, a trader at Molepolole.

38. Ibid., pp. 375–76, Sebele to Surmon (undated).

39. Ibid.

40. In Sebele to Ellenberger (undated, ibid.) the chief said that another reason that compelled him to marry Bautlwe was that the Kwena objected to a chief keeping a concubine.

41. Ibid., Wookey to Surmon, 3 May 1901.

42. Ibid., p. 379, Surmon to Sebele, 11 May 1901.

43. C. O. 879/76, pp. 271–72, Macholohelo to Ellenberger, 19 July 1901: "I am still leading the same miserable life owing to Sebele's action with Bautlwe."

44. Ibid., p. 271, Ellenberger to Surmon, 4 August 1901.

45. Ibid., pp. 270, 273, Sebele to Ellenberger, 9 August 1901. See also Acting Resident Commissioner to Milner, 8 August 1901 (ibid.).

46. Ibid., p. 275, Ralph Williams to Milner, 7 November 1901.

47. Jennings to Thompson, 16 June 1904, 28 July 1904, Ngamiland Report, 1905 (L.M.S.).

48. C. O. 879/52, African (South), no. 552, p. 197, Surmon to Imperial Secretary, 9 October 1897, Minute no. 1, 130, Native Marriages, enclosed in High Commissioner to Chamberlain, 175 of 25 October 1897. For example, in the same correspondence when the B.D.C. asked which marriages were valid in Botswana, M. W. Searle, a colonial officer at the Cape, advised that only those marriages contracted according to Tswana custom were invalid, for they were "repugnant to civilized laws," a condition that could hardly have been fulfilled by non-Christian members of Tswana chiefdoms.

49. Williams, in Molepolole Report, 1903, Box 3 (L.M.S.).

50. I. Schapera and D. F. Van der Merwe, *Notes an Tribal Groupings, History, and Customs of the Kgalagadi* (Communication from the School of African Studies; Series no. 13, University of Cape Town, 1945), p. 66.

51. As is suggested in "Poisoning of Africa Papers," *Africa Pamphlets* (1884–1895), 12: 542, Rhodes House, Oxford.

52. Lichtsenstein, *Travels*, 2: 370.

53. Emil Holub, *Seven Years in South Africa*, 2 vols., trans. Ellen E. Trewer (London: 1881), 1: 235–36; Holub, "On the Central South African Tribes from the South Coast to the Zambezi," *J.R.A.I.*, 5 (1884), p. 7, in which he reported that the Khoikhoi were addicted to brandy.

54. In 1850, J. Leyland (*see his Adventures in the Far Interior of South Africa* [London: 1866], p. 59), reported that the Tlhaping chief, Mahura, was fond of Cape brandy; C. J. Andersson (*see his The Okavango River: A Narrative of Travel Exploration and Adventure* [London:

1861], pp. 196–97) reported in the late 1850s that liquor was in great demand in Ngamiland; E. W. Smith, *Great Lion of Bechuanaland: The Life and Times of Roger Price* (London: 1957), p. 162; Mrs. E. Price (*see* Una Long, ed., *Journals*, pp. 153, 179) reported that a Mr. Hewitt sold large quantities of brandy at Shoshong in the 1860s and alleged that Sechele's unpredictable behavior was largely influenced by European liquor. For the 1870s, *see* works cited in footnote 53.

55. Minutes of the B.D.C. meeting held at Kuruman on 12 June 1877, enclosed in Mackenzie to Mullens, 22 June 1877 (L.M.S.).

56. Wookey to Mullens, 28 August 1877, Box 38, Jacket C, Folder 1 (L.M.S.).

57. The Rev. Ashton in a letter to *Diamond Field News*, 16 August 1878.

58. B.D.C. to Frere, 25 January 1879 (L.M.S.). Apparently their recommendation of 1877 (*see* footnote 55) had not been carried out. Licensing laws that were promulgated in southern Bechuanaland do not seem to have been rigorously enforced; *see*, for example, the Rev. John Brown to Robinson, 3 November 1885, 23 July 1888, Box 45, Jacket C, Folder 3 (L.M.S.), in which he complained that Africans were still obtaining liquor from canteens. In 1880 Captain Harrel reported (*see* Parliamentary Papers, 1883, C. 4194, 49: 23) that traders sold liquor in contravention to the law.

59. Una Long, ed., *The Journals of Elizabeth Price*, p. 218.

60. Parliamentary Papers, 1878–9, C. 2220, 52: 76, Alexander Bailie to Administrator of Griqualand West, 17 May 1877.

61. Una Long, ed., p. 461.

62. Ibid., p. 482. At about the same time Sechele's new bride, Kholoma (ibid., p. 473), could be said to have become a connoisseur of liquor, preferring champagne and wine to gin. For Sechele's marriage to Kholoma, *see* chapter 3.

63. Kgama to Barkly, 22 August 1876, Chief's Papers, no. 4, p. 121, Selly Oak Colleges Library.

64. W. C. Willoughby, "Khama: A Bantu Reformer," *International Review of Missions* (January 1924), pp. 74–76. *See also* Hepburn to Whitehouse, 11 May 1880, Box 40, Jacket B, Folder 4 (L.M.S.), in which he reported that Kgama resolved in his youth that he "would not rule over a drunken town and people."

65. *See*, for example, Chief's Papers, no. 7, Selly Oak Colleges Library, "Documents signed by some Europeans recently came on the station respecting intoxicating drinks," 21 January 1880, when traders pledged "to drop entirely the use of all intoxicating drinks." F. Arnot, *From Natal to the Upper Zambezi* (London: 1863), p. 26: "[in May 1882 Arnot did not see] any intoxicated person [at Shoshong] . . . which could not be said by anyone, for the same period, in any other town in Afrika, where the white man with his trade has access. The Chief, Kgama, has put down the drink traffic most effectively." The view that Kgama did not tolerate liquor traffic through his chiefdom is not wholly accurate, for F. H. Barber diaries show (in E. G. Tabler, *Zambezi and Matebeleland*

More Aspects of Tswana Transformation

in the Seventies [London: 1960], p. 70), that Kgama allowed them to pass through Shoshong with casks of brandy.

66. See "Khama and Drink Traffic," by J. Johnson et al., in *The League Journal*, Glasgow (9 October 1880). The authors criticized Britain at great length: "It is a matter of shame and deep humiliation that Christian Britain, which has sent to Africa the Gospel of Jesus Christ—the water of life—has sent along with it the water of death, and that the ships which have carried the Bible and the missionary have carried the rum cask and the liquor seller to your shores." In their enthusiasm to support African chiefs who opposed the introduction of liquor in their communities, antiliquor organizations in Europe did not always report accurately; *see*, for example, "Poisoning of Africa Papers," Rhodes House, p. 542, when Kgama was reported to be the "First Native Christian Chief in Africa." *See also "Inquisitor,"* [pseudo.] "Khama, the King."

67. Wookey to Thompson, 4 August 1888, Box 45, Jacket C, Folder 3 (L.M.S.).

68. J. D. Hepburn, *Twenty Years in Khama's Country*, p. 85.

69. Hepburn to Thompson, 7 March 1885, Box 43, Jacket B, Folder 1 (L.M.S.).

70. C. O. 879/30 pp. 2–4, Shippard to Robinson, 3 August 1888, enclosed in Robinson to Knutsford, 2 of 22 August 1888.

71. Thompson to James Good, 15 July 1886, Box 19; 15 January 1891, Box 23 (L.M.S.).

72. Kanye Report for 1889–90, in Good to Thompson, 6 April 1890, Box 23, (L.M.S.).

73. C. O. 879/33, p. 52, the Rev. J. Grant to Knutsford, 47 of 2 January 1891. *See also* ibid., p. 61, C. O. to the Rev. Grant Mills (of the N.R.L.T.U.C.) 57 of 17 January 1891 in which the British Government policy was enunciated: "With regard to your observations as to the views of Khama on this subject, I am to state that Khama has the full sympathy and support of Her Majesty's Government in his policy of preserving his people from demoralization by the liquor traffic." For the Brussels Act of 1890 *see* "Poisoning of Africa Papers," no. 12, Rhodes House, p. 543. To discourage liquor traffic, the Act imposed high tariffs: six pence per gallon in British colonies and 15 francs per hectalitre in French colonies.

74. For example, *see* the *Cape Argus*, 31 January 1890; C. O. 879/37, p. 27, J. S. Moffat to High Commissioner 6 October 1892, enclosed in Cameron to the Marquess of Ripon, 17 of 14 October 1892, in which Moffat reported that the new Kwena Chief, Sebele, was addicted to alcohol.

75. H. C. Juta, *The Laws of Bechuanaland Protectorate*, pp. 669–77 (chapter 84, Liquor Proclamation, (a), 4 April 1892). The Proclamation listed three types of native liquors (i.e., *kaffir* beer, *mokolane*, and *kabidikama* or *ila*) that were considered potentially dangerous.

76. *See*, for example, "Liquor and Native Labour," *The Bechuanaland News*, 16 February 1895. For views on the nutritious value of *kaffir* beer, *see* "The Beer Question, Kaffir Beer as a National Food and Beverage of

the African," *The South African Outlook*, 1 November 1941, in particular Dr. R. T. Bokwe, Thomas Nkosinkulu, et al. I assume that the formula and ingredients for making *kaffir* beer have remained more or less the same; H. M. Hole, *The Passing of the Black Kings* (London: 1932), pp. 266–67. Some Europeans believed (*see* Willoughby to Thompson, 31 December 1894, Box 51, Jacket C, Folder 2, L.M.S.) that *kaffir* beer cured scab.

77. "Liquor Problems and Legislation," *The Bechuanaland News*, 16 December 1893.

78. *See* footnote 97. Some white farmers at the Cape made brandy out of an indigenous plant described by a Swedish traveler as "a species of cactus of a considerable size." *See* Andrew Sparrman, *A Voyage to the Cape of Good Hope Towards the Antarctic Polar Circle and Around the World . . . From the Year 1772 to 1776* 2 vols. (London: 1786), 2: 345.

79. "Sensational Liquor Case," *The Bechuanaland News*, 27 April 1895.

80. "Notes from Palapye, "*The Bechuanaland News*, 16 November 1895.

81. Williams to Thompson, 5 January 1895, Box 52, Jacket A, Folder 1 (L.M.S.).

82. Williams to Thompson, 20 September 1895, Box 52, Jacket A, Folder 2 (L.M.S.). For Boyne's renewal of liquor licence, *see* Williams to Thompson, 7 January 1896, Box 52, Jacket A, Folder 2 (L.M.S.).

83. Raditladi, Mphoeng, et al., to Thompson, 16 March 1895, translated by J. S. Moffat, Box 52, Jacket A, Folder 1 (L.M.S.). For a discussion of Kgama's quarrels with his brothers, *see* chapter 5. Willoughby correctly (in a letter to Thompson, 16 March 1896), observed that the beer issue had been used as a stance to provoke political dissent. *See also*, Palapye Church to Thompson, 17 February 1896, Willoughby to Thompson, 30 March 1896, Box 52, Jacket A, Folder 1 (L.M.S.).

84. "Khama and His People, "*The Bechuanaland News*, 6 July 1895: "The Chief's power is considerably weakened and he feels he can no longer enforce his liquor laws. He had therefore removed the restriction on beer drinking. He has done it against his own wish. . . ." Later that year prohibition featured prominently in the discussions that went on (*see* A. Sillery, *Founding a Protectorate* [The Hague: 1965], chapter 18) between three Tswana chiefs and the British Government in London.

85. "Khama Interviewed," *The Bechuanaland News*, 24 October 1895.

86. "Beer Drinking at Palapye," *The Bechuanaland News*, 11 January 1896.

87. C. O. 879/47, African (South), no. 517, p. 158: "It is, I fear, perfectly true that the drinking of kaffir beer at Palapye has occasioned delays to traffic and inconvenience to the public."

88. Ibid.

89. Ibid. In January 1896, 500 transport riders petitioned Kgama to reenact liquor laws.

90. Williams to Thompson, 27 March 1896, Box 52, Jacket B, Folder 1 (L.M.S.). *See also* D. M. MacRae, *The Protectorate and Prevalent Diseases* (M. D. thesis, Glasgow University, 1920), p. 20, who said Sebele died of cirrhosis of the liver, a disease aggravated by alcohol.

More Aspects of Tswana Transformation

91. Williams to Thompson, 5 June 1896, Box 53, Jacket B, Folder 3 (L.M.S.).
92. Williams to Thompson, 12 October 1896, Box 53, Jacket B, Folder 3 (L.M.S.).
93. Williams to Thompson, 20 November 1896, Box 53, Jacket C, Folder 3 (L.M.S.).
94. Wlliams to Thompson, 22 April 1898, Box 55, Jacket B, Folder 1 (L.M.S.).
95. C. O. 879/47, pp. 378–79, Chief Kgama to N.R.L.T.U.C., 24 December 1896.
96. Kgama had said: "Here in our country there are Europeans who like liquor exceedingly, and they are not people who like to save a nation, but to seek that a nation may be destroyed by liquor; and they are not people who like to be persuaded in the matter of liquor," ibid.
97. For laxity in enforcing liquor laws the following letter to the editor (*The Bechuanaland News*, 5 May 1894) is revealing: "Are the government sincere in their professing to keep a strict supervision over the liquor brought into the Protectorate and beyond its borders? Or is it only a superficial action to blind the British public? If they are sincere, why do they not have a strict watch kept over the class of carrier loading it up north? . . . While writing these lines a native carrier is outspanned here [Palapye] on his way north with a load of liquor. . . . As for the Bechuanaland Border Police acting as customs officers, I am quite sure the collector of Customs will agree with me that it is the greatest farce out. Six regular customs officers under the direct control of the collector of Customs would be of more use than the 500 men of the B.B.P. acting as at present. Not that I for one moment insinuate that there are not good and true men in the B.B.P., but there seems a want of judgment in the selection of men sent on the outstations. Not always the most sober are chosen for that duty. It does not give you the most exalted idea of Her Majesty's acting excise officers when they come much the worse for liquor, and make a pretence of looking through your waybills, and wind up by asking you if you have not got a bottle of whiskey you can spare!" Also, for unruly behavior of the Sotho members of the B.B.P., see "Tragedy in the Kalahari," *The Bechuanaland News*, 4 February 1899.
98. Minutes of the B.D.C., enclosed in John Tom Brown to Thompson, 25 October 1900 (L.M.S.).
99. Minutes of the B.D.C. enclosed in John Tom Brown to Thompson 25 October 1900 (L.M.S.), section C of the Minutes merely suggested: "Without wishing in any way to add to the Society's rules and regulations, we would suggest the advisability of selecting such missionaries for our Becwana Mission as are total abstainers, so that no missionary may find himself in an anomalous position in carrying out" measures against excessive drinking. For irresolute missionary policy on prohibition, see Willoughby to Thompson, 9 March 1901, in which he said ". . . we never made it a *sine qua non* in church members . . . it does not require total abstinence. From imported spirits, and a new fangled brew of golden syrup brew . . . as strong as brandy, yes! From their own malt liquor,

no!" In John Brown, *Secwana Dictionary* (London: 1895), p. 37, *boyalwe* is defined as a "kind of weak beer."

100. Willoughby to Thompson, 23 December 1902 (L.M.S.).
101. Jennings to Thompson, 15 June 1904 (L.M.S.).
102. Lewis to Thompson, 1907 Molepolole Report, Box 4 (L.M.S.).
103. Gould to Thompson, 8 September 1904, 16 September 1904 (L.M.S.). Prohibition was one of the issues that led to the formation (*see* chapter 6) of the Ethiopian movement in Bechuanaland.
104. Jennings, Report on Ngamiland, 1905 (L.M.S.).
105. Lloyd to Thompson, 15 July 1908 (L.M.S.).
106. C. O. 879/76 African (South) no. 694, pp. 162–63, Mervyn Williams to Ralph Williams, July 1901, enclosed in Milner to Chamberlain, 121 of 4 October 1901.
107. C. O. 879/69, Africa (South) no. 659, pp. 374, 377, Surmon to Kitchener, 13 May 1901, enclosed in High Commissioner to Chamberlain, 260 of 7 June 1901, and the Rev. Alfred Wookey to Surmon, 3 May 1901.
108. R. H. Lewis, Molepolole Report, 1908, Box 4 (L.M.S.). Lewis noted that illicit liquor traffic was a lucrative enterprise that Proptectorate officials seemed to condone.
109. The Rev. Jennings, Serowe Mission Report, 1909, Box 4 (L.M.S.).
110. Elsewhere in Africa prohibition was not successful either. See, for example, "The Triumph of Gin," in E. A. Ayandele, *The Missionary Impact on Modern Nigeria, 1842–1914* (London: 1966), p. 307, passim; Robert I. Rotberg, *Christian Missionaries and the Creation of Northern Nigeria, 1880–1924* (Princeton, New Jersey: 1965), p. 127, passim. In a general sense European attitudes toward Tswana institutions was influenced by the prevailing cultural absolutism of the day, in contradistinction to the now widely held views on cultural relativism (popularized by Ruth Benedict, in *Patterns of Culture* [London: 1935]. See also H. Alan C. Cairns, *Prelude to Imperialism, British Reactions to Central African Society, 1840–1890* (London: 1965; reprinted, 1966), pp. 120–46, for a discussion of some aspects of cultural relativism.
111. See chapter 4.
112. See chapter 3.
113. Although no estimates of plows in the possession of the Kwena are given, the plow must have been widely used there, for in 1881 Sechele forbade its use as a punishment for his army's poor performance in their 1881 war with the Kgatla; see Price to Thompson, 14 December 1881, Box 40, Jacket D, Folder 1 (L.M.S.).
114. R. Wardlaw Thompson, "With the Boers and Blacks in South Africa," *Pall Mall Gazette*, 6 June 1884. The use of plows is confirmed by H. A. Bryden in *Gun and Camera in Southern Africa: A Year of Wandering in Bechuanaland, the Kalahari Desert, and the Lake River Country* London: 1893), p. 117 who observed that in 1890 the Bechuanaland Trading Association sold 300 American plows at £5 each in one day at their Shoshong store.
115. Alfred Wookey, "More News from Lake Ngami," L.M.S. *Chronicle*, October 1894, p. 238, in which he noted: "I went to one garden where some of them were learning both to train oxen and to plough at the same time.

More Aspects of Tswana Transformation

. . . They asked me to show them how to plough, but, though I tried, I don't think I helped them very much."

116. L.M.S. *Chronicle*, March 1895, p. 107.

117. In 1891 and 1892 the B.S.A. Company sank six wells along the route between Ramatlhabama and Ramontsa, while the British Administration sank four wells along the same route; see Parliamentary Papers, 1892, 68: 46. But R. W. Thompson gave an optimistic account of the irrigation potential of Bechuanaland. "As for the lack of water . . . that is entirely due to their failure or neglect to dig for water. . . ." See R. W. Thompson, "With the Boers and Blacks in South Africa," *Pall Mall Gazette*, 6 June 1884.

118. Bryden, *Gun and Camera*, p. 117. In 1893 (*see* Wookey to Thompson, 21 October 1893, Box 50, Jacket C, Folder 2 (L.M.S.)) maize was selling at £1 a bag in Ngamiland, while Boer meal was selling at one pound ten shillings (£1 10/-).

119. Willoughby to Thompson, 30 March 1896, Box 53, Jacket C, Folder 1 (L.M.S.).

120. Willoughby to Thompson, 12 October 1896, Box 53, Jacket D, Folder 2 (L.M.S.). *See also*, C. Van Onselen, "Reactions to Rinderpest in Southern Africa, 1896–97," *Journal of African History* 13, no. 3 (1972): 485, where corn meal is reported to have fetched £10 per bag of 200 pounds.

121. See Bryden, *Gun and Camera*, p. 261, who estimated that the expeditionary B.S.A.Co. force to Mashonaland in 1890 bought Ngwato produce worth £20,000. However, by 1893 (*see* J. S. Moffat to Thompson, 30 January 1893, Box 54, Jacket B, Folder 1 (L.M.S.) it was reported that the circulation of money had eased off, for there were not many Europeans going to the north.

122. C. O. 879/40, Africa (South), no. 461, pp. 209–226, Loch to Ripon, 133 of 12 March 1894. It is not clear how the figure of £1,100 was arrived at, for the men were reported to have been engaged for twenty-two days at the rate of one shilling each day, which should have amounted to £2,090.

123. Howard Williams to Thompson, 11 May 1900 (L.M.S.), in which he said cattle were selling at £25— £30 a herd; sheep and goats at £3 each. See J. Ellenberger, "The Bechuanaland Protectorate and the Anglo-Boer War, 1899–1902," *Rhodesiana* (Salisbury, Rhodesia: 1964), pp. 21–35.

124. See, for example, C. O. 879/78, *Africa (South)*, no. 702, pp. 439–40, 472, Milner to Chamberlain, 379 of 8 November 1902; Earl of Onslow to Milner, 398 of 11 December 1902, where Chief Sebele received £1,300 for the sale of timber.

125. See, for example, Ellenberger, "Boer War," p. 16, where Chief Bathoen is reported to have placed his dam at the disposal of Colonel Plumer's forces for two days at the rate of £25 a day.

126. See, for example, Lloyd to Thompson, 20 August 1909 (L.M.S.), where Kgama was reported to have received £1,728 for the service rendered by his subjects to British troops during the war.

127. Williams to Thompson, 11 May 1900 (L.M.S.).
128. Williams to Thompson, 11 May 1896, Box 53, Jacket A, Folder 2 (L.M.S.). *See also* Willoughby to Thompson, 28 June 1896; Williams to Thompson, 31 July 1896, Box 53, Jacket A, Folder 3 (L.M.S.).
129. Good to Cousins, 24 September 1897, Box 54, Jacket C, Folder 2 (L.M.S.), in which his report certainly exaggerated cattle losses because it claimed that all cattle had died.
130. Willoughby to Thompson, 29 June and 18 September 1896; Williams to Thompson, 15 May, 5 June, 26 June 1896, all in Box 53, Jacket A, Folder 2 (L.M.S.). *See also* C. Van Onselen, "Reactions to Rinderpest," p. 474.
131. Williams to Thompson, 31 July 1896, Box 53, Jacket A, Folder 3 (L.M.S.).
132. C. O. 879/52, African (South), no. 552, p. 112, Kgama to Milner 9 August 1897, enclosed in Milner to Chamberlain, 107 of 25 August 1897.
133. Ibid., p. 75, Bathoen to Ellenberger, 17 June 1897, enclosed in Milner to Chamberlain, 33 of 13 July 1897.
134. Lloyd to Cousins, 17 September 1897, Box 54, Jacket B, Folder 2 (L.M.S.). There were two relief committees, one set up by the L.M.S. in London, and another made up of L.M.S. agents and Protectorate officials in Bechuanaland.
135. Lloyd to Thompson, 22 September 1898, Box 55, Jacket B, Folder 2 (L.M.S.). Among the tribes that received rations were Rolong, Tlhaping, Tlharo, and some Kgalagadi who came from Lehututu.
136. Wookey to Thompson, 4 August 1898, Box 55, Jacket A, Folder 2 (L.M.S.), and Mary Partridge to Thompson, 8 September 1898, Box 55, Jacket B, Folder 2 (L.M.S.).
137. Wookey to Thompson, 29 December 1898, Box 55, Jacket D, Folder 2 (L.M.S.). *See also* Wookey to Thompson, 11 and 29 September, and 10 November 1898, Box 55, Jacket C, Folder 2 (L.M.S.). However, government and missionary reports are not clear if the same people received rations at the various times nor do they specify the time it took a recipient to consume a ration before he could come for the next ration.
138. C. O. 879/47, African (South), no. 517, p. 98, Chamberlain to Robinson, telegram, 16 April 1896.
139. Ibid., p. 147, Robinson to Chamberlain, 5 May 1896.
140. Ibid.
141. *See*, for example, Good in Kanye Report, 21 January 1898, Box 4 (L.M.S.), in which he reported that 1,500 people had died in Ngwaketseland the previous year.
142. C. O. 879/52, African (South), no 552, pp. 112, 118, Milner to Chamberlain, 107 and 113 of 25 and 27 August 1897.
143. *See* ibid., in which the De Beers Mining Company is reported to have shouldered half the cost of transporting timber and brushwood.
144. C. O. 879/52, African (South), p. 213, Milner to Chamberlain, 188 of 13 November 1897.
145. *See* "To Restock Bechuanaland," *The Bechuanaland News*, 23 September 1899.

More Aspects of Tswana Transformation 275

146. J. Falconer, "History of the Botswana Veterinary Services, 1905–66," *Botswana Notes and Records,* 3: 74.

147. Ibid. In August 1892 a Proclamation was issued to prevent the spread of a cattle disease called *foot and mouth, see* D. Ward, *Bechuanaland Protectorate Orders in Council and High Commissioner's Proclamations* (Cape Town: 1904), revised and brought up to date by Barry May, p. 29.

148. Annual Reports of Bechuanaland Protectorate, 57, 195, 190: 8–9. Government expenditure on veterinary services between 1901 and 1910 was as follows: 1901–2, £307; 1902–3, £398; 1903–4, £576; 1904–5, £98; 1905–6, £689; 1906–7, £721; 1907–8, £793; 1908–9, £1,039; 1910, £2,601; *see* Annual Reports, 73: 10; 53: 5; 68: 4; 57: 5; 57: 6–7; 64: 15.

149. Ellenberger, Notes on the Tawana, Willoughby Papers, Folder 796, no. 9 Ngami, Selly Oak Colleges; Tlou, "A Political History of Northwestern Botswana to 1906" (Ph.D. diss., University of Wisconsin, 1972, University Microfilms, Ann Arbor, Mich.), p. 235.

150. Thomas Tlou, p. 235; I. Schapera, *Migrant Labour and Tribal Life: A Study of Conditions in the Bechuanaland Protectorate* (London: 1947), p. 28.

151. Evidence of Kgama and Ellenberger, Minutes of S.A.N.A.C. 4: 251, 235.

152. Schapera, *Migrant Labour,* pp. 27–28, who also shows that over 1,000 herdsmen (all probably Sarwa) were employed by white farmers at Ghanzi. *See also* B.N.A., J. 978, S. 29/5/1, Paul Jousse to Assistant Commissioner at Francis Town, 13 March 1915, in which he said the Bechuanaland Trading Association stores employed 40 Africans.

153. Lloyd to Hawkins, 25 February and 17 August 1914, Box 76 (L.M.S.).

154. B.N.A., J. 978, S. 29/5/1, H. C. Sloley to Macgregor, 24 February 1916; and Bonar Law to High Commissioner, 14 February 1916.

155. C. O. 879/57, p. 195, Hamilton Goold-Adams to Milner, 4 October 1898, enclosed in Milner to Chamberlain, 111 of 27 March 1899.

156. A few of the recruits worked in Rhodesian mines and in Tati mines, *see* ibid., pp. 193–94, Proclamation of 15 March 1899; Schapera, *Migrant Labour,* pp. 26–27, 225, where he shows laborers from the Protectorate to the Witwatersrand to have been as follows: in 1902, 357; 1903, 2,730; 1904, 1,723; 1905, 2,944; 1906, 1,333; 1907, 299; 1908, 2,380; 1909, 1,538; 1910, 1,865. For earlier reference to Tati mines, *see* chapter 3.

157. C. O. 879/52, p. 117, Milner to Chamberlain, 113 of 27 August 1897.

158. Ellenberger, *Minutes of Evidence S.A.N.A.C.* 4: 245; C. O. 879/52 p. 117, where Tswana workers are reported to have earned about £2–£3 a month.

159. For a fuller study of this problem, *see* I. Schapera, *Migrant Labour and Tribal Life: A Study of Conditions in the Bechuanaland Protectorate* (London: 1947). *See also* "Labour Problems of Basutoland, Bechuanaland,

and Swaziland," *International Labour Review* 29, no. 3 (March 1934): 397–406.

160. See chapter 4.

161. See Ratshosa, "My Book," Rhodes House Library, p. 201, who says Kgama prevailed in spite of opposition from the tribe against the move; Kgama to Buxton, 28 March 1916, Box 79 (L.M.S.).

162. Kgama to Buxton, 28 March 1916, Box 79 (L.M.S.). Nevertheless, the chief paid, according to Ratshosa, several thousand herd of cattle to Garrett and Smith, see Ratshosa, "My Book", Rhodes House Library, p. 201; B.N.A., J. 978, S. 29/5/1, Garrett to Resident Commissioner, 29 February 1916, who said Kgama bought four houses for the use of his managers for £3,000. This suggests that Kgama was better off than an ordinary subject. See also B.N.A., no. J. 127. Kgama's will, 17 July 1907.

163. B.N.A., J. 978, S. 29/5/1, J. C. Macgregor to High Commissioner, 15 January 1916.

164. Correspondence on this issue is heavy; see, for example, B.N.A., J. 978, S. 29/5/1, R. M. Daniel to Government Secretary, Mafeking, 11 October 1913; Paul Jousse to Assistant Commissioner, 13 March 1915; E. Campbell to Panzera, 14 July 1915, 2 July 1915; Affidavit of A. H. Casalis, Manager of the Bechuanaland Trading Association stores, Serowe, 14 June 1915.

165. B.N.A., J. 978, S. 29/5/1, Herbert Sloley, Memorandum of decision of Sir Herbert Sloley, 10 December 1915; High Commissioner, 31 July 1916; E. C. F. Garraway to Kgama, 9 August 1916, Kgama to Buxton, 28 March 1916.

166. I prefer to use servitude in place of slavery, which most nineteenth-century observers used rather indiscriminately. However, Schulz was cautious: "When talking of slaves amongst natives, the term slave does not bear the same import as to the European mind . . . [the] position between master and slave is more one of relative domesticity than actual slavery," see A. Schulz and A. Hammar, *The New Africa* (London: 1897), p. 166. See also I. Schapera, *Tribal Innovators: Tswana Chiefs and Social Change* (L.S.E. Monographs on Social Anthropology, London, 1970), p. 83; G. B. Silverbauer and A. J. Kuper, "Kgalagari Masters and Bushmen Serfs: Some Observations," *African Studies* 25, no. 4 (1966): 171–72, who use serfdom instead of slavery.

167. Schapera, *Tribal Innovators*, p. 83.

168. *See*, "Organization of a Tribe," Willoughby Papers, Folder 761, Selly Oak Colleges Library.

169. London Missionary Society, *The Masarwa (Bushmen): Report of an Inquiry* (Tiger Kloof, South Africa: 1935), p. 4; I. W. Joyce, "Report on the Masarwa in the Bamangwato Reserve, Bechuanaland Protectorate, Geneva: *League of Nations Publications* 6, B, Slavery (C. 112, M. 98, 1938): 57–58.

170. Tlou, "A Political History," p. 154.

171. Schapera, *Tribal Innovators*, p. 89; "Chief's Taxes," Chief's Papers, Folder 798, Selly Oak Colleges Library.

172. Schapera, *Tribal Innovators*, p. 89; Schapera, *A Handbook*, pp. 251–52.
173. Lichtenstein, *Travels*, 2: 397.
174. Robert Moffat, *Apprenticeship at Kuruman*, ed. I. Schapera (London: 1951), p. 131. See also Samuel Broadbent, *A Narrative of the First Introduction of Christianity Amongst the Barolong Tribe of Bechuanas, South Africa* (London: 1865), p. 97. Yet Professor Monica Wilson says the Tswana did not sell human beings: see M. Wilson and L. M. Thompson, eds., *The Oxford History of South Africa*, vol. 1 (London: 1969), 1: 148.
175. W. C. Baldwin, *African Hunting and Adventure from Natal to the Zambezi including Lake Ngami, the Kalahari Desert. . . , From 1852–1860* (London: 1894), pp. 437–38. See also James Chapman, *Travels in the Interior of South Africa*, 2 vols. (London: 1868), 1: 51–52, where a child was offered for sale but he refused to buy it.
176. C. J. Andersson, "A Journey to Lake Ngami," *South African Commercial Advertiser and Cape Town Mail*, 22 May 1854; C. J. Andersson, *Lake Ngami: or, Exploration and Discoveries in the Wilds of South Western Africa* (London: 1856), p. 453; W. C. Oswell, "Extract of a Letter from W. C. Oswell dated 10 January 1850," *J.R.G.S.*, 20 (1851): 149; D. Livingstone, "Extract of a Letter from the Rev. D. Livingstone, 24 August 1850," *J.R.G.S.* (1851): 23; Andrew Geddes Bain, *Journals of Andrew Geddes Bain*, ed. M. H. Lister (Cape Town: The Van Riebeeck Society, no. 30, 1949), p. 136; R. G. Cumming, *The Lion Hunter of South Africa* (London: 1904), p. 197; John Mackenzie, *Day-dawn in Dark Places* (London: 1884), p. 63. The treatment included beating maiming, and death.
177. D. Livingston, *Livingstone's Missionary Correspondence, 1841–1856*, ed. I. Schapera (London: 1961), p. 37; D. Livingstone to MacLehose, 20 June 1843, National Library of Scotland, MS 656.
178. J. D. Hepburn, *Twenty Years*, pp. 85, 190–91.
179. Mackenzie, *Day-dawn*, pp. 58–59.
180. Hepburn to Thompson, December 1877, Box 1, (L.M.S.).
181. J. D. Hepburn, *Twenty Years*, p. 262; Wookey to Thompson, 3 December 1894, Box 51, Jacket C, Folder 2 (L.M.S.).
182. Wookey to Thompson, 3 February 1895, Box 52, Jacket A, Folder 1 (L.M.S.).
183. Mackenzie, *Day-dawn*, p. 59. See also Captain Harrel's Report, 27 April 1880, in Parliamentary Papers, 1883, C. 4194, 49: 13, who said the Sarwa "through the force of events, are gradually emerging from their thraldom, and getting in many instances compensation for their services, such as a share of the game they kill."
184. Schapera, *Tribal Innovators*, p. 89.
185. Kgama to Buxton, 28 March 1916 in Captain Patterson's Report of July 1878, enclosed in no. 78, Governor H. B. E. Frere to Sir Michael Beach, 14 September 1878, in Parliamentary Papers, C. 2220, 52: 235; "Chief Khama . . . does not permit them to be sold."
Folder 1 (L.M.S.).

186. Schapera, *Tribal Innovators*, pp. 46, 89–90.
187. Kgama to L. M. du Plessis, 11 March 1877, Bailie's Report, Parliamentary Papers, 1878–9, C. 2220, 52: 46.
188. C. O. 879/47, 119, Lloyd to Chamberlain, 7 April 1896.
189. Ibid., p. 140, Bathoen to Chamberlain, 3 April 1896.
190. Ibid., Goold-Adams to Graham Bower, 9 April 1896.
191. C. O. 879/52, Scholefield to Newton, 3 July 1897.
192. C. O. 879/57, p. 91, Goold-Adams to Ashburnham, 10 November 1898.
193. Ibid., p. 248, Goold-Adams to Milner, 12 April 1899. *See also* Wookey, Molepolole Report, 1900, Box 4 (L.M.S.), who observed that the treatment of "serfs, though better than it was years ago requires looking into."
194. A. E. Jennings, Report of a Visit to Lake Ngami District April to August, 1905, Box 4 (L.M.S.); "Inquisitor," "Khama, The King."

8
Conclusion

BY 1910 TSWANA CHIEFDOMS HAD HAD CONTINUOUS INTERcourse with Europeans for over sixty years. Although there were a little over 2,000 full members of the L.M.S. church in northern Bechuanaland out of a population of about 90,000,[1] the European impact upon the Tswana—in its social, economic, and political manifestations—was more profound than what the number of converts alone suggests. And in all chiefdoms a special feature of the outcome of interaction was diversity, a characteristic that was fostered as much by the different personalities of Tswana rulers as it was by the inhabitants of the respective chiefdoms.

In an attempt to convert persevering followers, L.M.S. missionaries introduced a system of education that interfered with traditional economic activities without offering the Tswana groups alternative ways of making a living. This created a lacuna that the L.M.S. belatedly tried to fill by introducing vocational education at the turn of the twentieth century. Yet viewed in the context of Tswana history, the introduction of vocational training was merely a restoration of a Tswana institution—in a European guise—that L.M.S. missionaries had put in abeyance, for the traditional initiation schools trained Tswana youths in the vital arts of warfare, homecraft, hunting, and farming.

Tswana intercourse with a variety of adventurers, missionaries, and Cape Colony government officials evinced a diplomatic expertise that proved invaluable during the last quarter of the nineteenth century. Armed with shrewd diplomacy, northern Tswana chiefs successfully used it as a weapon to ward off the more aggressive forms of European imperialism. Another manifestation of Tswana diplomacy was the advent of Ethiopianism. In this respect the less ascetic genre of Ethiopian, such as Mothowagae of Kanye, clearly used religious dissent to agitate for civil liberties that the new white rulers had circumscribed and that traditional authorities seemed unable to restore.

The advent of British rule was like a double-edged sword: it circumscribed Tswana autonomy as much as it guaranteed the chiefdoms some protection against their neighbors. In the changed circumstances, the Tswana could now afford to build their towns in places where water was more readily available; previously, military considerations compelled them to choose sites that were strategically safe from outside attacks, but were invariably far from water supplies.[2]

If it is difficult to measure with precision the degree of social change in any given community, there is little doubt that Tswana responses to European ideas were characterized by a delicate balance between the old and the new forces. The point that needs great emphasis is that the existence of two modes of life—one traditional and the other new—was conducive to tribal stability. Though by no means uniform in its manifestation, the balance ranged from Kwenaland, where the inhabitants could choose between Sechele (Christian) and his brother Kgosidintisi (traditionalist), to Ngwatoland, where Kgama's subjects were also able to choose between the old and the new in spite of the fact that the Chief and his next of kin were practicing Christians. This aspect of Tswana life was spelled out in 1897 when a missionary prodded Kgosidintsi to become a Christian. The archtraditionalist said:

> No, monare, I cannot allow it. I put no hindrance in the way of my children. As you know, most of my sons and some of my grandsons are members of the church. My wife attends the service regularly; but as for me, I shall die as I have lived, and God who knows my reasons, will judge me righteously.[3]

Finally, the two most effective agents of stability in northern Bechuanaland during the period under review were the institution of chiefship in general and Chief Kgama III in particular. In spite of colonial laws and imperious officers who undermined their power, Tswana chiefs retained a great deal of respect in the eyes of their subjects. This accounts for the clamor of support the chiefs commanded whenever they defied colonial officers in an attempt to restore some dignity to their office and chiefdoms. Above all, the pillar of stability was no doubt Chief Kgama III of the Ngwato. He endeared himself to a generation of traders, missionaries, and British government officials, who in turn regarded the Ngwato chief as an epitome of a progressive Christian ruler. This image of Kgama's was an asset to all northern Tswana chiefdoms, because it offset the more unguarded moves that his counterparts were apt to make in dealing with expanding white groups. Hence, when in 1895, Chiefs Kgama, Sebele, and Bathoen visited England to plead their country's case, the British public highlighted Kgama's ascetic character; temperance and philanthropic organizations actually equated the chiefs' campaign against annexation of Bechuanaland with a crusade for prohibition. And yet Sebele was not an abstainer, and both Sebele and Bathoen were known to defy British authority from time to time. The success of the 1895 mission can therefore be ascribed to Kgama's personality.

If Kgama was a successful diplomat, he was also a perceptive observer of Tswana life. When in 1900 a visitor noted that whites complained that the Ngwato were rather slow in absorbing European ideas, Kgama gave a terse reply that applied to all Tswana chiefdoms:

Ah! Monare; they see what we are; but they do not know what we were.[4]

NOTES FOR CONCLUSION

1. A. J. Haile, *Historical Survey of the London Missionary Society*, p. 29.
2. *See*, for example, C. O. 879/76, African (South), no. 694, p. 278, Kgama to Milner, 5 September 1901, in which he said he wanted to move his town to Serowe, adding: "Serowe is a place that cannot be easily defended against foes. . . . But now that there is only one King in South Africa, whether in Matebeleland or in the Transvaal, we have ceased to think of these things."
3. Williams, in *L.M.S. Chronical*, February 1897, p. 231.
4. W. C. Willoughby, "Decennial Review of Mission Work at Palapye," 1 January 1900, Box 3 (L.M.S.).

Genealogies of Chiefs in Four Tswana Chiefdoms, 1795-1925

KWENA	NGWAKETSE	NGWATO	TAWANA
Legwale (1795–1803)	Makaba II (1790–1824)	Kgama or Khama I (1795–1817)	Tawana (1795–1820)
(1803–05) Maleke	Segotshane (1824–45)	Kgari (1817–28)	Moremi II (1820–28)
Tshosa (1805–07)	Gaseitsiwe (1845–89)	Sedimo (1828–32)	Sedumedi (1828–30)
Motswasele II (1807–22)	Bathoen I (1889–1910)	Kgama or Khama II (1832–34)	Mogalakwe (1830–47)
Segokotlo (1822–29)	Seepapitso (1910–16)	Sekgoma I (1934–57)	Lecholathebe (1847–74)
Molese (1829–31)	Kgosimotse (1916–18)	Macheng (1857–58)	Meno (1875–76)
Sechele I (1831–92)	Malope (1918–19)	Sekgoma I (1858–66)	Moremi II (1876–90)
Sebele I (1892–1911)	Tshosa (1919–23)	Macheng (1866–72)	Dithapo (1890–91)
Sechele II (1911–18)	Gagoangwe (1923–24)	Kgama or Khama III (1872–73)	Sekgoma (1891–1906)
Sebele II (1918–31)	Ntebogang (1924–28)	Sekgoma I (1873–75)	Mathiba (1906–31)
		Kgama or Khama III (1875–1923)	
		Sekgoma II (1923–25)	

Bibliography

THE AFRICAN METHODIST EPISCOPAL CHURCH ARCHIVES, NEW YORK

The Archives have old copies of the Society's organ, *Voice of Missions*, which contain letters written by South African blacks.

ANNUAL REPORTS OF THE BECHUANALAND PROTECTORATE

1902–03; 1903–04; 1905	51 (LI) Cd. 2238–17
1904–05; 1906	73 (LXXIII) Cd. 2684–25
1905–06; 1907	53 (LIII) Cd. 3285–4
1906–07; 1908	68 (LXVIII) Cd. 3729–2
1907–08; 1909	62 (LXII) Cd. 4448–2
1908–09; 1909	62 (LXII) Cd. 4448–23
1909–10; 1910	64 (LXIV) Cd. 4964–26
1910–11; 1911	61 (LI) Cd. 5467–32

BOTSWANA NATIONAL ARCHIVES, GABORONE, BOTSWANA

Archival Series, No. 1331. S.42/3; No. J.1288. S.41/2; No. J.23. S.2/5; H.C. 5/12; No. 2384. S.178/1; H.C. 192/2; H.C. 6/38; No. T.1024. S.32/5. No. Serow 337. S.601/18, "Khama's Life," by Sekgoma Khama; No. 199. S.5/3; No. J. 127. S.4/1; No. 860. J. 860. S.25/8; No. 503. J.503. S.12/3; MS 1, Helmore: Letter and Journal, from A. J. Haile, Tiger Kloof, November 1946; J.978. S.29/5/1, Complaints by P. Jousse against Khama; 410. R.C.7/8, Church Dispute at Kanye; No. 715. R.C.10/11; S.1/2. H.C.48/1/2, No. 968/10.

BUTLER LIBRARY, COLUMBIA UNIVERSITY, NEW YORK

Correspondence of John Philip to the Society of Inquiry on Missions in the Theological Seminary, Princeton, New Jersey, 2 May 1833.

LONDON MISSIONARY SOCIETY ARCHIVES

Missionary Letters: Incoming, 1816–1926.
                       Annual Reports, 1866–1910.
Letters from the Directors: Outgoing, 1880–1910
Deputation Reports: R. Wardlaw Thompson, *Report of the Deputation to South Africa, Confidential, Printed for the use of Directors*, 4 September 1883 to 9 April 1884; August to October 1892; January to March 1898; F. H. Hawkins, *Report of the Deputation to South Africa, Confidential, November 1912 to March 1913*. Willoughby, W. C., "African Thought and Custom in Relation to Christianity," MS.
W. C. Willoughby, sundry papers.

METHODIST MISSIONARY SOCIETY, LONDON

Missionary Letters: Incoming, South Africa, 1868–1876
Box 18 (XVIII)
Transvaal, 1881–1886, 1886–1891
Clarkebury, 1881–1885
Wesleyan Missionary Society, Reports
Volume 22: 68, 1882–1884.
Volume 23: 72, 1886.
The Wesleyan Missionary Notices Relating Principally to the Foreign Missions under the Direction of the Methodist Conference, Fifth Series
Volume 7: for the year 1884.

THE NATIONAL LIBRARY OF SCOTLAND, EDINBURGH

David Livingstone Letters, MS 656, MS 7792.

PARLIAMENTARY PAPERS (BLUE BOOKS)

1878–9, 52 (LII), C. 2220, Correspondence relating to the mission of Alexander Bailie and Colonel Patterson to Bechuanaland, 1876–1878.

1883, 49 (XLIX), C. 4194, South Africa, Reports by Colonel Charles Warren, R.E.C.M.G., and Captain Harrel on the affairs of Bechuanaland, 3 April 1879, 27 April 1880.

1885, 1887, 72 (LXXII), C. 4194, C. 4588; 48 (XLVIII), C. 4839, 59 (LIX), C. 4890, C. 4956, further correspondence respecting the affairs of the Transvaal and adjacent territories.

1888, C. 5524, further correspondence respecting the affairs of Bechuanaland and adjacent territories.

1889, C. 9335, Correspondence respecting the African Liquor Traffic Convention signed at Brussels, 8 June 1899.

1892, 60 (LX), Report of the Assistant Commissioner for the Bechuanaland Protectorate for the period from 1 August 1890 to 31 March 1892; Annual Report of the Bechuanaland Border Police, 1891–92.

PUBLIC RECORD OFFICE, LONDON

Colonial Office, 417; Confidential Print, 879, 1885–1916.

RHODES HOUSE LIBRARY, OXFORD

Papers of the British Foreign Anti-Slavery Society and of the Aborigines Protection Society; Mackenzie Papers, on microfilm, Reels 1–6; Poisoning of Africa Papers; Manuscripts, Cecil J. Rhodes, [C. J. R.]; MS Afr. S. 1198 (3), Simon Ratshosa, "My Book on Bechuanaland Protectorate Native Custom, etc."

ROYAL COMMONWEALTH SOCIETY, LONDON

Reports of the Chief Native Commissioner, Southern Rhodesia, 1900–1912.

SELLY OAK COLLEGES LIBRARY, BIRMINGHAM, ENGLAND

Willoughby Papers in Folders: 274, 285, 317, 327, 354, 361, 374, 376, 457, 705, 715, 731, 743, 756, 761, 765, 767, 770, 775, 776, 778, 779, 783, 795, 796, 798, 804, 807, and 813; "With the Concessions Commission," MS (1893).

PERIODICALS AND NEWSPAPERS

Africa, London.
Africana Notes and News, Johannesburg.
African-Pamphlets, Rhodes House, (1884–1895).
The American Journal of International Law, Washington, D.C.
The Bechuanaland News and Vryburg, Mafeking, and Malmani Chronicle, Vryburg, South Africa.
Botswana Notes and Records, Gaborone, Botswana.
The Cape Argus, Cape Town.
Cape Monthly Magazine, Cape Town.
The Diamond Field Advertiser, Kimberley, South Africa.
The Diamond Field News, Kimberley, South Africa.

The Free Church of Scotland Monthly, Edinburgh.
International Review of Missions, London.
International Labour Review, Geneva.
Journal of African History, London.
Journal of the Royal Anthropological Institute, London.
Journal of the Royal Geographical Society, London.
Koranta Ea Becoana, Mafeking, South Africa, cuttings in Botswana National Archives, Gaborone, Botswana.
Kutlwana, Gaborone, Botswana.
The League Journal, Glasgow.
Michigan Law Review, Ann Arbor, Michigan.
The Pall Mall Gazette, London.
Rhodesiana, Salisbury, Rhodesia.
The South African Commercial Advertiser and Cape Town Mail, Cape Town.
The South African Outlook, Alice, South Africa.
The Sunday Times, Johannesburg.
The Sunday Times Magazine, London.
Voice of Missions, New York.

THESES

Chiepe, Gladys. "An Investigation of the Problems of Popular Education in the Bechuanaland Protectorate." Master's thesis, University of Bristol, 1957.

Coan, J. R. "The Expansion of Missions of the African Methodist Episcopal Church in South Africa, 1896–1908." Ph.D. dissertation, Hartford Seminary Foundation, 1961, University Microfilm, Ann Arbor, Michigan.

Dachs, A. J. "Missionary Imperialism in Bechuanaland, 1813–1896." Ph.D. dissertation, Cambridge University, 1968.

Legassick, M. "The Griqua, The Sotho-Tswana, and the Missionaries, 1780–1840: The Politics of a Frontier Zone." Ph.D. dissertation University of California at Los Angeles, 1969, University Microfilm, Ann Arbor, Michigan.

MacRae, D. M. "The Bechuanaland Protectorate, Its People and Prevalent Diseases." Doctor of Medicine thesis, Glasgow University, 1920.

Northcott, C. W. "The Life and Work of Robert Moffat, 1817–1870." Ph.D. thesis, University of London, 1962.

Parsons, Neil Q. "The Visit of the Chiefs to England." A dissertation for the Diploma in African Studies, University of Edinburgh, 1967.

Tlou, Thomas. "A Political History of Northwestern Botswana to 1906." Ph.D. dissertation, University of Wisconsin, 1972, University Microfilms, Ann Arbor, Michigan.

OTHER UNPUBLISHED WORKS

Atmore, Anthony. "Notes on Firearms Among the Tswana and Ndebele." African History Seminar paper, 22 January 1969, Institute of Commonwealth Studies, University of London.

Chirenje, J. M. "A Survey of the Acquisition and Role of Firearms in the History of the Tswana, 1801–1885." African History Seminar paper, Institute of Commonwealth Studies, University of London, 27 November 1968, 22 January 1969.

Haile, A. E., of Sussex, England, letter communication, 12 December 1968.

Hole, Hugh Marshall, Letter to David Chamberlain, managing editor of the *L.M.S. Chronicle*, 28 October 1932, kept in Hole's book, *The Passing of the Black Kings* (London: 1932), L.M.S. Archives.

Mudenge, S. I. "The Role of Firearms in South Central Africa in the 19th Century." African History Seminar paper, Institute of Commonwealth Studies, University of London, 22 January 1969.

Parsons, N. Q. "Independency and Ethiopianism Among the Tswana in the Late 19th and Early 20th Centuries." Seminar paper, "The Societies of Southern Africa in the 19th and 20th Centuries," Institute of Commonwealth Studies, 29 January 1970.

Schapera, I. "Uniformity and Variation in Chief-made Law: Tswana Case Study." Burg Wartenstein Symposium 1966 (copy kindly supplied by the author).

Syson, (Mrs. Lucy). Research Assistant, Surveys and Training for

Bibliography

Development of Water Resources and Agricultural Production, Botswana, letter communication, 10 October 1969.

PUBLISHED WORKS

Agar-Hamilton, J. A. I. *The Road to the North, South Africa: 1852–1886.* London: 1937.

Anderson, C. J. *Lake Ngami: or Exploration and Discoveries in the Wilds of South Western Africa.* London: 1856.

———. *Notes of Travel in South Africa.* Edited by J. Lloyd. London: 1875.

———. *The Okavango River, A Narrative of Travel Exploration and Adventure.* London: 1861.

Arbousset, T. *Narrative of an Exploration.* London: 1846.

Arnot, Frederick A. *From Natal to the Upper Zambezi.* London: 1883.

Ayandele, A. *The Missionary Impact on Modern Nigeria, 1842–1914.* London: 1966.

Backhouse, James. *A Narrative of a Visit to the Mauritius and South Africa.* London: 1844.

Baeta, C. G., ed. *Christianity in Tropical Africa.* London: 1968.

Bain, Andrew Geddes. *Journals of Andrew Geddes Bain.* Edited by M. H. Lister. Cape Town: The Van Riebeeck Society, no. 30, 1949.

Baines, Thomas, *Exploration in South West Africa: Being an Account of a Journey in the Years 1861 and 1862 from Walvish Bay on the Western Coast to Lake Ngami and the Victoria Falls.* London: 1864. *Journal of Residence in Africa, 1842–53.* Edited by R. F. Kennedy. Cape Town: 1964.

———. *The Northern Goldfield Diaries of Thomas Baines.* 2 vols. Edited by J. P. R. Wallis, London: 1946.

Baldwin, W. C. *African Hunting and Adventure from Natal to the Zambezi including Lake Ngami, the Kalahari Desert . . . From 1852–1860.* London: 1894.

Barrow, John. *A Voyage to Cochinchina in the Years 1792–1793 to which Is Appended an Account of a Journey to the*

Residence of the Chief of the Booshuana Nation. London: 1806.
Benedict, Ruth. *Patterns of Culture.* London: 1935. Reprinted 1966.
Berry, L. L. *A Century of Missions of the A. M. E. Church, 1840–1940.* New York: 1940.
Blackburn, A. E. *The International Convention Relating to the Liquor Traffic in Africa, Report.* London: 1921.
———. *Khama, King of the Bamangwato.* London: 1926.
Borcherds, P. B. *An Autobiographical Memoir.* Cape Town: 1861.
Brink, C. F. *The Journal of C. F. Brink.* Edited by E. E. Mossop. Cape Town: The Van Riebeeck Society, no. 28, 1947.
Broadbent, Samuel. *A Narrative of the First Introduction of Christianity Amongst the Barolong Tribe of Bechuanas, South Africa.* London: 1865.
Brown, John. *Secwana Dictionary.* London: 1895.
Brown, J. Tom. *Among the Bantu Nomads, A Record of Forty Years Spent Among the Bechuana.* London: 1926.
———. *The Apostle of the Marshes: The Story of Shomolekae.* London: 1925.
Bryden, H. A. *Gun and Camera in Southern Africa: A Year of Wanderings in Bechuanaland, the Kalahari Desert, and the Lake River Country.* London: 1893.
———. *How to Buy a Gun.* London: 1903.
Burchell, W. J. *Travels in the Interior of South Africa.* 2 vols. Edited by I. Schapera. London: 1822, 1824.
Cairns, H. Alan C. *Prelude to Imperialism, British Reactions to Central African Society, 1840–1890.* London: 1965.
The Cambridge History of the British Empire. Cambridge, England: 1963.
Campbell, John. *Journal of Travels in South Africa: Among the Hottentots and Other Tribes in 1812, 1813, 1814.* 2 vols. London: 1815.
———. *A Journey to Lattakoo in South Africa.* London: 1835.
———. *Life of Kaboo, a Wild Bushman by Himself.* London: 1830.
———. *Travels in South Africa Undertaken at the Request of the Missionary Society.* London: 1815.

Bibliography 293

———. *Travels in South Africa Undertaken at the Request of the Missionary Society.* 2 vols. Edinburgh: 1822.

Carnegie, David. *Among the Matebele.* London: 1894.

Chalmers, John A. *Soga, Tiyo: A Page of South African Mission Work.* Edinburgh: 1878.

Chapman, James. *Travels in the Interior of South Africa.* 2 vols. London: 1868.

Coillard, Francis. *On the Threshold of Central Africa; A Record of Twenty Years Among the Barotse of Upper Zambezi.* London: 1897.

Cooper-Chadwick, J. *Three Years with Lobengula and Experiences in South Africa.* London: 1894.

Cumming, R. G. *The Lion Hunter of South Africa.* London: 1904.

Curtis, S. J. *History of Education in Great Britain.* London: 1967.

Dean, H. (with North, S.) *Umbala.* London: 1929.

DeKiewiet, C. W. *A History of South Africa: Social and Economic,* Oxford: 1941. Reprinted, 1964.

Dolman, Alfred. *In the Footsteps of Livingston: Being the Diaries and Travel Notes Made by Alfred Dolman.* Edited by J. Irving. London: 1924.

du Plessis, J. A. *History of Christian Missions in South Africa.* Edinburgh: 1911.

Ellenberger, D. *History of the Basuto; Ancient and Modern.* Translated by J. C. Macgregor. London: 1912.

Fox-Bourne, H. R., ed. et al. *The South African Natives: Their Progress and Present Condition.* London: 1908.

Freeman, J. J. *A Tour in South Africa.* London: 1851.

Gabatshwane, S. M. *Introduction to the Bechuanaland Protectorate: History and Administration.* Morija, Lesotho: 1957.

Galton, Francis. *Narrative of an Explorer in Tropical South Africa.* London: 1853. 2d ed., 1889.

Gelfand, M. *Gubulawayo and Beyond: Letters and Journals of the Early Jesuit Missionaries to Zambezia.* London: 1968.

Gillmore, Parker. *The Great Thirstland: A Ride Through Natal, Orange Free State, Transvaal, and Kalahari Desert.* London: 1878.

Goodall, Norman. *A History of the London Missionary Society, 1895–1945.* London: 1954.

Haccius, Georg, ed. *Hannoversche Missionsgeschichte Insbesondere die Geschichte der Hermannsburger Mission.* Hermannsburg: 1910.

Haile, A. J. *A Brief Historical Survey of the London Missionary Society in Southern Africa.* London: 1951.

Harris, John C. *Khama, The Great African Chief.* London: 1922.

Harris, William C. *Narrative of an Expedition into Southern Africa, During the Years 1836 and 1837 from the Cape of Good Hope Through the Territories of the Chief Moselikatse, to the Tropic of Capricorn.* Bombay: 1838.

Hepburn, Elizabeth. *Jottings.* London: 1928.

Hepburn, J. D. *Twenty Years in Khama's Country.* Edited by C. Lyall. London: 1895.

Holden, W. C., ed. *History of the Colony of Natal, South Africa.* London: 1855.

Hole, H. M. *The Passing of the Black Kings.* London: 1932.

Holub, Emil. *Seven Years in South Africa: Travels, Researches, and Hunting Adventures, Between the Diamond Fields and the Zambezi, 1872–79.* 2 vols. Translated by Ellen E. Frewer. London: 1881.

Inglis, W. *Memoirs and Remains of the Rev. Walter Inglis, African Missionary and Canadian Pastor.* Edited by William Cochrane. Toronto: 1887.

Jaarsveld, F. A. Van. *The Afrikaaner's Interpretation of South African History.* Cape Town: 1964.

Jacottet, E. *The Native Churches and Their Organization.* Morija, Lesotho: 1905.

Jennings, A. F. *Bogadi: A Study of the Marriage Laws and Customs of the Bechuana Tribes of South Africa.* Tiger Kloof, South Africa: 1931.

Johnston, James. *Reality Versus Romance in Central Africa.* London: 1893.

Juta, H. C. *The Laws of the Bechuanaland Protectorate.* 3 vols. London: 1949.

Kerr, Walter M. *The Far Interior: A Narrative of Travel and Adventure from the Cape of Good Hope Across the Zambezi to the Lake Region of Central Africa.* 2 vols. London: 1886.

Kircherer, J. J. *Narrative of Mission to Hottentots.* London: 1806.

Bibliography

Knight-Bruce, Wyndham. *The Story of an African Chief: Being the Life of Khama.* London: 1893.
Leask, Thomas. *The Southern African Diaries of Thomas Leask, 1865–1870.* Edited by J. P. R. Wallis. London: 1954.
Leyds, W. J. *The Transvaal Surrounded.* London: 1919.
Leyland, J. *Adventures in the Far Interior of South Africa.* London: 1866.
Levaillant, Francois. *Travels into Interior Parts of Africa, by the Cape of Good Hope; in the Years 1780, 1781, 1783, 1784, and 1785.* 2 vols. Perth: 1796.
Lichtenstein, Henry. *Travels in Southern Africa in the Years 1803, 1804, 1805, and 1806.* 2 vols. Translated by Anne Plumptre. London: 1815.
Livingstone, David. *Family Letters, 1841–56.* 2 vols. Edited by I. Schapera. London: 1959.
———. *Livingstone's Missionary Correspondence, 1841–56.* Edited by I. Schapera. London: 1961.
———. *Missionary Travels and Researches in South Africa.* London: 1857.
———. *Private Journals, 1851–1853.* Edited by I. Schapera. London: 1960.
Lloyd, E. *Three Great African Chiefs.* London: 1895.
London Missionary Society. *The Masarwa (Bushmen): Report of an Inquiry.* Tiger Kloof, South Africa: 1935.
Long, Una, ed. *The Journals of Elizabeth Lees Price.* London: 1956.
Lovett, Richard. *The History of the London Missionary Society.* London: 1899.
Lutz, Jessie G., ed. *Christian Missions in China: Evangelists of What?* Lexington, Massachusetts: 1965.
Mackenzie, John. *Austral Africa, Losing It or Gaining It.* 2 vols. London: 1886.
———. *Day-dawn in Dark Places: A Story of Wanderings and Work in Bechuanaland.* London: 1884.
———. *Ten Years North of the Orange River.* Edinburgh: 1871.
Mackenzie, W. D. *John Mackenzie: South African Missionary and Statesman.* London: 1902.
Methuen, H. *Life in the Wilderness or Wanderings in Southern Africa.* London: 1846.

Mockford, Julian. *Khama: King of the Bamangwato.* London: 1931.
Moffat, J. S. *The Lives of Robert and Mary Moffat.* London: 1886.
Moffat, Robert. *Apprenticeship at Kuruman, 1820–1928.* Edited by I. Schapera. London: 1951.
———. *The Matebele Journals of Robert Moffat, 1829–1860.* 2 vols. Edited by J. P. R. Wallis. London: 1945.
———. *Missionary Labours and Scenes in South Africa.* London: 1843. New York: 1850.
Moffat, Robert U. *John Smith Moffat Missionary, C.M.O.: A Memoir.* London: 1921. Reprint ed. New York: 1969.
Mohr, Edward. *To the Victoria Falls of the Zambezi.* London: 1876.
Molema, S. M. *The Bantu, Past and Present.* Edinburgh: 1920.
———. *Montshiwa, Barolong Chief and Patriot.* Cape Town: 1966.
Musgrave, P. W. *Society and Education in England Since 1800.* London: 1968.
Northcott, Cecil. *Robert Moffat: Pioneer in Africa, 1817–1870.* London: 1961.
Oliver, R. *The Missionary Factor in East Africa.* London: 1965.
Omer-Cooper, J. D. *The Zulu Aftermath.* London: 1966.
Oswell, W. E. *William Cotton Oswell.* 2 vols. London: 1900.
Pauw, B. A. *Religion in a Tswana Chiefdom.* London: 1960.
Philip, John. *Researches in South Africa.* 2 vols. London: 1828.
Phillips-Wooley, C., ed. *Big-game Shooting.* London: 1894.
Pinto, Serpa. *How I Crossed Africa.* 2 vols. Translated by A. Elwes. Philadelphia: 1881.
Preller, Gustav S. *Day-dawn in South Africa.* Pretoria: 1938.
Plaatje, Solomon T. *Mhudi.* Lovedale, South Africa: 1930.
———. *Sechuana Proverbs with Literal Translations and Their Suropean Equivalents.* London: 1916.
Rotberg, Robert I. *Christian Missionaries and the Creation of Northern Rhodesia, 1880–1924.* Princeton, New Jersey: 1965.
Roux, E. *Time Longer than Rope.* London: 1948. Reprinted, Madison, Wisconsin: 1966.
Sargant, E. B. *No. 52, Report on Native Education in South*

Africa, Part III, Education in the Protectorates. Headley, Surrey, England: 1908.

Schapera, I., ed. *Ditirafalo tsa Merafe ya Batswana ba Lefatshe la Tshireletso*. Alice, South Africa: 1940.

——. *The Ethnic Composition of Tswana Tribes*. L.S.E. Monographs on Social Anthropology, no. 11. London: 1952.

——. *Government and Politics in Tribal Societies*. London: 1956.

——. *A Handbook of Tswana Law and Custom*. London: 1938. Reprinted 1955, 1970.

——. *Married Life in an African Tribe*. London: 1940.

——. *Migrant Labour and Tribal Life: A Study of Conditions in the Bechuanaland Protectorate*. London: 1947.

——. *Native Land Tenure in the Bechuanaland Protectorate*. Alice, South Africa: 1943.

——, with Van der Merwe, D. F. *Notes on the Tribal Groupings, History, and Customs of the Kgalagadi*. Communications from the School of African Studies. Series no. 13, University of Cape Town, 1945.

——. *The Political Annals of a Tswana Tribe: Minutes of Ngwaketse Public Assemblies, 1910–1917*. Communications from the School of African Studies, University of Cape Town, 1947.

——, ed. *Praise-poems of Tswana Chiefs*. Oxford: 1965.

——. *A Short History of the Bakgatla-baga Kgafela of Bechuanaland Protectorate*. Communications from the School of African Studies, University of Cape Town, 1942.

——. *Tribal Innovators: Tswana Chiefs and Social Change, 1795–1940*. L.S.E. Monographs on Social Anthropology, no. 43. London: 1970.

——. *Tribal Legislation among the Tswana of the Bechuanaland Protectorate*. L.S.E. Monographs on Social Anthropology, no. 9. London: 1943.

——. *The Tswana*. London: 1952.

Schulz, A., and Hammar, A. *The New Africa*. London: 1897.

Selous, F. C. *A Hunter's Wanderings in Africa*. London: 1881.

Shepherd, Peter M. *Molepolole: A Missionary Record*. Glasgow: 1947.

Sillery, A. *The Bechuanaland Protectorate.* Cape Town: 1952.
———. *Founding a Protectorate.* The Hague: 1965.
———. *Sechele.* London: 1954.
———. *John Mackenzie of Bechuanaland, 1835–1899.* Cape Town: A. A. Balkema, 1971.
Smith, Andrew. *The Diary of Doctor Andrew Smith, Director of the Expedition for Exploring Central Africa, 1834–36.* Edited by P. R. Kirby. Cape Town: The Van Riebeeck Society, 1939.
Smith, E. W. *Great Lion of Bechuanaland: The Life and Times of Roger Price.* London: 1957.
Smith, Thornley, ed. *Memoir of the Rev. Thomas Laidman Hodgson, Wesleyan Missionary in South Africa.* London: 1854.
———. *South Africa Delineated, or, Sketches, Historical and Descriptive of Its Tribes and Missions, and of the British Colonies of the Cape and Port Natal.* London: 1850.
South Africa: Report of the South African Native Affairs Commission. Lv. Cd. 2399. Cape Town: 1905.
South African Native Affairs Commission, 1903–5, Minutes of Evidence Taken in the Cape Colony. No. 4. Cape Town: 1904.
Sparrman, Andrew. *A Voyage to the Cape of Good Hope Towards the Antarctic Polar Circle, and Around the World ... From the Year 1772 to 1776.* 2 vols. London: 1786.
Steedman, A. *Wanderings and Adventures in Southern Africa.* 2 vols. London: 1835.
Stewart, James. *Lovedale Past and Present.* Cape Town: 1879.
Stow, George. *The Native Races of South Africa.* Edited by G. M. Theal. London: 1905.
Sundkler, Bengt. G. M. *Bantu Prophets in South Africa.* London: 1948.
Thomas, T. M. *Eleven Years in Central Africa.* London: 1872.
Thompson, George. *Travels and Adventures in Southern Africa.* London: 1827.
Thompson, L. M., ed. *African Societies in Southern Africa.* London: 1969.
Tabler, Edward G., ed. *The Far Interior.* London: 1955.
———., ed. *Zambezia and Matabeleland in the Seventies.* London: 1960.

Taylor, J. D., ed. *Christianity and the Natives of South Africa.* Lovedale, South Africa: 1925.
Vedder, H., ed. *The Native Tribes of South West Africa.* London: 1928.
Walker, E. A. *The Frontier Tradition in South Africa.* Oxford: 1930.
———. *The Great Trek.* 4th ed. London: 1960.
———. *A History of Southern Africa.* London: 1965.
Wallis, J. P. R., ed. *The Matebele Mission: A Selection from the Correspondence of John and Emily Moffat, David Livingstone, and Others.* London: 1945.
Ward, D. *Bechuanaland Protectorate Orders in Council and High Commissioner's Proclamations.* Revised by Barry May. Cape Town: 1904.
Wikar Jacob, ed. *The Journal of Hendrik Jacob Wikar (1779), With an English Translation by A. W. Van Der Horst, and the Journals of Jacobus Coetze Jansz (1760) and William van Ronen (1791), with an English Translation by Dr. E. E. Mossop.* Cape Town: The Van Riebeeck Society, 1935.
Williams, Ralph. *How I Became a Governor.* London: 1913.
Willoughby, W. C. *Native Life on the Transvaal Border.* London: 1900.
———. *Nature Worship and Taboo.* Hartford: 1932.
———. *Race Problems in the New Africa.* London: 1923.
———. *The Soul of the Bantu.* London: 1928.
Wilson, M., and Thompson, L. M., eds. *The Oxford History of South Africa.* Vol. 1. London: 1969.
Wright, R. R., et al. *The Encyclopedia of the African Methodist Episcopal Church.* Philadelphia: 1947.

ARTICLES

Anonymous. "Another Version: The Trouble in the Northern Protectorate . . . The Story of Sekgoma's Arrest." *Diamond Field Advertiser,* 10 August 1910.
Anonymous. "The Ngamiland Mission, 1906." *Diamond Field Advertiser Christmas Number,* 1906.

Anderson, C. J. "A Journey to Lake Ngami." *South African Commercial Advertiser and Cape Town Mail*, 22 May 1854.

Atmore, Anthony, et al. "Firearms in South Central Africa." *Journal of African History* 12, no. 4 (1971): 545–56.

Atmore, W. "Irrigation—What Hinders It?" *Cape Monthly Magazine* 2, no. 9 (September 1857): 129–37.

"Bangwaketze." *Koronta ea Becoana*, 2 December 1903.

Bent, Theodore. "Among the Chiefs of Bechuanaland." *British Museum Pamphlets* 121 (1892).

"The Beer Question: Kaffir Beer as a National Food and Beverage of the African." *The South African Outlook*, 1 November 1941.

"Beer Drinking at Palapye." *The Bechuanaland News*, 11 January 1896.

"To Bite the Year, A Native Ceremony." *The Bechuanaland News*, 25 July 1896.

Brown, John. "The Bechwana Tribes." *Cape Monthly Magazine* 11 (July 1875): 1–5.

Brown, J. Tom. "Circumcision Rites of the Becwana Tribes." *Journal of the Royal Anthropological Institute* 51 (1921): 419–27.

Brown, Richard. "External Relations of the Ndebele Kingdom." In *African Societies in Southern Africa*. Edited by L. M. Thompson. London: 1969, pp. 259–81.

Chirenje, J. M. "Chief Sekgoma Letsholathebe II: Rebel or 20th-Century Tswana Nationalist?" *Botswana Notes and Records* 3 (1971): 64–69.

———. "Portuguese Priests and Soldiers in Zimbabwe, 1560–1572: The Interplay Between Evangelism and Trade." *The International Journal of African Historical Studies* 6, no. 1 (1973): 36–48.

Edwards, R. "Traditions of the Bayeye." *Folklore Journal* 2 (1888).

Elbe, J. Von. "The Evolution of the Concept of the Just War in International Law." *American Journal of International Law* 33 (1939): 665–68.

Ellenberger, J. "The Bechuanaland Protectorate and the Anglo-Boer War, 1899–1902." *Rhodesiana* (1964), pp. 10–35.

Ellenberger, V. F. "History of the Batlokwa of Gaberones." *Bantu Studies* 13 (1939): 165–98.

Falconer, J. "History of the Botswana Veterinary Services, 1905–1966." *Botswana Notes and Records* 3 (1971): 74–78.

Fox-Bourne, H. R. "The Regulation of the Liquor Traffic in Africa." Paper read at the Seventeenth Conference of the Association for the Reform and Codification of the Law of Nations, October 1895, Brussels.

Galton, F. "Recent Expedition into the Interior of South Western Africa." 23 February and 26 April 1852, *Journal of the Geographical Society* 22 (1952): 140–63.

Green, F. G. "Narrative of a Journey to Ovamboland." *Cape Monthly Magazine* 1 (January 1857).

Hall, H. "Notes on Animal Life in South Africa." *Cape Monthly Magazine* 1 (January 1857): 6.

Henrici, M. "Growth of Veld Plants Under Arid Conditions of Bechuanaland." *South African Journal of Science* 23 (1926): 325–39.

How, Marion. "An Alibi for Mantatisi." *African Studies* 13 (1954): 65–76.

Holub, E. "On the Central South African Tribes from the South Coast to the Zambezi." *Journal of the Royal Anthropological Institute* 5 (1884): 1–16.

"Inquisitor" [pseudo]. "Khama, the King. Truth about the Bechuanas." *Central News Agency*, Johannesburg, 1914, being a compilation of articles that appeared in *The Sunday Times* (Johannesburg) on 4 January, 8 February, 15 February, 1 March and 22 March 1914.

Jackson, Brian. "100 Years of State Schools." *The Sunday Times Magazine* (London), 4 January 1970.

Jackson, Sonia. "The Long Haul." *The Sunday Times Magazine* (London), 4 January 1970.

Johnson, J., et al. "Khama and Drink Traffic." *The League Journal*, 9 October 1880.

Joyce, I. W. "Report on the Masarwa in the Bamangwato Reserve, Bechuanaland Protectorate." *General: League of Nations Publications* (vi.B.Slavery, c.112, M.98) 1938. Annexe b, pp. 57–76.

Kamokate, Chief. "Notes on the Khurutshe." *Botswana Notes and Records* 2 (1970): 14.
"Khama and His People." *The Bechuanaland News*, 6 July 1895.
"Khama Interviewed." *The Bechuanaland News*, 24 October 1895.
"Khane ea Bangwato." *Koronta ea Becoana*, 25 November 1903.
Knightley, Phillip. "Circumcision: The Blunted Knife." *The Sunday Times* (London), 5 July 1970.
"Labour Problems of Basutoland, Bechuanaland, and Swaziland." *International Labour Review* 3 (March 1934): 397–406.
Larson, T. J. "The Political Structure of the Ngamiland Mbukushu Under the Rule of the Tawana." *Anthropos* 60 (1965): 164–76.
Lea, A. "Native Separatist Churches." In *Christianity and the Natives of South Africa, a Yearbook of South African Mission.* Edited by J. D. Taylor. Lovedale, South Africa: 1928.
Legassick, Martin. "The Sotho-Tswana Peoples Before 1800." In *African Societies in Southern Africa.* Edited by L.M. Thompson. London: 1969.
Lerrigo, P. H. J. "The Prophet Movement in the Congo." *International Review of Missions,* April 1922, pp. 270–77.
"Liquor and Native Labour," *The Bechuanaland News*, 6 February 1895.
"Liquor Problems and Legislation." *The Bechuanaland News.* 16 December 1893.
Livingstone, D. "Extract of Letter from the Rev. D. Livingstone, 24 August 1850." *Journal of the Royal Geographical Society* 21 (1851): 18–24.
Loram, C. T. "The Separatist Church Movement." *International Review of Missions,* July 1926, pp. 476–82.
Lye, W. F. "The Difaqane: The Mfecane in Southern Sotho Area, 1822–24." *Journal of African History* 8, no. 1 (1967): 124–26.
———. "The Distribution of the Sotho People After the Difaqane." In *African Societies in Southern Africa.* Edited by L. M. Thompson. London: 1969.
MacCabe, Joseph. "The Great Lake Ngami." In *History of the Colony of Natal, South Africa.* Edited by W. C. Holden. London: 1855, pp. 413–35.

Bibliography

Mackenzie, John. "Bechuanaland and the Land of Ophir." Paper read to the British Association at Bath, September 1888, in British Museum, London.

Miers, Sue. "Notes on the Arms Trade and Government Policy in Southern Africa Between 1870–1890." *Journal of African History* 12, no. 4 (1971).

Mzimba, L. N. "The African Church." in *Christianity and the Native of South Africa.* Edited by J. D. Taylor. Lovedale, South Africa: 1928, pp. 86–95.

Nettleton, G. E. "History of the Ngamiland Tribes Up to 1926." *Bantu Studies* 8 (1934): 343–60.

"Notes from Palapye." *The Bechuanaland News,* 16 November 1895.

Nussbaum, A. "Just War—A Legal Concept?" *Michigan Law Review* 42 (1943–44): 453–79.

Onselen, C. Van. "Reactions to Rinderpest in Southern Africa, 1896–97." Journal of African History 13, no. 3 (1972): 473–88.

Oswell, W. C. "Extract of a Letter from W. C. Oswell Dated 10 January 1850." *Journal of the Royal Geographical Society* 20 (1951): 143–51.

———. "South Africa Fifty Years Ago." In *Big-game Shooting.* Edited by C. Phillips-Wooley. Vol. 1. London: 1894.

Parsons, N. Q. "Khama, Not Missionaries Initiated Trip for Negotiations." *Kutwano,* February 1972.

———. "The Image of Khama the Great—1868–1970." *Botswana Notes and Records,* 3 (1971): 41–58.

Pauw, B. A. "Some Change in the Social Structure of the Thlaping of the Taung Reserve." *African Studies* 19, no. 2 (1960): 49–76.

Ramoshoana, D. M. "The Origin of Secwana." *Bantu Studies* 3, no. 2 (1928): 197–98.

Ranger, T. "The Early History of Independency in Southern Rhodesia." *Religion in Africa,* Center of African Studies, University of Edinburgh (Edinburgh: 1964), pp. 52–74.

———. "The 'Ethiopian' Episode in Barotseland, 1900–1905." *The Rhodes-Livingstone Journal* 37 (June 1965): 26–41.

"Tragedy in the Kalahari." *The Bechuanaland News,* 4 February 1899.

"To Restock Bechuanaland." *The Bechuanaland News,* 23 September 1899.

Saunders, C. C. "Tile and the Thembu Church." *Journal of African History* 11, no. 4 (1970): 553–70.

Schapera, I. "Christianity and the Tswana." *The Journal of the Royal Anthropological Institute of Great Britain and Ireland* 88, no. 1 (January–June 1958): 1–9.

———. "Contract in Tswana Case Law." *Journal of African Law* 9 (1965): 142–53.

———. "Kinship and Politics in Tswana History." *The Journal of the Royal Anthropological Institute of Great Britain and Ireland* 93, no. 2 (July–December 1963): 159–73.

———. "Livingstone and the Boers." *African Affairs* 59, no. 235 (1960): 144–56.

———. "Notes on the History of the Kaa." *African Studies* 4, no. 3 (September 1945): 109–20.

———. "The Political Organization of the Ngwato of Bechuanaland Protectorate." In *African Political Systems.* Edited by M. Fortes and E. E. Evans Pritchard. London: 1940.

———. "Report and Recommendations Submitted to the Bechuanaland Protectorate Administration on the Native Land Problem in the Tati District, 1943." *Botswana Notes and Records* 3 (1971): 219–68.

———. "A Short History of the Bangwaketse." *African Studies* 1 (1942): 1–39.

———. "The Social Structure of the Tswana Ward." *Bantu Studies* 9 (1935): 203–24.

———. "The Sources of Law in Tswana Tribal Courts: Legislation and Precedent." *Journal of African Law* 1 (1957): 150–62.

———. "Tswana Legal Maxims." *Africa* 36, no. 2 (April 1966): 121–34.

Sebina, A. M. "Makalaka." *African Studies* 5, no. 2 (1947): 88–94.

"Sensational Liquor Case." *The Bechuanaland News,* 27 April 1895.

Shepperson, G. "Ethiopianism: Past and Present." in *Christianity in Tropical Africa.* Edited by C. G. Baeta. London: 1968, pp. 249–68.

Silberbauer, G. B., and Kuper, A. J. "Kgalagari Masters and

Bushmen Serfs: Some Observations." *African Studies* 25 (1966): 171-79.

Tabler, E. "The Tati Gold Rush." *Africana Notes and News* 12-13 (1956-59): 53-63.

———. "The Walvis Bay Road: Reitfontein to Lake Ngami." *Africana Notes and News* 12, no. 4 (December 1956): 123-29.

Thema, B. C. "On Role of L.M.S. in Tswana Education." *Kutlwano* 8, no. 12 (December 1969).

Thompson, R. Wardlaw. "With the Boers and Blacks in South Africa." *Pall Mall Gazette*, 6 June 1884.

"Tragedy in the Kalahari." *The Bechuanaland News*, 4 February 1899.

Tylden, G. "The Bechuanaland Border Police, 1885-95." *Army Historical Research* 19 (1940): 236-42.

"Veritus" [pseudo]. "Secheli and the Boers." *Cape Town Mail*, 12 March 1853.

Willoughby, W. C. "Khama: A Bantu Reformer." *International Review of Missions*, January 1924, pp. 74-83.

———. "Notes on the Relation of the Black and White Races in the Civilization of the World." In *Tracts on Natural History*. Cape Town: 1913.

———. "Notes on the Totemism of the Becwana." *Journal of the Royal Anthropological Institute* 35 (1905).

Wookey, Alfred. "Literature for the Bechuana: Its Preparation and Influence." *L.M.S. Chronicle* (January 1902), pp. 56-58.

———. "Missionary Work in Bechuanaland." *Diamond Field Advertiser*, 11 February 1907.

———. "More News from Lake Ngami." *L.M.S. Chronicle*, October 1894.

Index

African Methodist Episcopal Church, 204, 206, 207, 217, 220
African social institutions, 250
Afro-Americans, 206
Agriculture, 111
Alcohol, prohibition of, 243
Alcoholism, 241–42, 244
Andersson, Charles J., 61, 64
Anglo-Boer relations, 63
Anglo-Boer War, 178, 252
Angra Paquena settlement, 131
Arithmetic, teaching of, 184–85
Ashburnham, J. A., 149

Baanami (son of Kgari), 174
Backsliding, 236
Bailie, Alexander, 36, 108, 126–27, 242, 257
Bain, Andrew A., 30
Bain, Andrew Geddes, 37
Baines, Thomas, 95

Bakalahari, 263–64
Bakwena, 31
Baldwin, William, 64, 65, 66, 261
Balfour, Reginald, 180
Bamangwato Hills, 31
"Bantu balechulo" (people of the hunt), 53 n58
"Bantu balehuku" (people of the book), 53 n58
Baptism, 42, 104–5
Barber, Frederick Hugh, 110
Barter, 262
Basutoland (Morija), 203
Basutos, 31
Bathoen (Ngwaketse chief): and church schism, 208; and concessionaires, 147; death of, 219–20; and defiance of British, 282; and donation to Ngwaketse, 185; and drinking, 247; and Ethiopians, 205; and expulsion of missionary, 211; grant to, 148; and initiation

ceremonies, 231–32; and new missionary, 217–18; and prohibition of liquor, 244; and quarrel with Boers, 138; and servitude, 263; and tribal laws, 213; and visit to Cape Town, 137; and wife's illness, 209

Batlaping's monarchy, 129

Bautlwe, 238–39

Bechuana District Committee (BDC), 125, 160–61, 169, 177, 179, 182, 183, 188, 202, 206–21, 233, 234, 242, 248

Bechuanaland: annexation of, 142–43; Border Police, 271 n97; European settlement in, 256, 259; white visitors to, 31–32

Beelelwa (betrothal), 233

Beer drinking, 240–41, 245, 246

Behrens, Superintendent, 72

Bent, Theodore, 235

Bethanie converts, 73

Bible reading, 160

Biddulph, John B., 30

Bididi chief, 40, 41

Biltong (jerked meat), 110

Boers: aggression, 70, 71, 124–27; and British hunters and traders, 59; freebooters, 169; hostilities against the Tswana, 46, 61; and Joseph McCabe, 59; and the Kwena, 62; plundering activities of, 131

Bogadi (bride price), 233

Bogwera (circumcision rites, 45, 230–32, 265 n14. See also Circumcision; Initiation ceremonies

Boikgololo movement, 201–3, 215–17, 219–20, 222

Bojale (initiation ceremonies), 45, 230–34. See also Circumcision; Initiation ceremonies

Bolowane (rinderpest), 252

Boomu (heathenish customs), 44

Borcherds, Petrus, 28

Bosman, Isaac, 138

Botha, J. D., 126

Boundaries, 149, 150 n1

Boyne, Henry, 118, 242, 243, 245–47

Boys Boarding School, 161

Brandy, 267 n53, 268 n54

Bride price, 233–34

British rule, 123–49, 263, 280

British South Africa Company, 148

British sphere of influence, 118

Brown, John, 211, 248

Brussels Act, 244

Bubi, death of, 43

Bulilima Mangwe district, 174

Burns, James, 184

Bushmen, 261

"Bush" schools, 202

Campbell, John, 29, 34

Cape of Good Hope, 27

Carleton, Reverend, 217

Carrington, Captain, 136

Carson, Edward, 140–41

Cattle: bred by Bechuanas, 76 n19; disease, 252, 255; herding, 56, 162; raiding, 29; ritual use of, 74 n5; theft of, 61, 77 n29

Chamberlain, Joseph, 143, 248, 254

Chapman, James, 62, 63, 75, 91

Chartered Expeditionary Force, 252

Chase, W. H., 255

Children, sale of, 260–62

Christians, 231–33

Chukudu (Kgamane's father-in-law), 99

Church secessionists, 201–23

Church and state, 44, 168

Church Temperance Society, 245

Circumcision, 57, 105, 119 n103,

Index

120 n104, 229–30. *See also* Initiation rites.
Civil war of 1866, 94–97
Conversion, 36, 38, 52 n36
Coppin, J., 224 n24
Crime, punishment of, 108
Crop failures, 251
Cumming, Gordon, 63

Diamond fields, 257
Dimawa (Kwena capital), 61
Dingaka (witch doctors), 91, 253
Dinokana, school at, 72, 73
Dithakong, battle of, 30
Dithapo (son of Lecholathebe), 87
Dithejwane hills, 88
Dithubaruba, Germans expelled from, 85
Divorce, 233
"Doppers" (members of the Dutch Reformed Church), 124
Droughts, 56, 252–53
Drunkenness, 249–50
Dutch Reformed Church, 124
Dwane, James, 204

East Coast fever (cattle disease), 255
Education, 159–91
Edwards, Rogers, 34, 47
Elephants, 64, 109, 110
Ellenberger, Jules, 137, 210, 213–14, 239, 258
English language, teaching of, 184
Ethiopian Church, 203–6
Ethiopianism, 210, 215–22, 280
Europeans, 229
Evangelists, 160, 201–3

Farming, 256
"Fee-School," 176–77, 186

Firearms, 28, 63, 65–66
Food rations, 253–54
Freebooting, 130
Freeman, John, 47, 234
"Free-School," 176

Gabarone block farms, 257
Gabatshwane, Marcus, 217
Game hunting, 58, 64, 256
Garrett, Reginald P., 258–59
Gaseitsiwe (Ngwaketse chief): and alcoholism, 242; burial of, 265 n2; and Christianity, 103–4; and distrust of British, 135; fondness for tea and coffee, 66; and initiation ceremonies, 106; and land lease, 146; and protection by Mothowagae; and Protectorate, 134; and reading and writing; and serfs, 262; and traders, 69
German missionaries, 55–73, 127
German stations, 81–113
Ghanzi area, 139
Gilmore, Parker, 124
Girls' education, 162–63, 180–81
Gohakgosi (brother of Kgama), 134, 172
Gold, 100–101, 257
Good, James, 86, 103, 111, 146, 205, 208, 210
Goold-Adams, Captain, 64, 144, 263
Goshen community, 131, 133
Gould, Reverend, 215, 216
Griqualand, annexation of, 152 n29
Griquas, 30, 75 n13
Grobler, Piet, 142
Groening, William, 126

Hamilton, Evans, 35
Hamilton, Robert, 36
Hamilton, Roger, 35

Hardeland, Superintendent, 73
Heathen practices, 232
Hepburn, J. D., 87, 103, 111–12, 125, 162–63, 169–72, 231, 261
Hermannsburgers Society, 70, 72, 81–82
Hides and skins, 256, 260
Hohls, Karl, 85
Horses, 59
Hunters and traders, 58, 60–61
Hunting, 57–58, 109–10, 162
Hurutshe (people of the Transvaal), 144
Hurutsheland, 47, 72
Hygiene, 39

Industrial schools, 177, 180
Inglis, Walter, 47
Initiation ceremonies, 33, 57, 106, 229. See also Circumcision
Inyati station, 43
Ironwork, 56
Irrigation project, 36–37
Ivory, 48, 58, 59, 63, 64, 109–10, 144, 156 n95, 260

Jacobs, Pit, 64
Jennings, Reverend, 185, 187, 240, 249
Jensen, Reverend, 72, 73
Jousse, Paul, 257

"Kabomo," 213
Kaffir beer, 269 n76, 270 nn. See also Beer
"Kaga Mma Kgos" (concerning the mother of the chief), 34
Kalanga mission, 31, 171
Kanye, 161
Kanye church, 208, 210
Kanye Exporation Company, 146

Kanye station, 86
Karosses (skins), 63, 74 n2
Kebailele (brother of Kgama), 183
Kesieman, John, 177
Kgalagadi Desert, 125
Kgalagadi tribe, 61, 65, 104, 259–60, 263
Kgama (Ngwato chief): abdication of, 103; and acceptance of Protectorate, 135; and Bechuanaland District Committee, 183; and Boers, 124, 127, 169–72; and British traders, 128; and conflicts with Willoughby, 189; and diplomacy, 150 n5, 283; generosity of, 185; and Hepburn dispute, 170–72; and initiation rites, 196; and Macheng's removal, 102–3; and marital life, 236; and missionary, 194 n46; and opponents, 194 n51; and opposition to charity, 253–54; and position as chief, 29; as practicing Christian, 281; and Price, 88; and purchase of retail stores, 258–59; and servitude, 264; and Shoshong invasion, 103; as student, 94; and warning to Sebele, 247; and whites' attitude, 235
Kgama II, 97
Kgama III, 139, 206, 230, 281
Kgamane, 88, 94, 124
Kgari (Ngwato chief), 31, 97
Kgatla tribe, 37, 40, 66
Kgosidintsi (brother of Sechele), 30, 39, 41, 62–63, 67, 89, 92, 133, 231, 253, 281
Kgotla (chief's court), 30, 32, 57, 232
Khukwi Mogodi, 161, 168–69, 202
Khurutshe, 215, 216
Kimberley diamond fields, 257
King Edward Bangwaketse Mission Church, 212

Index

Kok, John, 34
Kololo tribe: and attack on the Tawana, 95; forays of, 49 n11; migration of, 29; mission, 87; and myth of unfriendly Africans, 47; and retreat into the Kgalagadi Desert, 30; war of 1823, 37
Korana tribe, 28
Kruger, Paul, 132
Kuruman, 30, 35, 37, 161
Kuruman Boarding School, 175, 176
Kuruman Institution, 130
Kwenaetsile, 209, 217
Kwena tribe: and assassination of Motswasele, 30; and Boers, 70; and Bubi, 38; and Christian morale, 67; defeat in 1852, 70; and Mathiba, 29; mission, 84; and Ndebele, 72, 98; opposition to Livingstone, 39–40; penal system, 66; population, 64, 161; and race relations, 62; raid on Ngwato cattle posts, 97; and Sechele, 38; traders, 75 n13, 110–11; traditional ceremonies, 231; truce with the Kgatla, 125

Laborers, 254
Land concessions, 144–48
Land disputes, 61
Land franchises, 144–45
Land laws, 128–29
Land tenure, 251
Lattakoo, 35–36
Leask, Thomas, 106–7
Lecholathebe (Tawana chief): and Andersson's gifts, 61, 64; inhospitality of, 67; and land concession, 145; and survivors of Kololo mission, 87; taken prisoner, 50 n16; and vaccination, 91; and war council

Lechulo (tribal war council), 32, 41, 53 n58, 95
Lee, G. W., 255
Legong, Sencho, 218
Lehuha (polygamy), 233–34
Lekhetko (serfdom and taxation), 57
Lewis, Haydon, 185, 186, 237, 249
Leyland, 68
Lichtenstein, Henry, 28, 241
Liquor, 134, 240–48, 268 nn, 269 nn, 271 nn), 272 nn
Liteyana station, 72
Livestock, British purchase of, 252
Livingstone, David, 37–41, 42, 43, 45–46, 261
Lloyd, Edwin, 161, 176, 177, 208–11, 217–18, 249, 257
Lobang (schoolteacher), 217
Lobatsi block farms, 257
Loch, Henry, 137, 145
London Missionary Society (LMS), 26–47, 80–113, 125, 139, 149, 159–91, 199, 201–17, 221, 240, 264, 279
Lopepe wells, 144
Lovedale school, 175, 176, 183, 192 n16, 203
Lutheran missionaries, 73
Lutherans, 82, 92

Mabe, 212
Mabotsa, 37
McCabe, Joseph, 60–61
Macheng, 71, 97, 98, 99, 100–102
Macholohelo (Sebele's wife), 237–38, 239
Mackenzie, John, 65, 84–85, 90, 91, 93, 96, 100, 112, 130–32, 143, 152 n36, 153 n38, 261, 262
Maghato, Reverend, 219
Maize, 251–57
Makabe (brother of Bathoen), 30, 213

Makaiitschoah (wife of Molehabangwe), 234
Malaria, 47
Mankurwane (Tlhaping chief), 131
Manye, Charlotte, 204
Marico District, 126
Marriage, 233, 234, 247, 265 n17, 267 n48
Mashonaland, 130
Massauw, David, 131
Mathiba (heir to Tawana chiefdom), 29, 138-40
Matlare, converts in, 73
Mauch, Karl, 101
Meat, 57, 58
Mebalwe, Paul, 44, 67, 82, 202
Medicine men, 90-92. *See also* Witchcraft
"Melao ea Ksogi" (Rights of the Chief), 57
Melville, Cape government agent, 36
Mfecane (nineteenth-century wars), 29, 34, 46, 49 n11, 58, 95
Migrant workers, 258
Migration of tribes, 29
Mineral concessions, 145, 147
Mining, 112
Mission schools, 196 nn
Mma-Kgama (Ggari's chief wife), 49 n12, 97
Moffat, Emily, 66
Moffat, John Smith, 82, 142-43, 164, 165, 172, 177, 230-31
Moffat, Robert, 30, 35, 37, 41, 45, 47, 62, 68, 70-73, 81, 83, 260-61
Mogodi, Khukwi, 87, 161, 202
Mokgokong (former wife of Sechele), 43, 47
Mokone, Mangena, 203, 204, 207, 222
Molehabangwe (Tlhaping chief), 28, 35, 72, 235

Molehani, Paul, 67
Molehani, David, 37
Molema, Silas, 188
Molepolole school, 161, 231, 236
Molomo (tasting first fruits of harvest), 232, 237
Montshiwa (Tshidi-Rolong chief), 106, 131, 132, 234-35
Moravians, 70, 81-82
Moremi, 29, 112, 168, 244, 261
Moremi II, 87
Morija (Basutoland), 203; school, 175, 176
Moshette (Rolong chief), 131
Moshupa school, 177, 217
Moshweshwe (Sotho chief), 42
Mothibi (Tlhaping chief), 30, 33, 35
Mothowagae (evangelist), 176, 177, 208-14, 217-22, 280
Motiki, Gaofhetoge, letters from, 187-88
Motswasele (Kwena chief), 30, 31, 49 n12
Mphoeng-Raditladi faction, 144, 172, 174
Multiracial schools, 197 n82
Murder, capital crime, 108
Mzimba, L. N., 228 n118

Namaqualand, 131
Native Advisory Council, 232
Native Races and Liquor Traffic United Committee, 244
Ndebele tribe, 30, 43, 70, 95, 96, 97, 171
Ngami, Lake, 29, 60
Ngamiland, 29, 43, 67, 168
Ngwaketseland, 133, 146, 160, 169, 244, 261
Ngwaketse tribe; and Andrew Bain, 30, 37; and initiation ceremonies,

231; and Kuruman evangelist, 43; and liquor, 242; location, 86; and Mothowagae, 214; population, 160; and Sechele, 62; and traders, 110–11; war with the Kololo, 30
Ngwatoland, 31, 186
Ngwato tribe: bargaining habits, 64; and cattle-post raids; and Christianity, 104; and civil war of 1866, 99; confllicts, 95–96; and Ethiopians, 218; and Kwena attack, 105; and liquor supplies, 243; and Livingstone, 43; main groups, 104; markmanship, 63; and *mfecane*, 31; and military troubles, 95; population, 63, 88, 110; schools, 183; separation from Tawana tribe, 29, 30; and shooting incidents, 142; and Tiger Kloof school, 181–82; and war of 1893
Ntare (chief of the Yei), 169

"Onze Veld," 59
Ornaments, 56, 58
Ostrich feathers, 58, 59, 63, 109–10, 144, 149, 256, 260
Oswell, W. C., 60
Oxen, 59

Palapye, 246
Palapye church, 170, 171
Palapye mission, 173
Palapye school, 173
Partridge, Miss (headmistress of school), 185–86
Philip, John, 33–34
Phuthego (tribal court), 32, 65, 206, 219
Pilgrim's Progress (Bunyan), 167
Pitso (tribal council), 32, 65, 107, 108, 205

Plaatje, Solomon, 188, 197 n91
Plows, 111, 251, 272 n114, 273 n115
Polygamy, 68, 233–34, 237
Pondoland, 207
Potchefstrom Landrost, 60
Pretorius, Andries, 69, 70
Price, Mrs., 82, 242
Price, Roger, 82, 85, 88, 92, 93, 104, 112, 166–67, 168
Prohibition, 240–48. See also Liquor
"Prophetess," 224 n20
"Prophets," 206

Railway lines, 254–55
Rainmaking, 33, 40–41, 44, 107, 120 n107), 233
Ratshosa, Simon, 182
Rauwe Sekoko, 215, 217, 235
Read, James, 35, 72, 88, 92, 160
Rebellion of 1878, 130–31
Rees, Cullen, 216
Religion, 67
Religious rites, 57
Rhodes, Cecil, 132, 142, 244
Richardson, James, 178–79, 248
Rideout, C. A. A., 206, 207
Rinderpest, 177, 251–53
Robinson, Hercules, 147, 254
Rolong group, 217
Rolongland, 133
"Royal herald," 108

Sargant, E. B., 184–85
Sarwa group, 52 n49, 61, 65, 259–60
Schapera, I., 144
Scholefield, Lieutenant, 264
School curricula, 163
Schroeder, Heinrich, 70, 71, 82, 84
Schulenburg, Heinrich C., 70, 72, 73, 83–84
Scottish Temperance League, 243

Scripture lessons, 41
Seapapitso (Ngwatse chief), 220, 221
Sebele (Kwena chief): and book learning, 181; and challenge to his authority, 174; and drunkenness, 242, 245, 246, 282; and gifts to a prophet, 219; and land concessions, 147; and police, 136–37; and polygamy, 236–39; and the Protectorate, 132–33; and tribal school, 186
Sebobi (evenagelist), 44, 67, 86, 166
Sebolai, Shomoloekae, 202
Secessionists, 201–22, 223–28 nn
Sechele (Kwena chief): afflicted by dropsy, 92, 107; appeal to Tswana chiefs, 61; and baptism, 42; and Boers, 61, 77 n27, 79 n62; character, 71, 73, 89; and church and state, 166–67; and constitutional government, 108; death of, 168; drunkenness, 242–43; education of, 161–62; and Germans, 85–86; and gunpowder restrictions, 62; and heathen practices, 104; and Henry Boyne, 118; and initiation ceremonies, 106; and Kholoma, 118; as kingmaker, 98; and knowledge of the Bible, 71, 162, 166–67; and Kwena politics, 30; and Livingstone, 38; and medical affairs, 91; and Molepolole mission, 84–85, 89; and monogamy, 42; and quarrel with Sebobi, 44–45; and release of Macheng, 98; and religious observances, 78–79 nn; response to Christianity, 47; and right to preach, 44; and South African politics, 69; and traders, 79; and traditional practices, 92, 231; and Tswana women, 111; visit to England; and whites, 70
Sedimo (Kgari regent), 97
Sehuba (tribute), 57
Sekgoma (Ngwato chief): and circumcision, 154; and British officials, 138–40; conversions, 93; estrangement of his sons, 96; and firearms, 88; failure at school, 195 n63; and ivory, 59; and Livingstone, 43; and offer of truce, 99; opposition to Christianity, 94; opposition to London Missionary Society, 261; and plot to poison water wells, 100; and his six wives, 68; and threat to kill Van Viljoen, 62
Selepeng church, 216
Serfdom, 260–61, 263
Setlagole outstation, 217
Servitude, 276 n166
Sex scandals, 238
Sharp, Ella, 183
Shashi-Motlotsi area, 171
Shippard, Sidney, 135–36, 141–42, 231
Shoshong mission, 73, 83–84, 110, 231
Slavery, 263, 276 n166
Smallpox epidemic, 90–91, 115 n34
Smith, Adolph G., 60, 258–59
Social life, Tswana, 240
Sorghum, 256
Sotho tribe, 29, 30
South African Confederacy, 60
South African Native Affairs Commission, 222
Southern Bechuanaland, 28
Special court, 109
Sprigg, Gordon, 207
Stellaland, 131, 132
Stewart, Mark, 248
Surmon, W. H., 136–37, 237–39

Tabler, Edward, 102
Tati Concessions Company, 216
Tati River area, 100–101, 109, 141, 174, 215, 216
Taung church, 205
Tawana tribe, 29, 62, 66, 87, 91, 95
Taxation, 57–58
Teacher-evangelists, 208, 215, 223 n3
Teachers, 175, 180
Ten Years North of the Orange River (Mackenzie), 101
Theft, 108
Thomas, Thomas Morgan, 86
Thompson, George, 30, 33
Thompson, R. Wardlaw, 163–64, 172, 178
Tiger Kloof school, 180, 181, 186–87, 189, 198 n101
Tlhalano (divorce), 233
Tlhaping tribe: apparel style, 78 n48; and cattle raiding, 29; and civil rights, 33; and firearms, 28; and Kololo, 30; and major split with Rolong, 49 n6; and missionaries, 130; preparations for war, 49 n8; uprising of 1878, 117 n59
Trade and commerce, 46
Traders, 32, 69, 111, 112
Trade schools, 192 n16
Transvaal, 203
Tribal councils (*pitso, lechulo, phthego*), 32, 33
Tribal life, 32
Tribal school, 186
Tribes, four principal, 48 n2, 283
Tribute (*legketho*), 260
Truter-Sommerville mission, 28
Tsetse flies, 47
Tshidi-Rolong group, 131, 235
Tsime (Bathoen's brother-in-law), 209
Tswana tribes (Kwena, Ngwaketse, Ngwato, and Tawana), 29, 283: agriculture, 56; alphobet, 39; business acumen, 65; and Boers, 61; and cattle, 75; chiefdoms, 129–30; chiefs, 32, 50 nn, 283; and Christianity, 72, 93; council proceedings, 65; customs, 50 n20; diplomacy, 125; economic activities, 31, 109; education, 159–91; and firearms, 31, 63–44, 95; hospitality, 66–67; and ivory, 76 n15; and land tenure, 128–29; and Livingstone, 43; and missionaries, 105; region, 205; religion, 41; schools, 94, 178–79; society, 27–28; students, 84; system of punishment, 108; systems of government, 107, 108; taboos, 69; traders, 69, 75 n13; transformations, 229–64; weaknesses, 29–30; and whites, 35; women, 69
Tuli block farms, 257
Tumedi group, 215, 216, 235
"Turkey incident," 106–7

Utensils, 56

Vaccination, 90–91
Van Niekerk, William, 131
Van Pitius, Gey, 131
Van Viljoen, Jan, 62, 64
Van Zyl, H. M., 145
Veterinary measures, 256
Victoria, Queen, 143
Vocational training, 280
Vryburg school, 178

Walvish Bay route, 61
Warren, Charles, 131, 132, 134, 135, 147

Waterboer, Andries, 44
Weapons, 56
Weavind, George, 204
White traders, 58, 59, 63–64, 65, 110, 262
Williams, Charles, 104, 109
Williams, Howard, 137, 165, 168, 236
Williams, Ralph, 140, 212, 214, 218, 231, 239–40
Willoughby, W. C., 33, 105, 143, 149, 172, 177, 187–89, 211, 235, 243, 249
Witchcraft, 39, 92, 105, 231, 260
Witwatersrand, 257
Wodehouse, Governor, 101

Women, 56, 69, 111, 181
Wookey, Alfred, 130, 139, 167, 230, 238, 242, 243

Xaba, Jacobus G., 204

Yakwe, Diphukwe, 87, 169, 202
Yei (Koba) group, 169
Young, Alice, 176

Zimmerman, Ferdinand, 70, 73, 82, 83

968.1
C541h

Chirenje, J Mutero.
  A history of Northern Botswana
  1850-1910